UNIVERSAL INDEX OF BIOGRAPHICAL NAMES
IN THE LANGUAGE SCIENCES

Volume 113

E.F.K. Koerner

Universal Index of Biographical Names in the Language Sciences

UNIVERSAL INDEX
OF BIOGRAPHICAL NAMES
IN THE LANGUAGE SCIENCES

E.F.K. KOERNER

Zentrum für Allgemeine Sprachwissenschaft,
Typologie und Universalienforschung, Berlin

JOHN BENJAMINS PUBLISHING COMPANY
AMSTERDAM/PHILADELPHIA

The paper used in this publication meets the minimum requirements of American National Standard for Information Sciences — Permanence of Paper for Printed Library Materials, ANSI Z39.48–1984.

Library of Congress Cataloging-in-Publication Data

Koerner, E. F. K.
 Universal index of biographical names in the language sciences / E.F.K. Koerner.
  p.   cm. -- (Amsterdam studies in the theory and history of linguistic science. Series III, Studies in the history of the language sciences, ISSN 0304-0720; v. 113)
Includes bibliographical references and index.
1. Linguists. 2. Philologists. I. Title.
P83.K64   2008
410.92'2--dc22
[B]   2008018664
ISBN 978 90 272 4604 2 (Hb; alk. paper)

John Benjamins Publishing Company • P.O. Box 36224 • 1020 ME Amsterdam • The Netherlands
John Benjamins North America • P.O. Box 27519 • Philadelphia, PA 19118-0519 • USA

For all co-travelers in the history of linguistics
on the occasion of the
Eleventh International Conference on the
History of the Language Sciences (ICHoLS XI)
Potsdam, Germany, 28 August–2 September 2008

BOOKS BY THE SAME AUTHOR

Bibliographia Saussureana 1870–1970: An annotated,
classified bibliography on the background, development, and actual
relevance of Ferdinand de Saussure's general theory of language
(Metuchen, New Jersey: The Scarecrow Press, 1972), 406 pp.

Contribution au débat post-saussurien sur le signe linguistique
Introduction générale et bibliographie annotée
(The Hague & Paris: Mouton, 1972), 103 pp.

Ferdinand de Saussure: Origin and Development of
His Linguistic Thought in Western Studies of Language.
A contribution to the history and theory of linguistics
(Braunschweig: Friedrich Vieweg & Sohn [Oxford &
Elmsford, N.Y.: Pergamon Press], 1973), xl, 428 pp.
— Translated into Hungarian (Budapest: Tankönyvkiadó, 1982); Japanese
(Tokyo: Taishukan, 1982), and Spanish (Madrid: Gredos, 1982) —

The Importance of Techmer's "Internationale Zeitschrift für Allgemeine
Sprachwissenschaft" in the Development of General Linguistics
(Amsterdam: John Benjamins, 1973), vii, 76 pp. in-4°.

Western Histories of Linguistics, 1822–1976
An annotated, chronological bibliography
(Amsterdam: John Benjamins, 1978), ix, 113 pp.

Toward a Historiography of Linguistics
Selected essays. Foreword by R. H. Robins
(Amsterdam: John Benjamins, 1978), xx, 222 pp.

(Together with Matsuji Tajima)
Noam Chomsky: A personal bibliography, 1951–1986
(Amsterdam & Philadelphia: John Benjamins, 1986), xi, 217 pp.

Saussurean Studies / Études saussuriennes
Avant-propos de Rudolf Engler
(Geneva: Éditions Slatkine, 1988), xxi, 207 pp.

Practicing Linguistic Historiography: Selected essays
(Amsterdam & Philadelphia: John Benjamins, 1989), xii, 454 pp.

Professing Linguistic Historiography
(Amsterdam & Philadelphia: John Benjamins, 1995), viii, 274 pp.

Linguistic Historiography: Projects & prospects
(Amsterdam & Philadelphia: John Benjamins, 1999), x, 236 pp.

Toward a History of American Linguistics
(London & New York: Routledge, 2002), x, 316 pp.

Essays in the History of Linguistics
(Amsterdam & Philadelphia: John Benjamins, 2004), x, 271 pp.

Jezikoslovna historigrafija: Metodologija i praksa Translated from the
English by Milica Lukšić. Edited by Zvonko Pandžić (Zagreb:
Tusculanae Editiones, 2007), 266 pp.

PREFACE & ACKNOWLEDGMENTS

Maybe this is the place to attempt a reconstruction of the genesis of the present compilation and to mention those who at one stage or another of its long history contributed to this list of names and dates. Those familiar with my work will have noticed that my penchant for bibliographical detail also has included an effort to provide the life-dates of authors. This is already in evidence in Part II of *Bibliographia Saussureana*, "Background sources of F. de Saussures's linguistic theory, 1816–1916" (Koerner 1972: 215-351). In fact, soon after I had switched from English and German philology to general linguistics in 1968, I began to compile bibliographies of all linguistic subjects, filling dozens of shoe boxes with 3x5 inch cards by the thousands (as I had done before in the fields of German and English literature from the earliest times to the mid-20th century and, especially, of Old and Middle English words and their Germanic, at times even noting their Indo-European roots, as was customary in German university curricula before the study of 'modern linguistics' largely replaced old-time *Sprachwissenschaft*).

Given this mania on my part, as some may call it, for collecting bibliographical information, and given my long-standing interest in history generally and the history of linguistics particularly, it was only natural to me that when I began editing *Historiographia Linguistica* in 1973, I required authors to provide such data as a matter of course. While I am sure that some of them were displeased for having to go back to the library and check out such details, I am inclined to believe that most of the contributors to *HL* as well as its companion monograph series "Studies in the History of the Language Sciences" (SiHoLS) have come to see the usefulness of such exercise: while providing such data may be cumbersome to some and not the 'meat' of their scholarly narrative, I strongly believe that it is a service to the profession that should not be underestimated as such biographical dates place an author at least in some chronological context.

Given this understanding of things, I have collected basic biographical information on linguists, philologists, and various other personages who have contributed to the understanding of language and languages in one way or another. As a result, the list may contain the names of people who few of us would expect to find therein. On the other hand, it will be easy for specialists in a particular area of interest to notice gaps and errors that have crept in during the twenty and probably many more years that I worked, on and off, on this list. As a matter of fact, I'd be the first to admit that the term 'universal' may sound a bit too grand. In fact, while the title of this list is intended to signal that it contains not only names and dates of Western persons in 'the language sciences', the present 280 odd pages do by no means include all and everybody who has contributed to the field, past and present. Indeed, very few scholars born after 1950 have been included, and the biographical various sources that have become available over the past fifteen and more years (e.g., Brekle et al. 1987–2002, Kürschner 1994, Koerner & Asher 1995: 483-494; Sasaki & Kihara 1995, Stammerjohann et al. 1996, Fernández Pérez et al. 1999) have not always been exhausted.[1] I trust tat there will be opportunities in the future to rectify this, although I'll gladly leave this to younger, more energetic people to do.

In the meantime, I decided that one has to find a point to stop and make information available where it is clear that the task will never be complete. However, I am hoping to find a good soul ready to take on the job of preparing the data here presented in such a manner that it could be placed on a web site accessible to everybody. If at all possible, means should be found to permit users to make additions, corrections and even deletions, if an entry was found to be spurious or undesirable.

I had been wondering how best to present the data in this bok. At first I had thought that I should arrange the names in a single column, thus providing sufficient extra space for additions and corrections. I had done so in Koerner (1989: 445-454). However, after consultation with several potential users, I decided on double columns, at the same time starting each new letter on a recto page (except for the letters Q and X), thus providing I hope, extra space for additions and corrections.

It is now impossible to recall who in particular contributed to the present list. However, several persons must be mentioned. Daniel Labonia (formerly of Ottawa, now residing in Montreal), sent me a list of names and dates culled from the *Bibliographie linguistique* for the years 1989–1997 which I had missed;[2] Jan Noordegraaf (Amsterdam) provided me information on especially scholars from the Low Countries on various occasions, and Kees Versteegh (Nijmegen) most generously helped me with the difficult Arabic

---

[1] For those lucky ones who have access to open stack libraries and the Library of Congress catalogs (also referred to as the Union Catalogue), I may add that I have found there in my student days and later in North America biographical dates of people who were otherwise impossible to trace. For the full references to the publications mentioned in this Preface, see the 'Remarks' (below). See also Bronstein et al. (1977) for a pioneering effort in biography.

[2] I added information gleaned from the years 1998–2002 of the same source only recently.

names and their transcription. None of these colleagues should be held responsible for the lacunae and inconsistencies — not to mention outright mistakes (references to which would be much appreciated) — that still remain. Yet I hope that their efforts will have been worth their while.

The above text had largely been drafted in September 2003, when I had had hopes of finding a publisher for this list without simply suggesting (as certain companies were ready to do) that I throw it open to everyone by having the data being put on their website. (I admit that having invested so many hundreds of hours of work on this 'projet de longue haleine', I was not quite ready to be that generous.) Happily, the up-coming Eleventh International Conference on the History of the Language Sciences (ICHoLS XI), scheduled to take place in Potsdam during 28 August – 2 September 2008, has provided the fortunate circumstance under which "my" publisher, John Benjamins of Amsterdam, did agree to invest their time and money to bring out this 'Universal List' in regular print, and indeed suggesting — something that I find extremely generous on their part — that participants in this year's ICHoLS meeting — thirty years after its first, nota bene — should receive a complimentary copy.

Since my relocation to Germany in 2002, I have continued to add to the list, which has grown to well over 15,000 names and dates by now. In that task I have profited, in addition to those colleagues mentioned earlier, from a number of persons who provided me with corrections and, especially, additions. I shall list them here in alphabetical order — with due apologies to anyone whom I may have unintentionally omitted:

> Cristina Altman (São Paulo), Josefa Dorta (Tenerife), Kurt R. Jankowsky (Washington, D.C.), John E. Joseph (Edinburgh), Douglas A, Kibbee (Champaign, Ill.), Jurij A. Kleiner (St. Petersburg), Zvonko Pandžić (Würzburg), Ekaterina Velmezova (Moscow & Lausanne), and Otto Zwartjes (Amsterdam).

In particular, while Kurt Jankowsky provided me with the list of linguists who have received an individual entry under his special editorship in charge of biographies (see Brown et al. 2006),[3] Josefa Dorta (see Dorta et al. 2007), Doug Kibbee (see Kibbee 2007), and Otto Zwartjes (see Zwartjes et al. 2007) each sent me electronic files of the name indexes that they had provided for their respective collective volumes. May they all receive our thanks.

Berlin-Prenzlauer Berg, Easter 2008   E.F.K.K.

---

[3] See the References at the end of the front matter for the respective bibliographical entries.

AFTERTHOUGHT

I realize, of course, that supplying names and life-dates of people is not all that much information that a historian of linguistics may want to know. I still have those shoe boxes with 3 x 5 inch cards carrying references to places where more on a certain author could be found (but hardly ever consult them nowadays). Apart from the internet, there are many printed sources available where biographical data can be found. For North America the *Directory of American Scholars* and its various editions would be a source; the *Who's Who* volumes in various formats and countries may be another one. But these places are rather selective and, at least in most instances, provide information on living scholars. only. On earlier ones, one may turn to such publications as Friedrich August Eckstein's (1810–1885) 1871 *Nomenclator Philologorum* (Leipzig: B. G. Teubner; repr., Hildesheim: Georg Olms, 1968) and Wilhelm Pökel's additions in *Philologisches Schriftsteller-Lexikon* of 1882 (Leipzig: Krüger; repr., Darmstadt: Wissenschaftliche Buchgesellschaft, 1974). Above (p. viii), I have referred to volumes like Brekle et al. (1987–2002), Kürschner (1994), and Stammerjohann et al. (1996) as much more recent sources, to which I should like to add the 3-volume *Internationales Germanistenlexikon 1800–1950* (König 2003) and of course the 700 or so entries in the *Encyclopedia of Language & Linguistics* (Brown et al., 2006). There are surely many more places one may look up for information.[4] I am thinking, for instance, of Robert A. Kaster's 525-page *Guardians of Language: The grammarian and society in late Antiquity* (Berkeley & Los Angeles: University of California Press, 1988), and I am sure that specialists in areas other than 19th and 20th century of linguistics will know where to find biographical data for their domain. Indeed, the ideal would be to have references to these biographical sources appended to the present list.

I have at least made a modest beginning, and owners of this *Universal Index* may want to add such references in their personal copies. I have added the following letters to a number of names and dates in the alphabetical list:

E stands for the above-mentioned *Encyclopedia* published by Elsevier;
K for Kürschner's two-volume *Linguisten Handbuch* (1994), and
S for Stammerjohann's 1,047-page *Lexicon Grammaticorum* (1996).

---

[4] Back in 2000, I served the *Encyclopedia Britannica* as advisor on (and reviser of) biographical entries of linguists, but I found that places like this are rather selective; on the lesser known scholars one rarely finds information in such reference works.

REMARKS ON THE ARRANGEMENT OF THE INDEX

Given that the present book consists of little else than an alphabetical list of names and dates, it makes little sense to provide a table of contents. However, the user is entitled to know about the ideas that guided my work and how to use this index most fruitfully.[1]

1. *Alphabetical ordering and transcription conventions*

Westerners are inclined to assume that ordering names by following the (Latin) alphabet has become universal, although they may be willing to concede that not all languages use the same kind of letters and scriptural conventions as they do. Yet still among languages that follow the Latin alphabet there are differences; one just has to look for words like *chupa* "waistcoat, jacket" in a Spanish dictionary and be frustrated not to find it under *C*. They will be glad that double *r* does not appear in initial position (since it would otherwise have been listed separately after the single *r*, like *ll* as in *llevar* "to carry, bear, wear, etc." for example, or *ñ*, which also is listed apart from *n*). Things become more difficult once one deals with Slavic names written in Cyrillic script. Here as in many other instances, I have followed the conventions of the *Bibliographie linguistique*, with one important difference: the digraph *ch* for the velar fricative, has been replaced by an *x*, with the result that, e.g., Russian names beginning with this consonant have been arranged together with the *x*, which admittedly more often than not stands for 'ks'. Where other consonants are concerned, again diacritics have been ignored in the alphabetical ordering, so that names beginning with Č, Š, or Ž (as well as Polish Ż, for example) have been listed like *C*, *S*, and *Z*, respectively, despite their obviously different phonetic values. Also, German *ß* has been treated as *ss*, not *sz* as in some pre-WW I texts.

At the risk of having been inconsistent, *ä*, *ö*, and *ü* have been interpreted (as is customary in German) as *ae*, *oe*, and *ue*, respectively; likewise, the ligatures *æ* and *œ* have been treated like *ae* and *oe*; however, *å* and *ø* have been arranged among the letters *a* and *o*; other diacritics concerning vowels (acutes, macrons, circumflexes, etc.) and signs for aspiration, too, have been ignored in the present alphabetic arrangement. Last but not least the definite article *al-* in Arabic and its various assimilatory variants (*az-*, *aš*, etc.) has been discounted and placed at the end of the (often very elaborate) name.

---

[1] See also (especialy page viii of) the Preface to the present book for information.

2. *Religious orders added to a variety of names in the list*

Given the great attention that 'Missionary Linguistics' — a subject pioneered by the late Victor Egon Hanzeli (1925–1991) in 1969 — has received in recent years (see Hovdhaugen 1996, Nowak 1999, Zwartjes & Hovdhaugen 2004, Zwartjes & Altman 2005, Zwartjes et al. 2007; also Bergunder 1999 concerning missionary activity n India),[2] a special effort has been made to add the adherence of a person to a religious order in cases where it has been ascertained (and as they are typically added to their — often religious — names).[3] Thus the following abbreviations can be found in the present list:

O.A.R. is sometimes used for Augustinian — not Franciscan — Recollects, an offshoot of the Augustinian Hermits, but see O.R.S.A. (below).

O.Carm. stands of course for any member of the medicant order of Our Lady of Mount Carmel, a Carmelite monk (also referred to as 'White Friar').

O.F.M. (Ordo Fratrum Minorum), i.e., Franciscans, among which one can find three independent branches: the Friars Minor (O.F.M.), the Friars Minor Conventual (O.F.M. Conv.), and the Friars Minor Capuchin (O.F.M. Cap.).

O.F.M. (Recollect) has been adopted for a distinct province of Franciscans.

O.M.I. (Order of Mary Immaculate), usually written in lower case o.m.i.

O.P. (Ordo Predicatorum "Order of Preachers"), which stands for in fact four mendicant orders commonly referred to as Dominicans.

O.R.S.A. (Order of Recollects of Saint Augustine); see also O.A.R.

O.S.A. (Order of Saint Augustine) marks Augustinian Canons as well as Augustinian Hermits.

S.J. (Societas Jesu "Society of Jesus") as regularly used by Jesuits (after the surnames).

Less frequently found are orders like the Spiritians, i.e., members of the Order of the Holy Spirit, abbreviated C.S.S.P., or the Sulpicians who bear the (unfortunate) abbreviation S.S. after their name; members of the Society of the Holy Word, a missionary order, would add SVD (Societas Verbi Divini) to their name. There are no doubt other orders that have escaped my notice.

---

[2] See the contributions by Cristina Altman, Manuel Breva-Claramonte, Sabine Dedenbach-Salazar Sáenz, Beatriz Garza Cuarón, Michael Mackert, Cristina Monzón, Elke Nowak, Richard Steadman-Jones, and others in Cram et al., eds. (1999: 71–174) as well as, more recently, Koerner (2002, 2004, 2005).

[3] This means that Protestant missionaries receive at best a Rev. in front of their first names; in most instances, these entries remain unmarked. This is a pity, since so many Protestant missionaries wrote at times excellent grammars and dictionaries, in particular of African languages (cf. Jungraithmayr & Möhlig 1983) and elsewhere in the world (see the recent papers by Tomalin (2006, 2008) and McGregor (2008), which have appeared in *Historiographia Linguistica*).

However, all these religious societies are Catholic,[4] and for those interested in Protestant orders involved in missionary work will note with regret that they cannot be identified in similar fashion. In a number of instances, they may hide behind a 'Rev.' in front of their (first) names in the present list, but they are few and far between. A perusal of Jungraithmayr & Möhlig's 1983 *Lexikon der Afrikanistik* for instance, which includes several scores of biographical entries, would indicate that, at least as far as Africa is concerned, the great majority of missionary linguists were in fact Protestants, many of which belonged to or were associated with the Church Missionary Society of London or religious organizations based in Switzerland or Germany. Among the latter, the Moravians, so-called after the geographic area from where some of those Hussites originate, who in 1722 were given a home and a new purpose under the leadership of Count Nikolaus Ludwig Zinzendorf (1700–1760) — although the name United Brethren (Unitas Fratrum) or, in German, after the name of the first place in Lusatia he had established, *Herrnhut* "the Lord's keeping", the Herrnhuter Brüdergemeine "Herrnhut Society of Brethren" would have been more correct. However, the name 'Moravian Brethren' has stuck, and so be it. Their main base in North America, since 1740, has been Bethlehem, Pennsylvania; David Zeisberger (1721–1803) and John Gottlieb Ernestus Heckewelder (1743–1823) are their best-known representatives whose work on Delaware has received much attention in the annals of Amerindian linguistics, probably because of their connection with Peter Stephen Duponceau (1760–1844). Much more recently, the Mahican Dictionary of the Herrnhut missionary Johann Jacob Schmick (1714–1778) was published,[5] but many other works by Moravian Brethren, not only by David Zeisberger, still linger in the Bethlehem archives. The present Index of Biographical Names does not reveal many of these missionaries; in a recent 450-page book on their work in the Upper Ohio Valley during a single decade (Wessel 1999) we would find at least a dozen of

---

[4] There is yet another order of which I first heard from William McGregor in conjunction with his recent paper (McGregor 2008). Founded in 1835 by a certain Vincent Pallotti (1795–1850), the Society of the Catholic Apostolate, more popularly known as the Pallottines, is an order largely devoted to missionary activity. In about 1891 a house committed to missionizing was established in Limburg, Germany, which established missions first in Cameroon, later in Australia. See further Brigida Nailon, *Nothing Is Wasted in the Household of God: Vincent Pallotti's vision in Australia 1901–2001* (Richmond: Spectrum, 2001), pp. 2-12.

[5] See *Schmick's Mahican Dictionary* ed. by Carl Masthay. With a Mahican Historical Phonology by David H. Pentland (= *Memoirs of the American Philosophical Society*, 197.) Philadelphia, 1991.

them who probably deserve more than footnote treatment in a history of missionary linguistics still to be written.[6]

3. *Closing remarks*

Upon reflection, I have decided to say little about my reasons for publishing this list and at this point in time beyond what I've already said in the Preface. That this book will serve me well as editor for as long as I shall be able to work in such capacity — books are portable, and so I won't have to turn on my computer each time I want to check a name or a date — is clear to me: still today I consult my personal, marked-up copy of *Bibliographia Saussureana* of 1972 on a number of occasions. I'd be the first to admit that the list is less than perfect, but then I'd like to argue with Dr Samuel Johnson who, in the preface to his famous *Dictionary* of 1755, suggested to his readers something to the effect that they should appreciate what is in it rather than deplore what has been left out. And so I trust that anyone interested in the history of linguistics will find some useful information in the present book.

REFERENCES

Bergunder, Michael, ed. 1999. *Missionarsberichte aus Indien im 18. Jahrhundert.* (= *Neue Hallesche Berichte,* 1.) Halle/S.: Verlag der Franckeschen Stiftungen zu Halle.

Brekle, Herbert E., Edeltraud Dobnig-Jülch, Hans Jürgen Höller & Helmut Weiß, eds. 1987–2004. *Bio-bibliographisches Handbuch zur Sprachwissenschaft des 18. Jahrhunderts: Die Grammatiker, Lexikographen und Sprachtheoretiker des deutschsprachigen Raums mit Beschreibungen ihrer Werke.* 8 vols. Tübingen: Max Niemeyer.

Bronstein, Arthur J., Lawrence Raphael & Cj Stevens, eds. 1977. *A Biographical Dictionary of the Phonetic Sciences.* New York: Press of Lehman College.

Brown, Keith et al., eds. 2006. *Encyclopedia of Language & Linguistics.* Second edition. 14 vols. Oxford–Amsterdam, etc.: Elsevier.

Cram, David, Andrew Linn & Elke Nowak, eds. 1999. *History of Linguistics 1996. Selected papers from the Seventh International Conference on the History of the Language Sciences (ICHoLS VII), Oxford, 12–17 September 1996).*

---

[6] Unfortunately, Wessel is a social historian and her book only mentions in passing some of the linguistic work of these missionaries when she discusses what languages of communication they used in their work (pp. 170-175). Typically, her reference to Schmick's Mahican Dictionary is buried in a footnote (p.171n.27), and not even listed in her bibliography where one also looks in vain for any linguistic work of Zeisberger, whose linguistic abilities she otherwise writes about at some length (pp. 171-173). – From a linguistic point of view Peter van Baarle's 38-page article, "Eighteenth Century Descriptions of Arawak [an indigenous language of coastal Surinam and British Guyana] by Moravian Missionaries" (in Nowak, ed. 1999.117-154) is much more informative.

Vol. I: *Traditions in linguistics worldwide*. (= *Studies in the History of the Language Sciences*, 94.) Amsterdam & Philadelphia: John Benjamins.

Dorta, Josefa, Cristóbal Corrales & Dolores Corbella, eds. 2007. *Historiografía lingüística en el ámbito hispánico: Fundamentos epistemológicos y metodológicos*. Madrid: Arco / Libros.

Fernández Pérez, Miagros, Francisco José Albertuz, Ana Mª Fernández Mella [et al.]. 1999. "El *Diccionario de lingüística: Autores*. Objetivos, estructura y muestras de su contenido". *Actas del I Congreso de la Sociedad Española de Historiografía Lingüística (A Coruña, 18–21 de febrero de 1997)* ed. by Mauro Fernández Rodríguez, Francisco García Gondar & Nancy Vázquez Veiga, 271-300. Madrid: Arco / Libros.

Hanzeli, Victor Egon. 1969. *Missionary Linguistics in New France: A study of seventeenth- and eighteenth-century descriptions of American Indian languages*. The Hague: Mouton.

Hovdhaugen, Even, ed. 1996. *... and the Word was God: Missionary linguistics and missionary grammar*. Münster: Nodus.

Jungraithmayr, Hermann & Wilhelm J. G. Möhlig, eds. 1983. *Lexikon der Afrikanistik: Afrikanische Sprachen und ihre Erforschung*. Berlin: Dietrich Reimer.

Kibbee, Douglas A., ed. 2007. *History of Linguistics 2005: Selected papers from the 10th Internatinal Conference on the History of the Language Sciences (ICHoLS X), Urbana-Champaign, Illinois, 1–5 September 2005*. (= *Studies in the History of the Language Sciences*, 112.) Amsterdam & Philadelphia: John Benjamins.

König, Christoph, ed. 2003. *Internationales Germanistenlexikon 1800–1950*. 3 vols. Berlin & New York: Walter de Gruyter.

Koerner, E.F.K. 1972. *Bibliographia Saussureana 1870–1970: An annotated, classified bibliography on the background, development, and actual relevance of Ferdinand de Saussure's general theory of language*. Metuchen, N.J.: Scarecrow Press.

Koerner, E.F.K. 1989. *Practicing Linguistic Historiography: Selected essays*. Amsterdam & Philadelphia: John Benjamins.

Koerner, E.F.K. 2002. "Toward a History of Americanist Linguistics". Chapter 2 of *Toward a History of American Linguistics* by Koerner, 17-38. London & New York: Routledge.

Koerner, E.F.K. 2004. "Missionary Linguistics in North America". Zwartjes & Hovdhaugen, eds. 2004.47-80.

Koerner, E.F.K. 2005. "Missionary Linguistics: The French Canadian Experience". *Actas del IV Congreso Internacional de la SEHL [= Sociedad Española de Historiografía Lingüística], La Laguna (Tenerife), 22 al 25 de octubre de 2003* ed. by Cristóbal Corrales Zumbado, Josefa Dorta Luis, Dolores Corbella Díaz et al., Tome I, 75-96. Madrid: Arcos / Libros, 2004.

Koerner, E.F.K. & R. E. Asher, eds. 1995. *Concise History of the Language Sciences: From the Sumerians to the Cognitivists*. Oxford & New York: Pergamon Press.

Kürschner, Wilfried, ed. 1994. *Linguisten Handbuch: Biographische und bibiographische Daten deutschsprachiger Sprachwissenschaftlerinnen und Sprachwissenschaftler der Gegenwart.* 2 vols. Tübingen: Gunter Narr.

McGregor, William B. 2008. "Missionary Linguistics in the Kimberley, Western Australia: A history of the first seventy years". *Historiographia Linguistica* 35:1/2.121-162.

Nowak, Elke, ed. 1999. *Languages Different in All Their Sounds ...: Descriptive approaches to indigenous languages of the Americas 1500 to 1850.* Münster: Nodus.

Sasaki, Tatsu & Kenzo Kihara, eds. 1995. *The Kenkyusha Biographical Dictionary of Linguistics and Philology.* Tokyo: Kenkyusha; numerous portraits. [See *HL* 26:1/2.250 (1999), for further information.]

Stammerjohann, Harro [et al.], ed. 1996. *Lexicon Grammaticorum: Who's who in the history of world linguistics.* Tübingen: Max Niemeyer.

Tomalin, Marcus. 2006. "'... to this rule there are many exceptions': Robert Maunsell (1810–1894) and the Grammar of Maori". *Historiographia Linguistica* 33:3.303-334.

Tomalin, Marcus. 2008. "Reassessing 19th-Century Missionary Linguistics on the Pacific Northwest Coast". *Historiographia Linguistica* 35:1/2.83-120.

Wessel, Carola. 1999. *Delaware-Indianer und Herrnhuter Missionare im Upper Ohio Valley, 1772–1781.* Tübingen: Max Niemeyer.

Zwartjes, Otto & Even Hovdhaugen, eds. 2004. *Missionary Linguistics / Lingüística misionera. Selected papers from the First International Conference on Missionary Linguistics, Oslo, 13–16 March 2003.* (= *Studies in the History of the Language Sciences*, 106.) Amsterdam & Philadelphia: John Benjamins.

Zwartjes, Otto & Cristina Altman, eds. 2005. *Missionary Linguistics II / Lingüística misionera II: Orthography and Phonology. Selected papers from the Second International Conference on Missionary Linguistics, São Paulo, 10–13 March 2004.* (= *Studies in the History of the Language Sciences*, 109.) Amsterdam & Philadelphia: John Benjamins.

Zwartjes, Otto, Gregory James & Emilio Ridruejo, eds. 2007. *Missionary Linguistics III / Lingüística misionera III: Morphology and Syntax. Selected papers from the Third and Fourth International Conferences on Missionary Linguistics, Hong Kong/Macau, 12-15 March 2005, Valladolid, 8-11 March 2006.* (= *Studies in the History of the Language Sciences*, 111.) Amsterdam & Philadelphia: John Benjamins.

A.

Aalholm, Niels Matthias (1811–1894)

Aalto, Pentti (1917–1998)

Aarhus, Jacob Madsen, *see* Madsen, Jacob

Aarsleff, Hans (Christian, b.1925)

Abbé d'Olivet, *see* Fabre d'Olivet

Aasen, Ivar Andreas (1813–1896)S, E

Aavik, Johannes (1880–1973)S

Abaev, Vasilij Ivanovič ("Vaso", 1900–2001)

Abakumov, Sergej Ivanovič (1890–1949)

Abbéville, Claude d', O.F.M. cap. (d.1616)

Abbon de Fleury (940/45–1004 A.D.)S

Abbott, *Rev.* Edwin (1838–1926)

Abboud, Peter F. (b.1931)

Abbt, Thomas (1738–1766)

Abe, Isamu (b.1919)

Abegg, Emil (1885–1962)

Abeghian, Artasches (1878–1955)

Abel, Carl (1837–1906)

Abel, Fritz (b.1939)K

Ābele, Anna (1881–1975)S

Abela, Leonard, Bishop of Sidon (d.1605)

Abelard, Peter (1079–1142)

Abeles, Ronald P. (b.1944)

Abel-Rémusat, *see* Rémusat, J. P. Abel

Abendana, Isaac (d.1699)

Abercrombie, David (1909–1992)E

Abernathy, Robert H. (b.1924)

Abhyankar, Kashinath Vasudev (1880–1976)

Abinal, *Père* Antoine (1829–1887)

Ablancourt, Nicholas Perrot d' (1660-1743)

Abraham, Roy Clive (1890–1963)E

Abraham, Werner (b.1936)K

Abraham de Balmes, *see* de Balmes

Abraham Ibn Ezra, *see* Ibn ᶜEzra, Avrāhām

Abrahamowicz, Roger D. (b.1933)

Abrahamowicz, Zygmunt (1923–1990)

Abramson, Arthur S(eymour, b.1925)

Abramson, Shraga (b.1915)

Abresch, Petrus (1736–1812)

Abreu y Bertodano, Félix José (1700–1775)

Abril, Pedro-Simón (1530–1600)S

Abū al-Aswad ad-Du'alī, Ẓālim ibn ᶜAmr (c.15/607–69/688)S

Abū l-Faraǧ, Gregory (*called* Bar Hebraeus, 1225/26–1286)

Abū l-Faraǧ, Hārūn, *see* Hārūn ibn al-Faraǧ

Abū ᶜAlī al-Fārisī, *see* Fārisī, Abū ᶜAlī al-

Abū ᶜAlī al-Qālī, *see* al-Qālī

Abudiente, Moseh (1602–1688)

Abū l-Feda (1273–1331)

Abū Ḥayyān, Aṯīr ad-Dīn Muḥammad ibn Yūsuf al-Andalusī al-Ǧarnāṭī (d.745/1344)S

Abū Isḥāq, *see* Ibn ᶜEzra, Avrāhām

Abū ᶜUbayd, al-Qāsim ibn Sallām (154/770–224/838)S

Abū ᶜUbayda, Maᶜmar ibn al-Muṯannā (210/738– 207/822 or 213/828)S

Ac(c)arisio, Alberto (*alias* degli
   Accarigi, c.1440–1523)S
Accursius, Francis (13th cent. A.D.)
Acevedo, Juan de, O.F.M. (1551–
   1624)
Ach, Narziß Kaspar (1870–1937)
Achard, Pierre (1943–1997)
Achillini, Giovanni Filoteo (1466–
   1538)
Ackermann, Paul (1812–1846)S
Acosta, Cristóbal de (fl.1587;
   d.1594?)
Acosta, José de, S.J. (1540–1600)
Acosta, José de (1911–1994)
A(c)quaviva, Claude (1542–1615)
Acuña, Cristobal de (*also* Cristoval,
   1597–1675)
Adair, James (c.1709–1783)
Adair, James, *see* Phillips, *Sir* Richard
Adam du Petit Pont, *see* Adam of
   Balsham
Adam of Balsham "Parvipontanus"
   (*alias* Adam du Petit-Pont, 1105?–
   ante 1159)S
Adam of Rotweil, *see* Rot, Adam
Adam of Veleslavín, Daniel (1546–
   1599)
Adam (Quirinus) Wodeham (1298?–
   1358)
Adam, Alexander (1741–1809)
Adam, (Quirin, François) Lucien
   (1833–1918)S
Adam, Nicolas (1716–1809)
Adamczewski, Henri (b.1929)E
Adamec, Přemysl (b.1931)
Adams, Daniel (pseud. Dudley
   Leavitt, 1773–1864)
Adams, Eleanor Nathalie (fl.1914–
   1917)

Adams, James, S.J. (1737–1802)
Adams, John Quincey, Jr. (6th
   President of the United States,
   1767–1848)
Adams, Richard N. (b.1939)
Adams, *Sir* Thomas (1586–*post*
   1625)
Adamska-Sałaciak, Arleta (b.1957)
Adamzik, Kirsten (b.1955)K
Adamson, James (1797–1875)
Addison, James (1672–1719)
Adelaar, W.F.H. (Willem, b.1948)
Adelard of Bath (c.1090–*post* 1160)
Adelung, Friedrich (Georg, von,
   1768–1842)
Adelung, Johann Christoph (1732–
   1806)S, E
Adler, Alfred (1870–1937)
Adler, Mortimer J(erome, 1902–*post*
   1992)
Admoni, Vladimir Grigor'evič
   (1909–1993)K
Adnes, Michel (b.1949)
Adodurov, Vasilij Evdoimovič (1709–
   1780)
Adōnīm ha-Lēwī, *see* Ibn Labraṭ
Adontz, Nikolaj (d.1942)
Adorno, Theodor W(iesengrund,
   alias Theodor Wiesengrün, 1903–
   1969)
Adrados, Francisco Rodriguez
   (b.1922)
Adrian, Johann Valentin (1793–18??)
Adriani, Nicolaus (1865–1926)
Aedler, Martin (*also* Edler, Eagle,
   Aquila, *possibly* Oettler, 1643–
   1724)
Äimä, Franz Gustaf (1875–1936)S

Aegidius Romanus, *see* Giles of
Rome
Aelfric (c.945–c.1020)S
Aelius Dionysius, *see* Dionysius of
Halicarnassus
Aelius Herodianus (2nd cent. A.D.)
Aeschylus (525/24–456 B.C.)
Ælfric of Eynsham (fl.987–1010)E
Æthelred (968?–1016)
Åfali, Tor (b.1955
Agard, Frederick B(rowning, 1907–
1993)
Agassiz, Louis (1807–1873)
Agata, Benedetto de (1754–1793)
Aggavaṃsa (12th cent. A.D.)S
Aggemark, Per (1905–1996)
Aginsky, Burt W. (b.1905)
Agreda, Antonio de (1714–1785)
Agrell, Jan (181–1947)E
Agrell, Sigurd (d.1942?)
Agricola, Georg (1494–1555)
Agricola, Mikael (Michel, *bishop*,
1510?–1557)
Agricola, Rodolphus (Rudolphus
Frisius, *alias* Roelof Huysman,
1443/44–1485)
Agrippa, Henry Cornelius (*alias*
Agrippa of Nettesheim, (Cornelius)
Heinrich, 1486–1535)
Agroecius (5th cent. A.D.)
Aguesseau, Henri François d'
(1668–1751)
Aguilar, Esteban de (1606–1668?)
Aguilar, Juan de (*vicecura*, fl.1690)
Aguilar, Juan Ignacio de, S.J. (1716–
1799)
Aguilar, Mosseh Rephael de (c.1625–
1679)

Aguilar, Tomás, O.P. (1618/19–
1676)
Aguilar y Claramunt, Simón (19th
cent.)
Aguilar y Lozado, Luis José
(anagram of Diego Antonio
degures supplied.J. (1715–1768)
Agustí, *Fray* Miquel (1560–1630)
Agustín, Antonio (Augustinus, 1517–
1586)
Aẖfaš al-Aṣġar, Abū l-Ḥasan ʿAlī ibn
Sulaymān, al- ("junior", 235/849–
315/927)S
Aẖfaš al-Awsaṭ, Abū l-Ḥasan Saʿīd
ibn Masʿada, al- ("middle", d.
c.215/830)S
Aẖfaš al-Kabīr ("senior", teacher of
Sībawayhi)
Ahl(e), Johann Rudolf (1625–1673)
Ahlqvist, (Carl) August (Engelbert,
1826–1889)S
Ahlqvist, Anders (b.1944)
Ahlström, Anna (1863–1943)
Ahlwardt, Christian Wilhelm
(d.1945?)
Ahmad, Yusof (1900–1980)
Ahn, Johann Franz (1796–1865)
Ahrens, Heinrich Ludolf (1809–
1881)
Ahrens, Wolfgang P(eter, b.1940)
Ahven, Heino (1919–1988)
Aichinger, Carl Friedrich (1717–
1782)S
Aickin, Joseph (fl.1693)
Aiken, Howard Hathaway (1900–
1973)
Aiken, Janet Ruth Rankin (1892–
1944)
Aikhenvald, Alexandra (b.1957)

Aimericus (fl.1086)S
Ainsle, Douglas (1865–1953)
Ainsworth, Henry (1571–1622?)
Ainsworth, William? (fl.1674–1687)
Airila, Martti (1878–1953)
Aisy, Jean (13th cent.)
Aisy, Jean d' (fl.1680s)
Aitchison, Jean (b.1938)
Aitken, Adam James ("Jack", 1921–1998)
Aizitarte, José Maria (1751–1809)
Aizkibel, José-Francisco (1798–1865)
Ajdukiewicz, Kazimierz (1890–1963)E
Ajetti, Idriz (b.1917)
Ājurrūm al-Samhājī, Ibn al- (1273–1323)
Akamatsu, Tsutomu ("Steve", b.1936)
Akattiyam (work attributed to Agastya, *see* HSK I, p.192)
Akinnaso, F. Niyi (b.1946)
Akira, Óta (b.1917)
Akiyashi, Toìdoì (b.1915)
Akmajian, Adrian (1944–1983)
Aksakov, Konstantin Sergeevič (1817–1860)
Alabaster, William (1567–1640)
Alain de Lille (1114–1202)S
Alajouanine, Théophile (1890–1980)
Alanus, Hans Jensen (1563–1631)
Alamán, Lucas (1792–1853)
Alarcos García, Emilio (1895–1986)
Alarcos Llorach, Emilio (1922–1998)E
Alardus of Amsterdam (fl.1539)
Albano Leoni, Federico (b.1941)
Alber(us), Erasmus (c.1500–1553)

Alberdi, Juan Bautista (1810–1884)
Alberdingk Thijm, Josephus Albertus (1820–1889)
Alberic de Paris (12th cent. A.D.)
Alberic of Montecassino (fl.1057–1088)
Albert the Great, *see* Albertus Magnus S
Albert of Saxony (c.1316–1390)S
Albert, Ethel Mary (b.1918)
Albertanus of Brescia (fl.13th cent.)
Alberti, Joannes (1698–1762)
Alberti, Leon Battista (1404–1472)
Alberti di Villanuovo, Francesco d' (1737–1800)
Albert(i)us, Laurentius (c.1540–1585)
Albert-Buisson, François (1881–1961)
Albertus Magnus (Albert von Lauingen, *Graf* von Bollstädt, 'Doctor universalis', c.1193–1280)S
Albinus (2nd cent. A.D.)
Albomoz, *Frei* Juan de, O.P. (17th cent.?)
Albrecht, Erhard (b.1925)
Albrecht, Heinrich Christoph (1763–1800)
Albrecht, Erhard (b.1925)K
Albrecht, Jörn (b.1939)K
Albrecht of Halberstadt (c.1180–post 1251)
Albright, Robert William (1913–1972)
Albright, William Foxwell (1891–1970?)
Alcalá, Pedro de, O.E.S.H. (b. c.1455; fl.1491–1505)

Alcalá, Venceslada, Antonio (1883–1955)

Alcázar, Bartolomé de (1648–1721)

Alcedo, *Coronel* Antonio de (fl.1786–1789)

Alciatus, Andreas (1492–1550)

Alcide de Bonnecase, Robert, sieur de Saint-Maurice (fl.1672)

Alcock, Rutherford (1809–1897)

Alcover, Antoni Maria (1862–1932)E

Alcuin (of York, *abbot* of Tours, c.735–804)S

Aldama y Guevara, Joseph Augustín de (17th cent.)

Alden, Abner (1758–1820)

Alden, Joseph (1807–1885)

Alden, Rev. Timothy, Jr. (1771–1839)

Aldhelm (c.700 A.D.)

Aldrete, Bernardo de (1565–1645)

Aldrete, José de, S.J. (1560–1641)

Aldrich, Henry (1647–1710)

Aldrisius, Robertus (*alias* Robert Aldridge, c.1495–1566)

Alea Abadía, *Abate* José Miguel (fl.1786–1826)

Aleksandrov, A(leksandr) I(vanovič, 1861–1917)

Alemán, Mateo (1547–1615)

Alemand, Louis-Augustin (1653–1728)

Alemany, Lorenzo de (1779–1855)S

Alemany Bolufer, José (1866–*post* 1921)

Alembert, Jean-Baptiste Le Rond, *dit* d' (1717–1783)S

Al-George, Sergiu (d.1982)

Alaverdov, Konstantin A. (1883–1946)

Alessandri d'Urbino, Giovanni Mario (fl.1560)

Alexander Nequam (Neckam, 1154–1220)S

Alexander of Aphrodisias (fl.198–211 A.D.)

Alexander of Hales (1175–1245)

Alexander of Villa-Dei, *see* Alexandre de Villedieu

Alexander, Caleb (1755–1828)

Alexander, Franz (1865–1964)

Alexander, Henry (1890–1975)S

Alexandre de Rhodes, le *Père* (1591–1660)S

Alexandre de Villedieu (= Alexander of Villa-Dei, c.1170–c.1250)S

Alexandre, Pierre (1922–1994)

Alexandrians, The (late 3rd–early 1st cent. B.C.)S

Alexi, Ioan (1801–1863)

Alffó, Ireneo (1741–1797)

Alfieri, Vittorio (1749–1803)S

Alfonso X of Spain ('el Sabio', 1221–1284)

Alford, Danny Keith Hawkmoon (*alias* Dan Moonhawk, 1946–2002)

Alford, Henry (1810–1871)

Alfred, *King* ('the Great', 848–899 A.D.)

Algarotti, Francesco (1712–1764)S

Algeo, James E(dward, b.1939)

Algeo, John (Thomas, b.1930)

Alger, Israel, Jr. (1787–1825)

Alibert, Jean Louis (1766–1837)

Alighieri, Dante, *see* Dante Alighieri

ᶜAlī Ibn Ḥamza, Abū l-Qāsim, (d.375/986)

Alisjahbana, Sutan Takdir (b.1908)

Alcalá-Zamora, Niceto (1877–1949)
Allain, Ernest, *chanoine* (1847–1902)
Allard, Jean-Paul (b.1940)
Allde, John (fl.1555–1592)
Allen, Alexander (1814–1842)
Allen, Cynthia Louise (b.1951)
Allen, Edward Archibald (1843–*post* 1897)
Allen, Harold Byron (1902–1988)S
Allen, Hope Emily (1883–1960)
Allen, John Patrick Brierley (b.1936)
Allen, Joseph Henry (1824–19??)
Allen, W(illiam) Sidney (b.1918)
Allerton, David J(ohn, b.1947)
Alliacus, Petrus, *see* Pierre d'Ailly
Allony, Nehemia (1906–*post* 1980)
Al-Marbawi, Mohammad Idris (1893–1989)
Allport, Floyd H. (1890–1978)
Allport, Gordon Willard (1897–1967)
Allouez, Claude Jean, S.J. (1613–1689)
Almenara, Juan Bardaxí y (d.1586)
Alonso de la Vera Cruz (fl.1572)
Alonso, Amado (1896–1952)S, N
Alonso, Dámaso (1898–1990)
Alonso, Juan, O.F.M. (16th cent.)
Alonso de Herrera, Fernand (c.1462–1527)
Alonso de los Ruyzes de Fontecha, Juan (1560–1620)
Alonso y Ocón, Juan (d.1638)
Alpatov, Vladimir Mixajlovič (b.1945)
Alquen, Richard d' (b.1933)K
Alsdorf, Ludwig (1904–1978)
Alsted, Johann Heinrich (1588–1638)
Alston, Robin C(arfrae, b.1933)

Altamirano, Christophe (d.1700)
Altbauer, Mosze (1904–1998)
Altenstaig, Ioannes (c.1470–*post* 1523)
Altenstein, Carl, *Freiherr* vom Stein zum (1770–1840)
Alter, Franz Carl (1749–1804)
Althamer, Andreas (d.1564)
Althaus, Hans Peter (b.1939)K
Althaus, L. H. (fl.1909–1914)
Altheim, Franz (1898–1976)
Althoff, Friedrich (1839–1908)
Althusser, Louis (1918–1990)
Altïnsarïn, Ibrahim (1841–1889)
Altman, Maria Cristina Fernandes Sales ("Cristina", b.1954)
Altmann, Gabriel (b.1931)K
Altoma, Salih J. (b.1929)
Alton, Reginald Ernest (1919–2003)
Alunno, Francesco (*alias* Francesco del Bailo, 1484?–1556)S
Alvar(-López), Manuel (1923–2001)E
Alvar Ezquerra, Manuel (b.1950)
Alvarado, *Fray* Francisco, O.P. (d.1603)
Alvarado, Lisandro (1876–1929)
Álvares, Emmanuel, S.J.(*or* Manuel, 1526–1582)
Alvares, Joseph, S.J. (d.1743)
Álvarez Rixo, José Agustín (1746–1883)
Alvarus of Cordoba (d.861)
Alverny, Marie Thérèse d' (1903–1991)
Alvre, Paul (b.1920)
Amacker, Réné (b.1942)
Amaduzzi, Giovanni Cristoforo (1740–1792)

Amama, Sixtinus (1593–1629)
Amano, Masachiyo (b.1950)
Amaral, Diego de (late 18th cent.)
Amaral, Prudêncio, S.J. (1675–1715)
Amarasiṃa (4th cent A.D.)S
Ambrogini, Angelo, *see* Poliziano
Ambrogio, Teseo (1469–c.1540)
Ambrosius, St. (Aurelius Ambrosius,
  c.340–397 A.D.)
Amelung, Arthur (1840–1874)
Amelung, Friedrich (1842–1909)
Amelung, Karl Ludwig (1769–1823)
Ament, Karl (Wilhelm, 1876–19??)
Amenta, Niccolò (1659–1759)S
Amiguet, Jerónimo (fl.1450)
Amirova, Tamara Aleksandrovna
  (b.1928)
Amman, Johann Conrad (1669–
  1724)E
Ammann, Hermann (1911–1970)
Ammann, Hermann (Joseph
  Ferdinand, 1885–1956)
Ammer, Karl (1911–1970)
Ammianus, Marcellinus (d. c.400
  A.D.)
Ammon, Ulrich (b.1943)K
Ammonius Hermiae (Gk. Ammónios
  Hermeíou, *ante* 445–517/526
  A.D.)S
Ammonius Sakkas (175–242 A.D.)
Amor Meilán, Manuel (1867–1933)
Amos, Ashley Crandell (1951–1989)
Ampère, Jean-Jacques (Antoine,
  1800–1864)S
Ampzing, Samuel (1590–1632)
Amsler, Mark E(ugene, b.1949)
Amsterdam, Nicolas of, *see* Nicolas
  of Amsterdam
Amsterdamska, Olga (b.1953)

Amthor, Eduard (1820–1884)
Amunátegui, Gregorio Víctor (1830–
  1899)
Amunátegui, Miguel Luis (1828–
  1888)
Amyot, Jacques (1513–1595)
Anan'ev, Boris Gerasimovič (1907–
  1972)
Anaximenes of Lampsakos (Gr.
  Anaximénēs ho Lampsakēnos,
  fl.4th cent. B.C.)S
'Anbārī, Abū Bakr Muḥammad ibn
  al-Qāsim, al- (271/885–328/940)
'Anbārī, Abū l-Barakāt ᶜAbd ar–
  Raḥmān ibn Muḥammad al-
  (d.577/1187)
Anchieta, José (Joseph) de, S.J.
  (1534–1597)E
Anchinoander (*alias* Wittmann?),
  Heinrich Cornelius (fl.1616)
Ancona, Paolo (20th cent.?)
Andersen, Dines (1861–1940)
Andersen, Henning (b.1934)
Andersen, Poul (Max Henrik, 1901–
  1985)S
Andersen, Vilhelm (1864–1953)
Anderson, Arthur J. O. (1907–1996)
Anderson, Benedict O'Gorman
  (b.1936)
Anderson, John M(athieson, b.1941)
Anderson, Keith O. (b.1934)K
Anderson, Nikolaj Ivanovič (1845–
  1905)
Anderson, Samuel W. (b.1929)
Anderson, Stephen R(obert, b.1943)
Andersson, Helge (1923–1997)
Andler, Charles (1866–1933)
Andrade, Antonio, S.J. (d.1732)
Andrade, Manuel Juan (1885–1941)S

Antinucci, Francesco (b.1947)
Antiochus of Ascalon (130/120–68
 B.C.)
Antipater (fl. 2nd cent. A.D.)
Antiphon (c.480 B.C.)
Antisthénes (444–368 B.C.)
Antoine, Gérald (b.1915)
Anton, Konrad Gottlob (1745–1841)
Antoni, Carlo (1896–1959)
Antonini, Annibale (1702–1755)
Antonio de Ciudad Real, see Ciudad
 Real, Antonio de
Antonio, Nicolás (1617–1684)
Antonius Gnipho, see Gnipho,
 Antonius
Antonsen, Elmer H(arold, b.1929)K
Antos, Gerd (b.1949)K
Anttila, Raimo (Aulis, b.1935)
Anusiewicz, Janusz (1946–2000)
Aoun, Joseph E. (b.1953)
Āpadeva (17th cent.)S
Aparicio, José (c.1848–c.1925)
Apel, Karl Otto (b.1922)
Apelt, Walter (b.1925)K
Apfelstedt, Friedrich (1859–1882)
Apion (Gk. Apíōn, 1st cent. A.D.)
Apollodorus of Athens (c.180–c.120
 B.C.)S
Apollodorus of Pergamon (c.105 –23
 B.C.)S
Apollonius Dyscolus (c.110–175
 A.D.)S
Appel, Karol (Julianovič, 1857–1930)
Appendini, Franceco Maria (1769–
 1837)
Applegate, Joseph R. (b.1925)
Appleyard, John Whittle (1814–
 1874)
Apresjan, Jurij D(erenikovič, b.1930)

Aptekar', Valerian Borisovič (1899–
 1937)
Apuleius (120–155 A.D.)
Aquaviva, Claudio, S.J. (1585–1629)
Aquila, Antonio de, O.F.M. (d.1679)
Aquila, Romanus (4th cent. A.D.)
Aquinas, St. Thomas, see Thomas
 Aquinas
Aquino Cortés, Gerónimo Tomàs de
 (17th cent.?)
Ara, Fray Domingo de, O.P. (fl.1545;
 d.1572)
Arabski, Janusz (b.1939)
Aragona , Alonso de (Aragão, Afonso
 de), S.J. (1585–1629)
Aralica, Ivan (b.1930)
Araujó, Antonio de, S.J. (1566–1632)
Araujo, Fernando (1857–1914)
Araujo, Lourenço, S.J. (d.1745)
Araujo y Gómez, Fernando (1857–
 1915)
Arbolí, Juan José (1795–1863
Arbois de Jubainville, (Marie) Henri
 d' (1827–1910)S
Arbouse-Bastide, Paul (1899–19??)
Archaimbault, Sylvie (b.1957)
Archbell, James (1798–1866)
Archenholtz, Johann Wilhelm von
 (1745–1812)
Archivolti, Samuel (1515–1611)
Arct, Michal (1840–1916)
Arct, Stanislaw (1818–1900)
Arden, A. H. (1841–1897)
Arct, Stanislaw (1884–1963)
Arends, Jacobus Tarcisius Gerardus
 ("Jacques", 1952–2005)
Arendt, Carl (1838–1902)
Arendt, Hannah (1902–1991)
Arens, Hans (1911–2003)K

Arensberg, Conrad M(aynadier, b.1910)
Aresti Martínez de Aguilar, Cristóbal, O.S.B. (bishop of Asunción, 1629–1635)
Aretino, *see* Bruni Arentino, Leonardo
Arewa, E. Ojo (b.1935)
Argote, Jerónimo Contador de (1676–1749)S
Argote de Molina, Gonzalo (1548–1596)
Arias Montano, Benito (1527–1598)
Aribov, Vasil (1789–1947)
Arigov, Tojan (1870–1939)
Arisaka, H. (1908–1952)
Aristar, Anthony (Manuel) Rodrigues (b.1936?)
Aristarchus (of Samothrace, c.217–c.145 B.C.)S
Ariste, (Elhunyt) Paul(s) (1905–1990)S
Aristeides (2nd cent. B.C.)
Aristippus, Henricus (archdean of Catania, c.1100–1170)
Aristonicus (fl. 1st cent. B.C.–1st cent. A.D.)
Aristophanes (of Byzantium, c.257–180 B.C.)S
Aristotle (of Stageria, 384–322 B.C.)S
Arithmaeus, Valentin (1587–1620)
Armstrong, Edward (1846–1928)
Armstrong, Lilias Eveline (1882–1937)E
Armstrong, Robert Gelston (1917–1987)E
Arnauld (or Arnault), Antoine (1612–1694)S

Arndt, Ernst Moritz (1769–1860)
Arndt, Horst (b.1929)K
Arndt, Johannes (1555–1621)
Arngart, Olof (1908–1997)
Arnold, Andreas (1656–1694)
Arnold, Christian (1627–1685)
Arnold, Friedrich August (d.1869)
Arnold, George Feversham (b.1914)
Arnold, Johann Franz (fl.1826–1847)
Arnold, Matthew (1822–1888)
Arnold, Theodor (1683–1761)
Arnold, *Rev.* Thomas Kerchever (1800–1853)
Arnoldi, Bartholomäus, *see* Bartholomäus de Usingen
Arnolfini, Marcos Antonio (1674–1748)
Arnoud, Émile (Jule François, 1898–1977)
Arnovick, Leslie K. (b.1957)
Arntz, Helmut (1912–1985?)
Aron, Albert William (1886–1945)
Arona, Juan de (pseud. of Pedro Paz Soldán Unánue)
Aronson, Howard Isaac (b.1936)
Aronstein, Philipp (1862–1942)
Arps, Bernard ("Ben", b.1961)
Arriaga, Emiliano (1844–1919)
Arrivé, Michel (b.1936)
Arronchos, João, O.F.M. (fl.1739)
Ars Ambianensis (anon. Lat. grammar, 8th-9th cent.)S
Ars Ambrosiana (anon. Lat. commentary, *ante* 700 A.D.)S
Ars Bernensis (anon. mid-8th cent. grammatical ms.)S
Ars Berolinensis (anon. Lat. commentary, 9th/10th cent.)S

Ars Brugensis (anon. Lat. commentary, 11th/12th cent.)S

Ars Laureshamensis (anon. Lat. commentary, 10th cent.)S

Arsac, Jean (1932–1994)

Artabe, Gabriel de (fl.1732)

Arthur, *Prince* (1486–1502)

Artopaeus, Petrus (*alias* Becker, Peter, 1520–1566)

Artrey, Jean-Louis (Ratier *dit)* d' (1883–1938)

Artsrouni, Georges (d.1960?)

Artymovyč, Agenor (1879–1935)

Arumaa, Peeter (1900–1982)

Arunmuka, Návalar (1822–1879)

Arveiller, Raymond (1914–1997)

Arzápalo Marín, Ramón (b. c.1948)

Ascham (Ask[e]ham), Roger (1515–1568))S

Asclepiades (of Myrlea, 1st cent. B.C.)S

Ascoli, Graziadio Isaia (1829–1907)S, E

'Ašʿarī, ʿAlī al- (874–936)

Asenova, Petja (.1941)

Ash, John (1724?–1779)

Ash, Mitchell (b. c.1945)

Asher, David (1818–1890)

Asher, James Edward (b.1931)

Asher, R(onald) E(aton, "Ron", b.1926)E

Ashmole, Elias (1617–1692)

Askedal, John Ole (b.1942)K

Asklebiades of Myrlea (1st cent. B.C.)

Ashmole, Elias (1617–1692)

Ashworth, E(arline) J(enny, b.1939)

Asín Palacios, Miguel (1871–1944)

Askedal, John Ole (b.1942)

Asklepiades of Myrlea (c.150–50 B.C.)

Aslakssøn, Cort (*alias* Cunradus Aslacus Bergensis, 1564–1624)

Aṣmaʿī, Abū Saʿīd ʿAbd al-Malik ibn Qurayb al- (122/740–213/828)S

Ašmarin, Nikolaj (1881–1937)

Ašnin, F. D. (1922–2000)

Asper (Lat. Asporius, c. 600 A.D.)S

Ast, (Georg Anton) Friedrich (1778–1841)

Astarabāḏî, Raḍī d-Dīn Muḥammad ibn al-Ḥasan al- (c.624/1226–c.700/1300)S

Astarloa y Aguirre, Pedro Pablo de (1752–1806)

Aster, Ernst von (1880–1948)

Aston, William George (1841–1911)S

Astore, Francesco Antonio (1742–1799)

Ašxamaf, Dant Alijevič (d.1946)

Athenaeus (c.200 A.D.)

Atkins, Samuel De Coster (b.1910)

Atkinson, Harold Waring (1868–1946)

Atkinson, James Blakely (b.1934)

Atran, Scott (b.1952)

Atwood, Elmer Bagby (1906–1963)S

Aubert de Sorgue, Esprit (fl.1633)

Aubery, Joseph, S.J. (1673–1755)

Aubertin, Simon Alexandre Ernest (1825–1865)

Aubin, Hermann (1885–1969)

Aubin, Joseph Marius Alexis (1802–1891)

Aubin, Michel (1923–1996)

Aubreton, Robert Henri (1909–1980)

Aubrey, John (1626–1697)

Auden, Wystan Hugh (1907–1973)
Audouin, Édouard (1864–19??)
Audran, Prosper-Gabriel (1744–1819)
Audumbarāyaṇa (*ante* 5th cent. B.C.)S
Auerbach, Erich (1892–1957)
Auerbach, Felix (1856–1933)
Aufrecht, (Simon) Theodor (1821–1907)S
August, Ernst Ferdinand (1795–1870)
Augustine of Canterbury, St. (d. c.604)
Augustinus, Antonius (fl.1554)
Augustinus, Aurelius, St. ("of Hippo", 354–430)S
Aulus Gellius, *see* Gellius, Aulus
Auraicept na nEces (anon. Irish 7th or 8th cent. text)S
Aureol, Pierre (c.1280–1322)
Aurifaber, Andreas (*alias* Goldschmidt, 1512–1559)
Aurifaber, Johannes (14th cent.)
Aurispa, Giovanni (c.1375–1459)
Aurivillius, Carl (1717–1786)
Auroux, Sylvain (b.1947)
Austerlitz, Robert (Paul, 1923–1994)E
Austin, John Langshaw (1911–1960)S, E
Austin, William (Mandeville, 1914–1968)
Autenrieth, Georg (fl.1899)
Avanesov, Ruben Ivanovič (1902–1982)S
Ávarezu Rixo, José Agustín (1796–1883)

Avenarius, Johannes (*alias* Johann Habermann, 16th cent.)
Avenarius, Richard (Heinrich Ludwig, 1843–1896)
Avendaño, Joaquín de (1812–*post* 1871)S
Aventin(us), Joannes (*alias* Turmair, Johannes, 1477–1534)S
Averroes (1126–1198)
Avicenna (ibn Sīna, 980–1037)
Ávila, Francisco de, O.F.M. (17th cent.?)
Avis, Walter Spencer (1919–1979)S
Avolio, Corrado (1843–1905)S
Awaka, Kiyoshi (1936–1988)
Avram, Mioara (fl.1950–1997)
Ax, Wolfram (b.1944)
Axelos, Kostas (b.1924)
Axmanova, Ol'ga Sergeevna (1908–1991)
Axutina,Tat'jana N. (b.1941)
Axvlediani, Georgi (1887–1973)
Ayala, Manuel de (fl.1673)
Ayala Manrique, Juan Francisco (d.1753)
Ayer, *Sir* Alfred (Jules, 1910–1989)
Ayer, Nicolas-Lous Cyprien (1825–1884)
Ayliff, John (1797–1862)
Aymard, André (1900–1964)
Az, Aḥmad al- (282/895–370/980)S
Azkue, Resurrección Maria (1888–1919)
Azpilicuento Navarra, *see* Navarra, Martin de Azpilicuento

B.

Baader, Emil O. (d.2004)

Babcock, Earle Brownell (1881–1935)

Babić, Stjepan (b.1925)

Babin, Jean (1905–1978)

Babington, Benjamin Guy (1794–1866)

Babukič, Vjekoslav (1812–1875)

Bacchini, Benedetto (1651–1721)

Bach, Adolf (1890–1972)S

Bach, Emmon W(erner, b.1929)

Bachelard, Gaston (1882–1962)

Bachellery, Édouard (1907–1988)

Bacher, Wilhelm (Vilmos, 1850–1913)

Bachmann, Albert (1863–1934)

Bachmann, Andreas (1600–1656)

Bachmann, Armin (b.1906)

Bachmann, Konrad (1572–1646)

Bachmann, Luděk (1931–1987)

Backer, Aloys de (1823–1883)

Backer, Augustin de (1809–1873)

Bacmeister, Hartwig Ludwig Christian (*alias* Ljudwig Ivanovič, 1730–1806)

Bacon, Francis (*Lord* Verulam and *Viscount* St Albans, 1561–1626)S, E

Bacon, Leonard (1887–1954)

Bacon, Nicholas (1509–1579)

Bacon, Roger, *see* Roger Bacon

Bacquet, Paul (Henri Charles Louis, b.1925)

Bacqueville de la Potherie de Roy, Claude Charles (1663–1736)

Băčvarov, Janko (b.1932)

Bade, Josse (Jodocus Badius Ascensius, 1642–1535)

Badawi, el-Said Muhamed (b.1929)E

Baden, Jacob (1735–1804)

Bader, Françoise (*née* Bernard, b.1932)

Badge, George Percy (fl.1840)

Bäbler, Johann Jakob (1836–1900)

Badía y Leblich, Mariano (1766?–1818?)

Baecker, Louis Benoît Désiré de (1814–1896)

Baer, Seligman Isaac (1825–1897)

Baerentzen, Per (b.1940)K

Baeteman, *Father* Joseph Émile (1880–1938)

Baggesen, Jens (1764–1826)

Baggioni, Daniel (1945–1998)

Bahder, Karl von (1856–1932)

Bahl, Kali Charan (b.1927)

Bahner, Werner (b.1927)K

Bahnsen, Julius Friedrich August (1830–1881)

Baier, Hieronymus (c.1545)

Bailey, Beryl Loftman (1920–1977)S

Bailey, Charles-James N(ice, b.1926)K

Bailey, (*Sir*) Harold (Walter, 1899–1996)

Bailey, Nathan(iel) (*ante* 1691–1742)S

Bailey, Richard Weld (b.1939)

Bailey, (Thomas) Graham (1872–1942)

Bailey, Rufus William (1793–1863)

Bailey, Samuel (1791–1870)

Baillarger, Jules Gabriel François (1806–1891)
Baillet, Auguste (1834–1923)
Bailly, Anatole (c.1830–1913)
Bailly, Louis (1796–1869)
Bails, Benito (1730–1797)
Bain, Alexander (1818–1903)
Bainbridge, John (b.1612?)
Baird, George (18th cent.)
Baird, Spencer (1823–1887)
Baissac, Charles (1831–1892)
Baist, Gottfried (1853–1920)
Bajerowa, Irena (b.1921)
Bąk, Piotr (1911–2000)
Bak, Stanislaw (1900–1981)
Bakalla, Mohammed Hasan (b. c.1950)
Bake, John (1787–1864)
Baker, Carl L(eroy, "Lee", 1939–1997)
Baker, *Rev. Sir* Henry William (1821–1877)
Baker, James Addison (b.1925)
Baker, Mark Cleland (b.1959)
Baker, Richard (1568?–1645)
Bakhtin, M. M., *see* Baxtin, M. M.
Bakker, Dirk Miente (1934–1985)
Bakó, Elmér (1915–2000)
Bal. Józef (1928–1992)
Bal, Willy (b.1916)
Balassa, Ivan (1917–2002)
Balassa, József (1864–1945)
Balázs, János (1914–1989)
Balbi, Antonio (*alias* Adriano, 1781–1848)
Balbi, Giovanni, *see* Johannes Balbus
Balbín, Bohuslav (1621–1668)E
Balbín de Unquera, Antonio (1842–1916)

Balch, William Stevens (1806–1887)
Balčíkonis, Juozas (1885–1969)S
Bald, Wolf-Dietrich (b.1942)K
Baldaeus, Pilippus (1632–1672)
Balde, Jacob (1604–1668)
Baldi, Philip (Harold, b.1946)
Baldinger, Kurt (b.1919)
Baldwin, Caleb Cook (fl.1871)
Baldwin, John Denison (1809-1883)
Baleczky, Emil (1919–1981)
Balhared, Gerhard (d.1996)
Balibar, Renée (1915–1998)
Balkevičius, Jonas Zemvaldas (1923–2000)
Ballanche, Pierre Simon (1776–1847)
Ballesteros, Juan Manuel (fl.1827–1845)
Ballot, José Pablo (c.1760–1821)
Balmes, Jaime (1810–1848)
Balmont, Konstantin Dmitri'evič (1867–1943)
Baldwin, James Mark (1861–1934)
Baldwin, William (fl.1547)
Bales, Robert Freed (b.1916)
Ballagi, Mór, *see* Bloch, Moritz
Ballard, Harlan Hoge (1853–1934)
Ballot y Torres, José Pablo (1760?–1821)S
Bally, Charles (1865–1947)
Bally, Gustav (1893–1966)
Baltaxe, Christiane Anna Maria (b.1934)
Balmes, Jaime (1810–1848)
Balmes y Urpiá, Jaime Luciano (1810–1848)S
Ballweg, Joachim (b.1946)K
Balzac, Guez de (fl.1624–1630)
Bamgbose, Ayo (b.1932)
Bammesberger, Alfred (b.1938)K

Bartsch, Karl Friedrich (1832–1888)
Bartsch, Renate (b.1939)
Bartschat, Brigitte (b.1937)K
Baruël, Euchaire (1849–1901)
Barwise, Jon (1942–2000)
Barxudarov, Stepan Grigorevič (1894–1983)
Barzana (Bárcena, Barzena), Afonso de, S.J. (1528–1598)
Bárzana, Afonso de, S.J. (1528–1598)
Barzizza, Gasparino (1360–1430)
Basalenque, *Fray* Diego de (1577–1651)
Basalenque, *Frei* Diego de, O.S.A. (1577–1651)
Basara, Anna (b.1931)
Basara, Jan (b.1929)
Basedow, Johann Bernhard (1723–1790)
Basehart, Harry (Wetherald, b.1910)
Basham, Arthur Llewelyn (1914–1986)
Basile, Giambattista (c.1575–1632)
Basilio, Tomás, S.J. (1582?–1654)
Basilius the Great (c.330–390)
Basilius, Harold Albert (1905–c.1990)
Basire, Issac (1607–1676)
Baskakov, Nikolaj Aleksandrovič (1905–1996)
Baskervill, William Malone (1850–1899)
Bašindžagjan, Levon Gevorkovič (1893–1938)
Baskerville, Alfred (fl.1853–1896)
Baskin, Wade (fl.1959; d. c.1990)

Bassaeus, Nicolaus (d.1599)
Basset, André (1895–1956)
Basset, René (1855–1924)
Basso, Ellen B. (b.1942)
Basso, Keith H. (b.1940)
Bastard, George (1851–1884)
Bastero y Lledó, Antonio (1652–1737)
Bastian, (Philipp Wilhelm) Adolf (1826–1905)
Bastide, Roger (1898–1974)
Bastin, *Abbé* Joseph (1870–1939)
Batalyūī, Abū Muḥammad ᶜAbdallāh ibn Muḥammad ibn as-Sīd al- (444/1052–521/1127)S
Batchelder, William H(oward, b.1940)
Batchelor, John (1854–1944)S, E
Batchelor, Thomas (fl.1809)
Bately, Janet Margaret (b.1932)
Bates, John L. (1910–1995)
Bateson, Gregory (1904–1980)E
Bateson, William (1861–1926)
Bathe, William, S.J. (1564–1614)S
Bathodius, Lukas, the elder (fl.1525)
Bathurst, Ralph (1602–1704)
Batokw, Harun (1889–1949)
Bátori, István S. (b.1935)K
Battaglia, Salvatore (1904–1971)S
Batteux, *Abbé* Charles de (1713–1780)S
Battisti, Carlo (1882–1977)S
Baudoin, Jean (1564–1650)
Baudelaire, Charles (1821–1867)
Baudet, Pierre Joseph (1778–1858)
Baudiš, Josef (d.1948)
Baudius, Dominicus (1561–1613)

Baudouin de Courtenay, Jan (Ignacy Niecisław, = Boduèn de Kurtenè, Ivan Aleksandrovič, 1845–1929)S, E

Baudusch, Renate (*née* Walker, b.1929)K

Bauer, Friedrich (1812–1874)S

Bauer, Gerhard (b.1929)K

Bauer, Gleb M. (1925–1989)

Bauer, Hans (1878–1937)

Bauer, Heinrich (1773–1846)

Bauer, Jaroslav (1924–1969)S

Bauer, (Johann) Heinrich (Ludwig, 1773–1846)S

Bauersfeld, Helmut (1907–*post* 1957)

Baugh, Albert Croll (1891–1981)

Baugh, John (b.1949)

Bauhinus, Casparus (1560–1614/1624)

Bauman, Richard (b.1940)

Baumeister, Karl August (1830–1922)

Baumgärtner, Klaus (b.1931)

Baumgarten, Alexander Gottlieb (1714–1762)

Baumgarten, Hans (19th cent.)

Baumgartner, Alexander, S.J. (1841–1910)

Baunack, Johannes (Fürchtegott, 1854–19??)

Baunack, Theodor (1861–19??)

Baur, Franciscus Johannes (*alias* Frank, 1887–1969)

Baur, Gerhard W. (b.1932)K

Barbeau, Marius (1883–1969)

Bausani, Alessandro (1921–1988)

Bausch, Karl-Heinz (b.1941)K

Bausch, Karl-Richard (b.1939)K

Bavoux, François-Nicolas (1774–1848)

Bawden, Henry Heath (1871–*post* 1910)

Baxter, Richard (1615–1691)

Baxter, William (1650–1723)

Baxtin, Mixail Mixajlovič (1895–1975)E

Bayer, Gottlieb Siegfried (1694–1738)

Bayle, Pierre (1647–1706)E

Bayly, Anselm (1719–1794)

Baynes, Ralph (1505–1559)

Bazán, Bernardo Carlos (b.1939)

Bazell, C(harles) E(rnest, 1909–1984)

Bazin, Antoine Pierre Louis (1799–1863)

Bazin, Louis (b.1920)

Beaglehole, John Caute (1901–1971)

Beaglehole, Pearl (1910–1985?)

Beale, John (1603–1683?)

Beals, Ralph L. (1901–1985)

Beames, John (1837–1902)S

Beardslee, John Walter III (b.1914)

Beattie, James (1735–1803)S, E

Beatty, John (1828–1914)

Beatty, Willard (1891–1961)

Beaufront, Louis (*marquis*) de (1855–1938)

Beaulieux, Louis (1876–1965)

Beaumont, Francis (1584–1616)

Beaumont, Jeanne-Marie Leprince de (1771–1780)

Beauzée, Nicolas (1717–1789)S, E

Bebel(ius), Heinrich (Henricus, c.1472–1518)

Bébian, Auguste (1789–1839)

Becan, Jan (*alias* Joannis Goropius Becanus, 1518–1572)

Beccaria, Cesare (*Marchese* de Bonasena, 1738–1794)S
Bech, Gunnar (1920–1981)S
Becher, Johann Joachim (1635–1682)
Bechert, Johannes (1931–1994)K
Becherer, Johann (fl.1596; d.1616)
Bechstein, Reinhold (1833–1894)
Bechtel, Friedrich (*or* Fritz, 1855–1924)S
Beck, Cave (1623–1706)S
Beck, Johann (1706–1777)
Bečka, J. V. (1903–1992)
Becker, Alton L. (b.1932)
Becker, Carl Heinrich (1876–1933)
Becker, Carl L(otus, 1873–1945)
Becker, Howard S. (b.1928)
Becker, Johann Nikolaus (1773–*post* 1829)
Becker, Karl Ferdinand (1775–1849)S, E
Becker, Marshall H. (1940–1994)
Beckh, Christoph Eugen Hermann 1875–1937)
Beckers, Hartmut (b.1938)K
Bede (Baeda), the Venerable (673–735 A.D.)S
Bedell, George Dudley (b.1940)
Bedell, William (1571–1642)
Bédier, (Charles Marie) Joseph (1864–1938)
Bedingfield, *Sir* Thomas (d.1613)
Bedwell, William (c.1562–1632)S
Beecher, Catharine Esther (1800–1878)
Beedham, Christopher (b.1952)K
Beeke, Hermann von der, *see* Torrentiuis, Hermannus

Beekes, Robert S(teven) P(aul, b.1937)
Beelen, Joannes Theodorus (1807–1884)
Beeler, Madison Scott (1910–1989)
Beer, Johann (1655–1700)
Bees, Nikos Athanasiu (1883–1958)
Beeston, Alfred (Felix Langdon, 1911–1995)
Beets, Nicolaas (1814–1903)
Begemann, Wilhelm (fl.1873–1874)
Behaegel, Pieter (1783–1857)
Behaghel, Otto (1854–1936)S
Behler, Ernst (b.1928)
Behn-Eschenburg, Hermann (1814–1873)
Behnsch, Ottomar (1813–*post* 1862)
Behourt, Jean (d.1620/21)
Behre, Frank (1896–1981)
Behrens, Dietrich (1859–1929)S
Behrns, Johannes Henricus (1803–1883)
Beijer, Jan Coenraad (1786–1866)
Beiler, Benedictus (fl.1731)
Beinhauer, Werner (1896–1983)
Beißner, Friedrich (1905–1977)
Beito, Olav T. (1901–1989)S
Béke, Ö. (1883–1964)
Békésy, Georg von (*alias* György, 1899–1972)
Bekker, (August) Immanuel (1785–1871)
Bekkum, W(outer) Jacques van (b.1954)
Belardi, Walter (b.1928)
Belasco, Simon (b.1918)
Beleckij, Andrej Alexandrovič (1911–1995)
Belić, Aleksandar (1876–1960)S

Bělić, Jaromir (1914–1977)
Bělić, Oldřich (1920–200)
Beling, Ernst Ludwig (1866–1932)
Belinskij, Vissarion Grigor'evič
(1811–1848)
Bell, (Alexander) Graham (1847–
1922)E
Bell, Alexander Melville (1819–
1905)S, E
Bell, Goodloe Harper (1832–1899)
Bella, *Padre* Ardelio della (1654–
1737)
Belleforest, François de (1530–1583)
Bellermann, Johann Joachim (1754–
1842)
Bellermann, Johann Friedrich (1795–
1874)
Belletti, Adriana (b.1954)
Belli, Giuseppe Gioachino (1791–
1863)S
Bellin, Johann (1618–1660)
Bellini, Giovanni Maria (1618–1660)
Bellman, Beryl L. (b.1941)
Bellmann, Günther (b.1929)K
Belmar, Francisco (fl.1897)
Bello, Andrés (1781–1865)S, E
Bellot, Jacques (fl.1580–1590)
Bellugi-Klima, Ursula (b.1931)
Belošapkova, Vera Arsen'eva (1917–
1996)
Belostenec, Ivan (1594–1675)
Bel'skaja, Izabella Kuz'minična
(1928–1964)
Beltrame, Giovanni (1824–1906)
Beltran, Sergio F. (2nd half of 20th
cent.)
Bem, Alfréd Ljudvigovič (1886–
1945)
Bembo, Pietro (1470–1547)S

Ben-Asher, Aharon (10th cent. A.D.)
Benavente, Álvaro de, O.S.A. (1646–
1709)
Ben-Bal'ām, Yehuda (*alias* Abū
Zakariyyā Yaḥyaì ibn Bal'ām, 2nd
half of 11th cent.)
Ben-David, Joseph (1920–1986)
Benary, Albert Agathon (1807–1861)
Benavente, Álvaro de, O.S.A. (1646–
1709)
Benavides, Miguel (Dominican,
1550–1605)
Bendel, Joachim (fl.1585)
Bender, Byron (Wilbur, b.1929)
Bender, Ernest (b.1919)
Bender, Harold Herman (1882–1951)
Bender, Marvin Lionel (b.1934)
Bendor-Samuel, David H. (b.1931)
Bendor-Samuel, John T(heodore)
(b.1929)
Bendsen, Bende (1787–1875)
Bene of Florence (It. Bene da
Firenze, fl.1218; d. *ante* 1242)S
Benecke, Georg Friedrich (1762–
1844)
Benedict, Paul K(ing, 1912–1997)
Benedict, Ruth Fulton (1887–1948)
Benedikt, Vavrinec (1555–1614)S
Benediktsson, Hreinn (b.1928)
Benello, Julian (1962–1988)
Beneš, Eduard (b.1911)K
Benevoglienti, Bartolomeo (d.1486)
Benfey, Theodor (1809–1881)S, E
ben Hanesi'ah, Moses ben Isaac
(13th cent.)
Beni, Paolo (1552?–1625)S
Benito de San Pedro, *padre* Feliu
(1732–1801)

Berreman, Gerald D. (b.1930)
Berry, Francis (b.1915)
Berry, Jack (1918–1982)
Berry, Margaret (b.1940?)
Bertalanffy, Ludwig von (1901–1972)
Berteloot, A. (b.1950)
Bertelsen, H. Hendrik A. (1874–1933)
Bertheau, Ernst (1812–1888)
Berthelot, Pierre Eugène Marcel(l)in, *prieur* de Saint Éloi (1827–1907)
Berthier, Ferdinand (1803–1886)
Berthold, Luise (1891–1983)
Berthold of Regensburg (c.1210–1272)
Berthold von Holle (c.1250)
Bertoldi, Vittorio (1888–1953)S
Berthollet, Charles-Louis, *comte* de (1748–1822)
Bertoni, Giulio (1878–1942)E
Bertoni, Moises (1857–1929)
Bertonio, (Antonio) Ludovico, S.J. (1552–1625)
Bertram, Charles (1723–1765)
Bertrand, Jean-Baptiste (1764–1830)
Bertuch, Friedrich Justin (1747–1822)
Bertūlis, Reinis (1937–1994)
Berynda, Pamvo (1555/60–1632)S
Berzelius, Jons Jacob (1779–1848)
Besarović, Gordana (1936–2000)
Besch, Werner (b.1928)K
Bescherelle, Henri Honoré (1804–1887)
Bescherelle, Louis-Nicolas (1802–1883)S
Beschi, Constanino Giuseppe, S.J. (1680–1747)E

Beslais, Aristide (1888–1973)
Besnier, Pierre, S.J. (1648–1705)
Besold, Christoph (1577–1638)
Best, Karl-Heinz (b.1943)K
Best, Richard Irvine (1872–1959)
Bešta, Theodor (1920–1996)
Besten, Hans den (b.1948)K
Betanzes, *Fray* Pedro de, O.FM. (d.1570)
Beth, Evert Willem (1908–1964)
Betham, *Sir* William (1779–1853)
Betten, Anne (Marie, b.1943)
Bettendorff, João Filippe, S.J. (*alias* Johann Philipp, 1625–1698)
Betti, Emilio (1890–1962)S
Bettinelli, Saverio (1718–1808)S
Betz, Werner (1912–1980)
Beutterich, Peter (1545?–1587)
Bever, Thomas Gordon (b.1939)
Bexterev, Vladimir Mixajlovič, 1857–1927)
Beyer, Franz (1849–c.1935)
Beyer, Klaus (b.1929)K
Beyerman, Hugo (1791–1870)
Beylsmit, Johannes Jurrian (1921–1986)
Beytan, Hermann (1875–*post* 1945)
Bèze, Théodore de (1519–1605)
Bezlaj, France (1910–1993)
Bezold, Carl (1859–1922)
Bezsonov, Petr Alekseevič (1828–1898)
Bezzenberger, Adalbert (1851–1922)
Bhaldraithe, Thomas de (1916–1996)
Bhandarkar, Ramkrishna Gopal (1837–1925)E
Bhartṛhari (c.450–510 A.D.)S, E
Bhaṭṭojīdīkṣīta (late 16th–early 17th cent.)S

Bhāmaha (7th cent. A.D.)
Bhaṭṭojí, Díkṣita (17th cent.)
Bianchetti, Giuseppe (1791–1872)S
Bianchi, Bianco (1839–1896)
Bianchi, Isidoro (1733–1807)
Biard, Pierre, S.J. (1568–1622)
Bibbesworth, see Walter of
    Bibbesworth
Biber, Johann (fl.1566; d. ante 1576)
Bibliander, Theodor (alias Georg
    Buchmann, 1504–1564)
Bichat, Marie-François-Xavier
    (1771–1802)
Bickell, Gustav (1838–1906)
Bickerton, Derek (b.1926)E
Bidez, Joseph (1867–1945)
Bidney, David (b.1906)
Bieder, Gabriel (1410/1415–1495)
Bidwell, Charles Everett (b.1923)
Bielenstein, August Johann Gottfried
    (Latvian: Augusts Bilensteins,
    1826–1907)S
Bieler, Ludwig (1906–1981)
Bielfeld, Hans Holm (1907–1987)
Bielmeier, Roland (b.1943)K
Bierbach, Christine (b. c.1950)
Bierwisch, Manfred (b.1930)K
Biester, Johann Erich (1749–1816)
Biet, Antoine (b.1620)
Biffi, Giovanni Ambrogio (fl.1606)
Biggs, Bruce G. (1921–2000)
Biggs, Lucy T. (d.1994)
Bignon, abbé Jean-Paul (1662–1743)
Bilderdijk, Willem (1756–1831)
Bilec'kyj, Andrij Oleksandrovič
    (1911–1995)
Biligiri, H. S. (b.1925)
Billet, Pierre Paul (fl.1673–1707)
Billeter, Gustav (1873–19??)

Billingham, Richard, see Richard
    Billingham
Billingsley, Martin (fl.1618–1637):
Binchy, Daniel Anthony (1899–
    1989)
Binet, Alfred (1857–1911)
Bingham, William (1835–1873)
Bini, Vincenzi (1775–post 1828)
Bingham, Caleb (1757–1817)
Binnick, Robert I(ra, b.1945)
Binns, John (1772–1860)
Bin-Nun, Jechiel, see Fischer, Jechiel
Binz, Gustav (1865–1951)
Biondelli, Bernardino (1804–1886)S
Biondo, Flavio (of Forli, 1392–
    1463)S
Biran, François-Pierre Gonthier
    Maine de, see Main de Biran,
    François
Birch, Thomas (1705–1766)
Birch-Hirschfeld, Adolf (1849–1917)
Bird, Isaac (fl.1864)
Birdwhistell, Raymond (b.1918)
Binet, Alfred (1857–1911)
Birkeland, H. (1904–1961)
Birken, Sigmund von (1626–1681)
Birlinger, Anton (1834–1891)
Birnbaum, Henrik (b.1925)
Birnbaun, Nathan (1860?–19??)
Birnbaum, Solomon Asher (1891–
    1990)
Birt, Theodor (1852–1933)
Bisang, Walter Alfred (b.1959)
Biscarrat, Félix (19th cent.)
Bischoff, Bernhard (1906–1991)
Bischoff, Karl (1905–1983)
Bischoff, Ludwig Friedrich Christian
    (1794–1867)
Bischoff, Wilhelm (1822–1888)

Bloch, Julia (1903–19??)
Bloch, Moritz (*alias* Mór Ballagi, 1815–1891)
Bloch, Oscar (1877–1937)
Bloch, Sören Nicolaus Johann (1772–1862)
Blok, Dirk Peter (b.1925)
Blommart, Jan (b.1961)
Blondel, Charles Aimé Alfred (1876–1939)
Blondheim, David Simon (1884–1934)
Blondin, Jean-Noël (1753–1832)
Blooah, Charles G. (b. c.1905)
Bloomfield, Leonard (1887–1949)S, E
Bloomfield, Maurice (*alias* Moritz Blumenfeld, 1855–1928)S
Bloomfield, Morton Wilfred (1913–1987)
Blount, Ben(ny) G(arell, b.1940)
Blount, Thomas (1618–1679)
Blümel, Rudolf (1876–1945)
Blümel, Wolfgang (b.1949)K
Blum, Léon (1872–1950)
Blumenbach, Johann Friedrich (1752–1840)
Blumenthal, Arthur L. (b.1936)
Blumer, Herbert (1900–1987)E
Blumstein, Sheila E. (b.1944)
Blund, John (d.1248)
Blund, Robert, *see* Robert Blund
Blundeville, Thomas (fl.1561)
Blust, Robert A. (b.1940)
Bluteau, *Padre* Rafael (1638–1734)
Boag, John (1775–1863)
Boak, Arthur E. R. (1888–1962)
Boas, Franz (1858–1942)S, E
Boas, Hans Ulrich (b.1940)K

Boaistuau, Pierre de (d.1566)
Bobrinsky, George V. (1901?–1985)
Bobrovskij, M. K. (1785–1848)
Boccaccio, Giovanni (1313–1375)
Bochart, Samuel (1599–1667)
Bocheński, Innocentius M(aria, S.J., 1901–1995)
Bochorizh, Adam, *see* Bohorič, Adam
Bock, Carl Alfred (1849–1898)
Bock, Hellmut (1897–1962)
Bocthor, Ellious (1784–1821)
Bodelsen, Carl Adolf (1894–1978)
Bodenstedt, Friedrich (1819–1892)
Bodman, Nicholas C(leaveland, 1913–1997)
Bodin, Jean (1530?–1596)
Bødtker, Adam (Frederik) Trampe (1866–1944)
Bodmer, Johann Jakob (1698–1782)
Boduèn de Kurtené, Ivan Aleksandrovič, *see* Baudouin de Coutenay, Jan
Boeck, Louis B. de, C.I.C.M. (1914–1966)
Boeckh, (Philipp) August (1785–1867)E
Boeckh, (Georg Friedrich) Richard (1824–1907)
Böckler, Georg Andreas (1620?–1687)
Boeder, Winfried (b.1937)
Bödey, József (1918–1998)
Bödiker, Johannes (1641–1695)
Bødtker, Adam Fredrik Trampe (1866–1944)
Boehme, Erich (1879–1937?)
Böhme, Jacob (1575–1624)
Boehmer, Eduard (1827–1906)

Böhtlingk, Otto (Nicolaus von, 1815–1904)S

Boekenoogen, G. J. (1868–1930)

Boer, Cornelis de (1880–1957)

Boer, Henri Gans (1838–1898)

Boerhaave, Herman(n)us (1668–1738)

Böschenstein, Johannes (1472–1540)

Boethius of Dacia (1240/50–*post* 1277)S, E

Boethius (Anicius Manlius Torquatus Severinus, 475–524 A.D.)S

Böhtlingk, Otto von (1815–1904)E

Boetticher, Paul Anton (*pseud.* Lagarde, Paul Anton de, 1827–1891)

Bogatyrev, Petr Grigor'evič (1893–1971)

Bogdan, Joan (1894–1919)

Bogdanov, Aleksandr (1873–1928)

Bogdanov, V. V. (1868–1949)

Bogdanovič, Dimitrije (1930–1986)

Bogorodickij, Vasilij Alekseevič (1957–1941)S

Bogorov, Ivan (1821–1892)

Bøgholm, Niels (1873–1957)

Bogoraz, Vladimir Germanovič (*alias* Waldemar Bogoras; pseud. N. A. and V. C. Tan, 1865–1936)

Bogorodickij, V(asilij) A(lekseevič, 1857–1941)

Bogrea, Vasile (d.1926)

Boguraev, Branimir K. (b.1950)

Boguslavskij, Igor' Mixajlovič (b.1950)

Bogusławski, Andrzej (b1931)

Bohas, Georges (b.1947)

Bohlen, Peter von (1796–1841)

Bohnert, Herbert G(aylord, b.1918)

Bohorič, Adam (c1520–1598)

Bohse, August (1661–1730/42)

Boil y Valero Ramírez, Antonio (1671–1744)

Boileau (Despráux), Nicolas (1636–1711)

Boindin, Nicolas (1676–1751)

Boineburg, Johann Christian, *Freiherr* von (Elector of Mainz, 1622–1672)

Boinvilliers[-Desjardins], Jean Étienne, *dit* Judith Forestier (1764–1830)S

Boirac, Émile (1851–1917)

Boisacq, Émile (1865–1945)

Boisregard, André de (b.1688)

Boissiers de Sauvage, Pierre Augustin (1710–1795)

Boiste, (Pierre) Claude (Victoire, 1765–1824)S

Bokadorova, Natalija (b.1948)

Bolaños, Luis, O.F.M. (d.1629)

Boldyrev, Aleksej V. (1780–1842)

Bolelli, Tristano (1913–2001)

Boléo, Manuel de Paiva (1904–1992)

Boole, George (1815–1864)E

Borfoni, Folchino dei (c.1350–*post* 1401)

Bolhuis, Lambertus van (1741–1826)

Bolinbroke, Henry (1678–1751)

Bolinbroke Mudie, Harold (d.1916)

Bolinger, Dwight L(eMerton, 1907–1992)S

Bolkestein, A. Machtelt (1944–2001)

Bollack, Léon (Moïse, 1859–1919)

Bolland, Gerardus Johannes Petrus Josephus (1854–1922)

Bollée, Annegret (b.1937)K

Boller, Anton (1811–1869)

Bolles, Robert C. (b.1928)
Bolling, George Melville (1871–1963)
Bolocan, Gheorge (1925–2000)
Bologna, Maria Patrizia (b.1951)
Bolognino, Guilielmus (1590–1669)
Bolton, Ralph (b.1939)
Boltz, August (1819–c.1878)
Bolzanio, Urbano Valerino (1442–1524)
Bolzano, Bernard (Placidus Johann, 1781–1848)
Bomberg, Daniel (1483–c.1549)
Bomhard, Allan R(obert, b.1944)
Bonald, Louis Gabriel Ambroise, *vicomte* de (1754–1840)
Bonamy, Pierre-Nicolas (1694–1770)
Bonaparte, Napoléon (Napoléon I, 1769–1821)
Bonaparte, Louis-Lucien (*Prince*, 1813–1891)
Bonaventura, St. (Johannes (of) Fidanza — 'Doctor Seraphicus', 1217–1274)
Bonaventure de Roquefort, Jean Baptiste (1777–1834)
Bondarko, Aleksandr Vladimirovič (b. c.1930)
Bonelli, Luigi (1865–1947)
Bonet, Juan Pablo (1574–1633)
Bonfante, Giuliano (1904–2005)
Bonghi, Ruggiero (1826–1895)S
Boniface, Alexandre (1785–1841)
Boniface, Saint (*alias* Wynfreth, c.675–754)S
Boniface of Savoy, *Archbishop* of Canterbury (d.1270)
Bonitz, Herrmann (1814–1888)
Bonifaz, Luiz, S.J. (1578–1644)

Bonilla y San Martín, Adolfo (1875–1926)
Bonitz, Hermann (1818–1888)
Bonivard, P. (1493–1570)
Bonnard, Henri (1915–2004)
Bonnefoy, Yves (b.1923)
Bonnell, Eduard (1802–1877)
Bonnerot, Louis (1897–1974)
Bonnet, Charles (1720–1793)
Bonn(us), Hermann(us, 1504–1548)
Bonus Accursius (Bonaccorso da Pisa, c.1400–c.1478)
Booch-Árkossy, Friedrich (*also* Frigyes, c.1820–1902)
Boodberg, Peter Alexis (*alias* Baron von Budberg; in Russian Pjotr Alekseevič Budberg, 1903–1972)
Boole, George (1815–1864)
Boone, Lalia Phipps (1907–1990)
Boons, Jean-Paul (1933–2006)
Booth, Andrew D(onald, b.1918)
Booth, David (1766–1845)
Booth, Kathleen H(ylda) V(alerie, *née* Britten, b.1922)
Boothe Luce, Clare (1903–1987)
Bopp, Franz (1791–1867)S, E
Boquillon, Nicolas (1795–1814)
Borba, Francisco da Silva (b.1932)
Borao, Jerónimo (1821–1878)
Borbolla y Gárate, Joaquín María de la (18th cent.?)
Borch(ius), Olaus (*alias* Ole or Oluf Clausen, 1626–1690)
Borchardt, Rudolf (1877–1945)
Borchling, Conrad (1872–1946)S
Bordázar de Artazú, Antonio (fl.1728–1737)
Borde, Andrew (1490?–1549)
Bordier, Henri (fl.1853–1874)

Bordin, Charles Laurent (d.1835)
Borecki, Marian (1928–1999)
Borek, Henryk (1929–1986)
Borecký, Bořivoj (1922–1995)
Borel, Adam (*also* Boreel, 1603–1667)
Borel, Pierre (1620?–1671)
Borer, Hagit (b.1952)
Boretzky, Norbert (b.1935)K
Borgaras, Waldemar (1865–1936)
Borgeaud, Willy (1913–1989)
Borger, Riekele (*alias* Rykle, b.1929)K
Borghini, Vincenzio (1515–1580)S
Borgstrøm, Carl Hjalmar (1909–1986)S, E
Borheck, August Christian (1751–1816)
Borinski, Karl (1861–1922)
Borinski, Ludwig (1910–1999)
Borner, Kaspar (c.1492–1547)
Borovko, Nikolaj Afrikanovič (1863–1913)
Boroxov, Ber (1881–1917)
Borrelly, Jean-Alexis (1738–c.1810)
Borri, Cristoforo, S.J. (1583–1632)
Borromee (Borromaeus), Charles (1752–1798)
Borroff, Marie Edith (b.1932)
Borrow, George (1941–1989)
Borst, Arno (b.1925)K
Bos, Lambertus (1670–1717)
Bosák, Ján (b.1938)
Bosanquet, Bernard (1848–1923)
Boscán, Juan (c.1490–1542)
Bosch, Dirk Willem (fl.1836–1861)
Bosch-Gimpera, Pedro (1891–1970?)
Bosilkov, Konstantin (1941–1989)
Bošković, Radosav (1907–1983)

Bosquet, Jean (c.1530–c.1595)
Bosscha, Joannes (1797–1874)
Bossert, Helmuth Theodor (1889–1961)
Bossong, Georg (b.1948)K
Bossuet, Jacques-Bénigne (évêque de Condom, 1627–1704)
Bossut, Charles (1730–1814)
Bostel, Nicolai von (1670–1704)
Boswell, James (1740–1795)
Boswell, (*Sir*) William (c.1583–1649)
Bosworth, Joseph (1789–1876)
Botero, Giovanni (c.1543–1617)
Botha, Rudolf P. ("Rudie", b.1942)
Bothmer, Bernard V. (1912–1993)
Botin, Anders af (1733–1705)
Botin, Anders (af, 1756–1830)
Bøtker, Adam Fredrik (1866–1944)
Bottiglioni, Gino (1887–1963)S
Bouchardy, François (1889–1974)
Boucher de Crèvecoeur de Perthes, Jacques (1788–1868)
Boucherie, Anatole (1831–1883)
Bouchet, A. (1877–1948)
Bouchot, *abbé* Léopold (d.1766)
Boudinot, Elias (1803?–1839)
Boudon, Raymond (b.1934)
Boudot, *père* Jean (c.1631–1706)
Bougainville, Louis-Antoine de (1729–1811)
Bouhours, Dominique, S.J. (1628–1702)S
Bouillet, Marie Nicolas (1798–1864)
Bouillaud, Jean Baptiste (1796–1881)
Boulé, *père* Étienne Marie (*alias* Hilaire de Barenton, 1864–1946)
Boulle, Jacques (1931–1996)
Bouquet, Simon (b.1954)

Bouquiaux, Luc (b.1934)
Bourbon Busset, Gabriel (*alias* Bourbon-LeBlanc, 1775–1862)
Bourbourg, *abbé* Charles Étienne Brasseur de, *see* Brasseur de Bourbourg, *abbé* Charles Étienne
Bourchier, John (*Lord* Berners, 1467–1533)
Bourciez, Édouard (Eugène Joseph, 1854–1946)
Bourcier, Georges (b.1930)
Bourdelin, *abbé* (1725–1783)
Bourdieu, Pierre (1930–2002)
Bourdon, Benjamin (Bienamé, 1860–1937)
Bourgade, *abbé* François (1806–1866)
Bourgoing, Charles-Paul Amable de (1791–1864)
Bourquin, Guy (b.1928)
Bourquin, Theodor (1833–1914)
Bourquin, Walther (1879–1957)
Bourzeys, Amable de (1606–1672)
Boussi, François-Narcisse (1795–1868)
Boutière, Jean (1899–1967)
Boutkan, Dirk Ferdinandus Henricus (1964–2002)
Bouton, Charles Pierre (1926–1996)
Boutroux, Émile (1845–1921)
Bouvier, Jean-Claude (b.1935)
Bovelles, Charles (de, 1479–1567)S, E
Bovillus, Carolus, *see* Bovelles, Charles
Bowdich, Thomas Edward (1791–1824)
Bover, José Maria (1877–1954)
Bowen, Jean Donald (1922–1989)

Bowers, Alfred W. (1901–19??)
Boxhorn(ius), Marcus Zuerius (1602–1653)E
Boyadijev, Jivco (*alias* Živko Bojadžiev, 1936–2007)
Boyanus, Simon Charles (1871–1952)
Boyce, William Binnington (1803–1889)
Boyd, Julian (b.1931)
Boyer, Abel (1664–1729)
Boyer, Paul (Jean Marie, 1864–1949)
Boyle, David (1842–1911)
Boyle, Robert (1627–1691)
Boym, Michael (1612–1659)
Boynton, David (b.19??)
Boynton, Percy Holmes (1875–1946)
Bozveli, Neofit Archimandrite (1785–1848)
Braccini, Giovanna Princi (b.1940)
Bracciolini, Gian Francesco ("il Poggio", 1380–1459)
Brachet, Auguste (1845–1898)S
Brack, Wenzeslaus (2nd half of 15th cent.)
Bracton, Henry de (d.1268)
Bradeau, Michel (b.1946)
Brademann, Albert (1871–1952)
Bradke, Peter von (1853–1897)
Bradley, Charles (1789–1871)
Bradley, Francis Herbert (1846–1924)
Bradley, Henry (1845–1923)S
Bradley, Joshua (1773–1855)
Bradwardine, *see* Thomas Bradwardine
Bräuer, Herbert (1921–1989)K
Bräuer, Rolf (b.1933)K
Braga, Theophilo (1843–1924)

Brahe, Tycho (1546–1601)
Braille, Louis (1809–1852)E
Braine, David (b.1940)
Braine, Martin D. S. (1926–1996)
Brajerski, Tadeusz (1913–1997)
Brainerd, Barron (b.1950?)
Brainerd, David (1718–1747)
Brainerd, John (1720–1781)
Braissai, Sámuel (1797/1800–1897)
Braithwaite, Richard B. (1900–1990)
Brajerski, Tadeusz (1913–1997)
Bram, Joseph (1904–1974)
Brambore, Josef (d.1980)
Brame, Michael K. (b.1944)
Branca, Sonia (b.1947)
Brâncuş, Grigore (b.1928)
Brandão (Brandônio), Ambrósio
    Fernandes (17th cent.?)
Branden, Lode van den (1923–1981)
Brandenstein, Wilhelm (1898–1967)
Brandi, Karl Maria Prosper Laurenz
    (1868–1946)
Brandl, Alois (1855–1940)S
Brands, Jan Lourens Andries (1857–
    1905)
Brandstetter, Renward (1860–1942)
Brandt, R. F. (1853–1920)
Brandt, Roman (1853–1902)
Branner, David Prager (b.1962)
Brant, Sebastian (1458–1521)
Brantomer, Piere de Bourdeille,
    Seigneur de (c.1540–1614)
Braswell, Laurel N. (b.1931)
Brasseur de Bourbourg, abbé Charles
    Étienne (1814–1874)S
Brassicanus, Joannes (post 1470–
    1514)
Bratranek, Frantiszek Tomasz (1815–
    1884)

Bratuscheck, Ernst (1837–1883)
Braudel, Fernand (1902–1985)
Brault, Geard Josph (b.1929)
Braun, Friedrich (alias Fedor
    Aleksandrovič, 1862–1942)
Braun, Heinrich (1732–1792)
Braune, Wilhelm (Theodor, 1850–
    1926)S, E
Brauner, Siegmund (b.1934)K
Braunholtz, Gustav (fl.1925–1952)
Braunmüller, Kurt (b.1948)K
Brauns, Karl Eduard (1793–1846)
Bravmann, Max Meir (1909–1977?)
Bravo, Bartolomé, S.J. (1540–1607)
Bravo de Lagunas, Frei Juan Bautiste,
    see under Lagunas, Juan Bautista
Bray, R. G. A. (1912–1993)
Brazeau, Jacques (b.1923)
Bréal, Michel (Jules Alfred, 1832–
    1915)S, E
Brébeuf, Jean de, S.J., saint (alias
    Héchon, 1593–1649)
Bredsdorff, Jakob Hornemann
    (1790–1841)S, E
Bree, Cor van (b.1932)
Bree, Germaine (b.1907)
Bregail, Gabriel (d.1929)
Bréhier, Émile (1876–1952)
Breidak(a)s, Antons (Antuonas,
    1932–2002)
Breidenbach (Breydenbach), 1440?–
    1497)
Breithaupt, Christian (1689–1749)
Breitinger, Heinrich (1832–1889)
Breitinger, Johann Jacob (1701–
    1776)
Brekle, Herbert Ernst (b.1935)K
Breloer, Bernhard (1894–1947)
Breloer, Bernhard (1894–post 1940)

Breme, Ludovico Arborio Gattinara di (1780–1820)
Bremer, Otto (1862–1936)
Brend, Ruth M(argaret, 1927–2002)
Brenes Mesén, Roberto (1874–1947)
Brenner, Oskar (1854–1920)
Brentano, Franz (Clemens, 1838–1917)
Brereton, John (fl.1602)
Brerewood, Edward (c.1565–1615)
Bresnan, Joan (Wanda, b.1945)
Bresnier, Louis-Jacques (1814–1869)
Bressani, Giuseppe, S.J. (1612–1672)
Bresson, François (1921–1996)
Bret, Antoine (1717–1792)
Bretke, Johann (in Lithuanian: Jonas Bretkūnas, 1536–1602)
Breton, Raymond (1609–1679)S
Breton, Raymond (b.1931)
Breton, Raymond, S.J. (1609–1679)
Bretonneau, Guy (d.1756)
Bretschneider, Anneliese (1898–1984)
Brett, Arthur (c.1635–1677)
Brett, Richard (1560–1630)
Brettschneider, Johannes, see Placotomus, Ioannes
Breuil, Ernest (1870–post 1936)
Breva Claramonte, Manuel (b.1942)
Brevik, Leiv Egil (b.1944)
Brewer, Derek Stanley (b.1923)
Brewster, (Sir) David (1781–1868)
Brewster, Francis Augustus (1817–1890)
Brewster, Kingman (b. c.1920)
Brewster, William (c.1560–1644)
Breymann, Hermann (Wilhelm, 1843–1910)

Breza, Edward (b.1932)
Bricker, Victoria Reifler (b.1940)
Bridel, Philippe-Sirice (1757–1845)
Bridges, Robert (Seymour, 1844–1930)
Bridgman, Elijah Coleman (1801–1861)
Bridgman, Percy Williams (1882–1961)
Brie, Friedrich (1880–1948)
Brière, de (alleged pseud.of Count Pierre Louis Roederer [d.1835], fl.1827–1841; d. c.1862)
Briggs, Charles L. (b.1953)
Briggs, Henry (1561–1630)
Bright, James Wilson (1852–1926)S
Bright, Timothy (1551–1615)S
Bright, William O(liver "Bill", 1928–2006)
Brightland, John (d.1717)
Brill, Abraham (1874–1948)
Brill, Willem Gerard (1811–1896)
Bringuier, Octavian (1820–1875)
Brink, Bernhard ten (1841–1892)
Brink, Daniel (Theodore, 1940–1997)
Brink, Jan ten (1834–1901)
Brinker, Klaus (b.1938)K
Brinkley, see Richard Brinkley
Brinkmann, Hennig (1901–2000)
Brinkmann, Karl Gustav von (1764–1847)
Brinsley, John (1566–c.1630)S
Brinsley, John (1600–1665)
Brinton, Daniel Garrison (1837–1899)
Brisson, Mathurin Jacques (1723–1806)
Brito, Radulphus, see Radulphus Brito

Britton, John (d.1275)
Broadbent, (*Sir*) William Henry, 1st
  bart. (1835–1907)
Broberg, Richard (1910–1988)
Broca, (Pierre) Paul (1824–1880)S
Broch, Joseph (fl.1771–1811)
Broch, Olaf (1867–1961)
Brock, Reginald Walter (1874–1935)
Brockelmann, Carl (1868–1956)E
Brockes, Barthold Heinrich (1680–
  1747)
Brockhaus, Hermann (1806–1877)
Brockie, William (1811–1890)
Brodnjak, Vladimir (1922–1992)
Broek, Paul van den (b.1955)
Broecke Hoekstra, Albert ten (1765–
  1828)
Bröcker, Wilhelm (1902–19??)
Broens, Otto (1887–19??)
Broglie, Louis Victor Pierre
  Raymond, *duc* de (1892–1987)
Bromberger, Sylvain (b.1924)
Bromby, Charles Henry (Bishop of
  Tasmania, 1814–1907)
Bronckart, Jean-Paul (b.1946)
Brøndal, Viggo (*alias* Rasmus
  Hansen, 1887–1942)S, E
Brøndum-Nielsen, Johannes (1881–
  1977)
Brøndum-Nielsen, Johannes (1881–
  1977)S
Bronisch, Gotthelf Matthias (1868–
  1937)
Bronn, Georg Heinrich (1800–1862)
Bronowski, Jacob (1908–1974)
Bronstein, Arthur J(ordan, b.1914)
Brook, George Leslie (1910–1987)
Brosin, Henry (Walter, b.1904)
Brosses, Charles de (1709–1777)S, E

Brosset, Marie-Félicité (1802–1880)
Brotanek, Rudolf (1870–1944)
Brough, John (1917–1984)
Brougham, Henry (1778–1868)
Broughton, Hugh (1549–1612)
Broukhusius, Janus (1649–1707)
Broussais, François-Joseph-Victor
  (1771–1838)
Brouwer, Dédé (b.1947)
Brouwer, Luitzen Egbertus Jan
  (1881–1966)
Brown, Anthony F(razer) R(itchie,
  b.1929)
Brown, Carleton (1869–1941)
Brown, Cecil (b.1943)
Brown, Gillian (b.1937)E
Brown, Goold (1791–1857)
Brown, H. Douglas (b.1941)
Brown, James ('grammarian',
  fl.1815–1856)
Brown, Keith (b.1935)
Brown, Nathan (1807–1888)
Brown, Norman (Oliver, b.1913)
Brown, Roger Langham (b. c.1940)
Brown, Roger (William, 1925–
  1997)E
Brown, Thomas (1778–1820)
Brown, Thomas Julian (1923–1987)
Brown-Sequard, Charles-Édouard
  (1817–1894)
Browne, *Sir* Thomas (1605–1682)
Browne, Richard (fl.1700)
Browne, Wayles (b.1941)
Browning, Robert (1812–1889)
Broz, Ivan (1852–1893)
Brožek, Josef Maria (b.1913)
Bruce, James (1730–1794)
Bruche-Schulz, Gisela (b.1943)

Bruchmann, Kurt (Guido, 1851–1928)

Brucidi, Antonio (c.1495–1566)

Brucioli, Antonio (c.1495–1566)

Bruckner, Johannes (pseud. Cassander, 1726–1804)

Brücke, Ernst (Wilhelm, *Ritter* von, 1819–1892)E

Brückner, Alexander (1834–1896)

Brückner, Aleksander (1856–1939)

Brückner, Jacob (fl.1620)

Brütsch, Louis, *see* Brutsch, Louis

Brueys, Claude (1570–1636)

Brugmann, (Christian) Karl (Friedrich, 1849–1919)S, E

Brugsch, Heinrich (c.1850–c.1930)

Brugsma, Berend (1797–1868)

Brûlé (Bruslé), Étienne (c.1592–1633)

Brun, Auguste (1881–1961)

Brun, L. (1890–1971)

Bruneau, Charles (1883–1969)E

Bruner, Edward M. (b.1924)

Bruner, Jerome (b.1915)E

Brunet, Pierre (1893–1950)

Brunetière, Fedinand (1849–1906)

Bruni (Aretino), Leonardo (1369–1444)S

Brunn, Henrich (1822–1894)

Brunet de Presle, ? (1809–1875)

Brunner, David B. (1835–1903)

Brunner, Hellmut (b.1913)K

Brunner, Johann (fl.1460–1468)

Brunner, Karl (1887–1965)S

Brunner, Rudolf (1907–1989)

Brunnhofer, Hermann (1841–1916)

Bruno, Giordano (Filippo, 1548–1600)S

Brunot, Ferdinand (Eugène, 1860–1938)S, E

Brunswik, Egon (1903–1955)

Brusch, Heinrich (1827–1894)

Brusciotto, Giacinto (Hyacinthus brusciottus a Vetralla, c.1600–*post* 1659)

Brusendorff, Aage (1887–1922)

Bruto, Giovanni (1515?–1594?)

Brutsch, Louis (1891–1967)

Bruyas, Jacques, S.J. (1635–1712)

Bryan, Francis (d.1550)

Bryan, George B. (1939–1996)

Bryan, William Frank (1879–19??)

Bryant, James Churchill (1812–1850)

Bryant, Margaret M. (1900–*post* 1990)

Brzeziński, Jerzy (1923–1990)K

Brzeziński, Władysław (1922–1998)

Brzuski, Witold Kazimierz (1935–1987)

Bubak, Józef (1934–1999)

Buben, Viktor (1888–1956)

Buber, Martin (1878–1965)

Bublitz, Wolfram (b.1947)K

Bubrix, D. V. (1890–1949)

Buča, Marin (b.1936)

Buccardus, Ioannes Franciscus, *see* Pylades

Bucer, Martin (1491–1551)

Buch, Tamara (1923–1970)

Buchanan, James (fl.1753–1773)S

Buchanan(us), George (Georgius, fl.1542)

Buchenröder, Johannes Nicolaus Carl (fl.1762–1785)

Bucher, Urban Gottfried (fl.1723–1772)

Bucherelli, Luis Maria (1684–1749)

Buschinger, Danielle (b.1936)
Buschmann, Johann Carl Eduard
(1805–1880)
Bush, Vannevar (1890–1974)
Buslaev, Fedor Ivanovič (1818–
1897)S
Busleiden, Jerome de (1470–1517)
Busse, Thomas Valentine (1941–
1986)
Busse, Winfried (b.1942)K
Bussing, Caspar (d.1732)
Bußmann, Hadumod (b.1933)K
Bustamente, Carlos Maria de (1774–
1848)
Būstanī, Buṭrus b. Būlus al- (1819–
1883)S
Busto, Barnabé del (first half of 16th
cent.))S
Butcher, Samuel Henry (classicist;
fl.1904)
Butet, Pierre Roland François (*dit*
Butet de la Sarthe, 1769–1825)
Buteux, Jacques, S.J. (1600–1652)
Butler, Charles (1560–1647)S
Butler, Inez (d.2000)
Butler, Nicholas Murray (1862–
1947)
Butler, Noble (1819–1882)
Butler, Samuel (1612–1680)
Butler, William (fl.1380–1410)
Butschky, Samuel (von, 1612–1678)
Butorov, Viktor Dmitrievič (d.1998)
Butt, David G. (b.1950)
Butter, Henry (1794–1885)
Butterfield, (*Sir*) Henry (1900–1979)
Butters, Ronald R(ichard, b.1940)
Buttler, Danuta (1930–1991)
Buttmann, Philipp Karl (1764–
1829)S

Butz, Kilian (1943–1990)
Buxarin, Nikolaj (1888–1938)
Buxton, Johann, the elder (1564–
1629)
Buxtorf, Johann (1564–1629)
Buyssens, Eric (1900–2000)
Buzacott, Aaron, the Elder (1800–
1864)
Buzetti, Dino (b.1941)
Buzuk, Petro Opanasovyč (1891–
1943)S
Byck, Jacques (1897–1964)
Byington, Cyrus (1793–1868)S
Bynon, James (b.1933?)
Bynon, Theodora ("Thea", b.1934?)
Byrne, James (1820–1897)
Bystroń, Jan (1860–1902)
Bystroń, Jan Stanisław (1892–1964)
Byvanck, Alexander Willem (1884–
1970)
Bywater, Ingram (fl.1897)
Bzdęga, Andrzej Z. (b.1927)K

C.

Caballero, Lucas, O.F.M. (18th cent.)
Cabanis, Pierre-Jean Georges (1757–1808)
Çabej, Eqrem (1908–1980)E
Cabeza de Vaca, Alvar Núñez (1490?–1559?)
Cabezas, Joaquín (pseud. of Jacobo Saquenzia, 1790?–1828?)
Cabrera, Ramón (1754–1833)
Cabrera de Córdoba, Luis (1559–1623)
Cá(r)ceres, *Fray* Pedro de, O.F.M. (fl.1582)
Cachedenier, Daniel (d.1612)
Cadaval, Álvaro de (1500–1575)
Caecilius of Calacte (1st cent. B.C.)S
Caesar, Gaius Julius (100–44 B.C.)
Caesar, Christophorus (1540–1604)
Caesarius, Ioannes (c.1460–1551)
Caetano de Almeida Nogueira, Batista (1826–1882)
Caffee, Nathaniel Montier (b. c.1910)
Cagareli, Aleksandre (1844–1929)
Cahannes, Gion (1872–1947)
Cahen, Maurice (1884–1926)
Caille, Louis (1884–1962)
Caillois, Roger (1913–1978)
Caix, Napoleone (1845–1882)S
Caix de Saint-Aymour, Amédée de (1843–1920)
Cajanus, Eric (1675–1737)
Calado, Manuel (1584–1654)
Calagius, Andreas (1549–1609)

Calandrelli, Matías (1845–1919)
Caland, Wilhelm (1859–1932)
Calderón, Juan (1791–1854)S
Calderoni, Mario (1879–1914)S
Caldwell, Robert (1814–1891)E
Calepi(n)o, Ambrogio (*alias* Giacomo, c.1435–1511)S
Callahan, Catherine A. (b.1931)
Callander of Craigforth, John (d. 1789)
Callaway, Henry (1817–1890
Callaway, Morgan, Jr. (1862–1936)
Calle, Antonio de la (1843–1889)
Calleberg, Axel (1891–1959)
Calleja, Juan Manuel (b. c.1780; fl.1818)S
Callenberg, Johann Heinrich (1694–1760)
Callery, Joseph Marie (Calleri, 1841–1862)
Calligaris, Louis (1808–1871)
Callin, F. A. (fl.1840–1867)
Calmet, Augustin (1672–1757)
Calmeta, Il (*alias* Colli, Vincenzo, 1460?–1508)
Calogero, Guido (1904–1986)S
Calonge, Julio (b.1914)
Calphurnius, Johannes (1443–1503)
Calverton, Victor Francis (1900–1940)
Calvet, Louis-Jean (b.1942)
Calvin, Jean (1509–1564)
Calvino, Italo (1923–1985)
Calvinus, Johannes (*alias* Johann Kahl, 1550–1614)
Calvisius, Seth(us) (*alias* Kallwitz, 1556–1615)
Calvo, Pedro, O.P. (fl.1550)
Calvo Fernández, Vicente (b.1967)

Calvo Pérez, Julio (b.1946)

Camaj, Martin (1925–1992)K

Camaño, *Padre* Joaquín, S.J. (1737–1820)

Câmara, Joaquim Mattoso, Jr., *see* Mattoso Câmara, Joaquim

Cambel, Samo (1856–1909)

Camden,William (1551–1623)

Camerarius, Joachim (1500–1574)

Camerarius, Joachim (1534–1598)

Camerarius, Philipp (1537–1624)

Cameron, Angus Fraser (1941–1983)

Cameron, Deborah (b.1958)

Camilli, Camillo (d.1615)

Caminda, Marc Alexandre (*dit* Caminade-Chatenay or 'le Citoyen Caminade', 1746–1830?)

Caminha, Pero Vaz de (c.1449–1500)

Camões, Luis Vas de (1524/25–1580)

Campanella, Tommaso (*or* Thomas, 1568–1639)S, E

Campanile, Enrico (1936–1994)

Campbell, Alexander Duncan (1789–1857)

Campbell, Alistair (1907–1974)

Campbell, Archibald (1787–18??)

Campbell, Douglas (Brian, b.1956)

Campbell, George (1719–1796)S

Campbell, Jeremy (b.1931)

Campbell, John Lorne (1906–1996)

Campbell, Lyle (R., b.1942)

Campe, Joachim Heinrich (1746–1818)S, E

Campensis, Johannes (*alias* Jan de Campen, d.1538)

Camper, Pieter (1722–1789)

Campori, Matteo (fl.1892)

Campos, Ramón (1760–1808)

Camproux, Charles (1908–1994)

Campsall, Richard, *see* Richard of Campsall

Canal, Pietro (1807–1883)

Candlin, Christopher (b.1940)

Candolle, Alphonse de (1806–1893)

Candolle, Augustin Pyramus de (1778–1841)

Candragomin (probably 5th cent. A.D.)S

Camello, Ugo Angelo (1848–1883)

Canellada Llavona, María Josefa (1912–1995)

Cañes, Francisco, O.F.M. Desc. (1730–1795)

Canguilhem, Georges (1904–1995)

Canini(us), Angelo (1521–1557)

Can(n)cat(t)im, Bernardo Maria de (late 18th–early 19th cent.)

Cankaranamacivávar (18th cent. A.D.)

Cankof, *see under* Kiriak Cankof

Cannecatim, Bernardo Maria de, O.F.M. Cap. (fl.1804–1859)

Cantemir, Dimitrie (1663–1723)

Cantera Burgon, Francisco (18th–early 19th cent.)

Cantineau, Jean (1899–1956)S

Cantor, Moritz Benedikt (19th cent.)

Canz, Israel Gottlieb (1690–1753)

Capart, Jean (1877–1947)

Capek, Karel (1890–1938)

Capell, Arthur (1902–1986)

Capelle, Guy (b.1946)

Caper, Flavius (late 2nd cent. A.D.)

Caper, Flavius (Caprus, 5th cent. A.D.)

Capesius, Bernhard (1889–1981)

Carreras Roure, Juan de Dios (1855–
post 1901)
Carreter, Fernando Lázaro (1924–
2003)
Carroll, John B(issell, "Jack",
b.1916)
Carroll, Lewis (pseud. for Charles
Lutwidge Dodgson, 1832–1898)
Carroll, Mitchell (1870–1925)
Carstens, Renate (b.1938)K
Carstensen, Broder (1926–1992)K
Cartagena, Alfonso de (1384–1456)
Cartellieri, Wilhelm (1860–1908)
Carter, Charles William (1928–1988)
Carter, Michael G(eorge, b.1938)
Cartier, Alice (1927–1991)
Cartier, Jacques (1494–c.1556)
Carus, Carl Gustav (1789–1869)
Carus, J(ulius) Victor (1823–1903)
Carus, Paul (1852–1919)
Carvajal, *Frei* Gaspar de, O.P. (1504–
1584)
Carvalhão Buescu, Maria Leonor
(1932–1999)
Carvalho, Luis, S.J. (d.1732)
Carver, David John (*pseud.* Chia-
Hua, d.1969)
Carver, Jonathan (1732–1780)
Casacchia, Giorgio (b.1949)
Casadesús Vila, José (1865–19??)
Casadio, Claudia (b.1955)
Casagrande, Jean (b.1938)
Casagrande, Joseph Bartholomew
(1915–1982)
Casalegno, Paolo (b.1952)
Casanova, José de (1615/16–*post*
1650)
Casanova, Maurice (1925–1995)
Casares, Julio (1878–1964)

Casas, Cristóbal de las, *see* Las Casas
Casaubon(us), Isaac (1559–1614)
Casaubon, Méric (1599–1671)
Cascales, Francisco (1564?–1642)
Casella, Mario (1886–1956)
Cascese, Patrizio (*or* Caxesi, *ante*
1567–1612)
Cairi, Niguel (1710–1792)
Caso, Alfonso (1896–1970)
Cass, *Gen.* Lewis (1782–1866)
Cassato, Umberto (*alias* Moshe
Daniel, 1863–1951)
Casserio, Julio (c.1552–1616)
Casserius, Julius (1732–1807)
Cassidy, Frederic G(omes, 1907–
2000)
Cassiodoro de Reina, *see* under
Reina, Cassiodoro
Cassiodorus (Flavius Magnus Aure-
lius Cassiodorus, *Senator*, c.490–
583 A.D.)S
Cassirer, Ernst (1874–1945)S, E
Cassius, Bartolomaeus, *see under*
Kašić, Bartul
Casson, Ronald W. (b.1942)
Castalio, Sebastiano (1515–1563)
Castañeda, Carlos (1935?–1998)
Castañeda, Leonardo Manrique, *see*
Manrique C., Leonardo
Castell, Edmund (1606–1685)S
Castellesi, Adriano (c.1460–1521)
Castelli, Nicolo di (= Christoph
Heinrich von Freiersleben?, 1661–
1728)
Castellesi, *Cardinal* Adrien
(Hadrianus Castellensis, c.1461–
1518)
Castelvetro, Luodovico (1505–
1571)S

Castiglione, Baldassarre (1478–1529)S
Castiglioni, Carlo Ottavio (1784–1849)
Castilho, Pêro de, S.J. (1572–1642)
Castille, Jean-Baptiste (1747–1816)
Castillo, Martín el (d.1680)
Castorena y Ursua, Juan Ignacio (1668–1733)
Castrén, Matthias Alexander (1813–1852)S, E
Castro, Adolfo (1823–1898)
Castro, Américo (1885–1972)
Castro, Francisco de, S.J. (1567?–1632)
Catach, Nina (1923–1997)
Catach, Irène, *see* Rosier, Irène
Catalá y Bayer, Joaquín, OCist (1744–1816)
Catalán, Diego (b.1928)
Cate, Abraham Pieter ten (b.1946)K
Catford, John Cunnison ("Ian", b.1917)
Catherine of France, *Queen* (1401–1437)
Catherine II, *Empress* of Russia (1729–1796)
Cathey, James Ernest (b.1940)K
Cato (3rd/4th cent. A.D.)
Cato, Dionysius, *see* Pseudo-Cato
Cattaneo, Carlo (1801–1869)S
Cattell, James McKeen (1860–1944)
Cauchie, Antoine (c.1530–1601?)
Cauchon de Maupas, Charles, *baron* du Tour (1566–1629)
Caucius, Antonius (*alias* Kuyck, Anthonis van, 1535–*post* 1600)
Cauer, (Paul Eduard) Ludwig (1854–1921)

Caumont, Arcisse de (1802–1873)
Caussin de Perceval, Amand-Pierre (1795–1871)
Caussin de Perceval, Jean-Jacques-Baptiste Antoine (1759–1835)
Cavaignac, Godefroy (1801–1845)
Cavalcanti, Bartolomeo (1503–1562)S
Cavalli-Sforza, Luigi Luca (b.1922)
Cavan, Sherri E. (b.1938)
Cavendish, John (d.1381)
Cavendish, Lucy Caroline Lyttleton (1841–1925)
Cavigneaux, Antoine (b.1948)
Cawdry, Robert (fl.1600–1609)S
Cawley, Arthur Clare (1913–1993)
Caxton, William (c.1422–1491)E
Caylus, A. Tubières de Grimoard, *comte* de (1692–1765)
Cayrou, Gaston (1880–1966)
Cazacu, Boris (1919–1987)
Cazaubon, Méric (1599–1671)
Cazden, Courtney B(orden, b.1925)
Cazeneuve, Pierre de (1591–1652)
Ceccato, Silvio (1914–1997)
Ceci, Luigi (1859–1927)S
Cecil, William (*Lord* Burghley, 1520–1598)
Cecioni, Cesare G. (b. c.1930)
Cedergren, Henrietta (b.1940)
Cegielski, Hipolit (1815–1869)
Cejador y Frauca, Julio (1864–1926)
Cejpek, Jiří (1921–1986)
Cejtin, Grigorij Samuelovič (fl.1958)
Čelakovsky, František (Ladislav, 1799–1852)
Cela, Camilo José (1916–2002)
Celaya, Juan de (fl. c.1516)

Cisneros, Diego de, OCarm (*alias*
Fray Diego de la Encarnación,
fl.1624–1635)S
Cisneros, Francisco Jiménez de,
cardinal (1436–1517)
Citolini, Alessandro (c.1500–c.1583)
Cittadini, Celso (1553–1627)S
Ciudad Real, *Fray* Antonio de,
O.F.M. (1551–1617)
Civañána Munivar (c.1725–1785)
Čiževskij, Dimitrij Ivanovič (*alias*
Dmytro I. Čiževśkyj, 1894–1977)
Cizikova, Ksenija (b.1933)
Claes, Fran(ciscu)s M(aria)
W(ilhelmus), S.J. (b.1928)
Claflin, Edith Frances (1875–1953)
Clahsen, Harald (b.1955)K
Clain, Samuil (*alias* Micu, 1745–
1806)
Clairmont, Carl Gaulis (1795–1850)
Clajus, Johann(es, 1535–1592)S
Clancy, Patricia (b.1950)
Claparède, Édouard (1873–1940)
Clapin, Sylva (1853–1928)
Clarac, Charles-Othon-Frédéric-Jean-
Baptiste, *Comte* de (1777–1847)
Clark, Cecily (1926–1992)
Clark, Donald Thomas (1911–1993)
Clark, Eve (Vivienne, b.1942)
Clark, Herbert H. (b.1940)E
Clark, James (1836–1895)
Clark, Stephen Watkins (1810–1901)
Clark, T. W. (b.1904)
Clark, Terry N. (b.1940)
Clark, William (1770–1838)
Clarke, Benjamin (1813–1850)
Clarke, David D. (b.1949)
Clarke, Hyde (1815–1895)
Clarke, John (1687–1734)

Clarke, Samuel (1675–1729)
Clauberg, Johann(es, 1622–1665)
Claude, Charles (1798–1863)
Clausen, John A. (b.1920)
Claver, Martín, O.S.A. (d.1646)
Claver y San Clemente, Ignacio, S.J.
(1637–1699)
Clavería, Carlos (1909–1974)
Clavijero (Clavigero), Francesco
Javier (Saverio), S.J. (1731–1787)
Clavijo y Fajardo, José Gabriel
(1726/30–1806)
Clavius, Christopher (1538–1612)
Clédat, Léon (1822–1916)S
Clédat, Léon (1851–1930)
Cledonius (mid-5th cent. A.D.)
Cleland, John (1709–1789)
Clemen, Wolfgang (1909–1990)
Clemens of Alexandria (c.150–215
A.D.)S
Clemens Scottus (9th cent. A.D.)S
Clement (fl.857–874 A.D.)
Clément, Catherine (b.1939)
Clément, Danielle (b.1943)K
Clement, Dorothy (b.1944)
Clement, John (d.1572)
Clément de Boissy, Athanase
Alexandre (1716–1793)
Clemoes, Peter (1920–1996)
Clenardus, Nicola(u)s (Cleynaerts,
Nicolaes, c.1494–1542)S
Cleochares (c.300 B.C.)
Clerc, Jean le (1657–1736)
Clerico, Geneviève (b.1941)
Clerk of Eldin, John (1728–1812)
Clerke, Bartholomew (1537–1590)
Clermont-Ganneau, Charles Simon
(1846–1923)

Clodius, Johann Christian (1676–1745)

Cloeren, Hermann Josef (b.1934)

Cloëtta, Wilhelm (1857–1911)

Cluver(ius), Philipp(us) (*alias* Clüver, 1580–1623)

Clyne, Michael (George, b.1939)K

Cnapius, Gregorius, *see* Knapski, Grzegorz

Coate, Howard (1910–2002)

Coates, Jennifer (b.1942)

Cobbett, William (1763–1835)S, E

Coblin, W(eldon) South (b.1944)

Cobo, Juan (Dominican, d.1592/93)

Cocheris, Hipolyte François Jules Marie (1829–1882)

Cochleus, Johannes (1479–1552)

Cocke, John (b.1925)

Coc(h)l(a)eus, Joannes (Noricius), *see* Cochleus, Johannes

Cocker, Edward (1631–1675)

Cockeram, Henry (*fl.*1623–1650)

Coco, Francesco (1926–1997)

Cocoran, Timothy (1871–1943)

Codret, Hannibal (1525–1599)

Coëffetau, Nicolas (1574–1632)

Coelestin, Johann Friedrich (*alias* Himmlisch, d. *post* 1577)

Coelho, Francisco Adolpho (1847–1919)S, E

Coëtanlem de Rostiviec, Pierre-Joseph-Jean (1749–1827)

Coetsem, Frans van (1919–2002)K

Coeurdoux, *le père* Gaston Laurent, S.J. (1691–1779)E

Coffin, Charles (1667–1749)

Coghill, Nevill (Henry Kendal Aylmer, 1899–1980)

Cohen, Antonie (1922–1996)

Cohen, David (b.1925)

Cohen, Gerald Leonard (b.1941)

Cohen, L. Jonathan (b.1923)

Cohen, Marcel (Samuel Raphael, 1884–1974)S

Cohen, Morris Raphael (1880–1947)

Cohen de Lara, David (c.1602–1674)

Cohn, Georg (1866–1942?)

Colao Agata, Diego (1732-*post* 1774)

Colbeck, Charles (1847–1903)

Colbert, Jean-Baptiste (1619–1704)

Colburn, Warren (1793–1833)

Colby, Benjamin N. (b.1931)

Colden, Cadwallder (1688–1776)

Coldeway, John C. (b.1944)

Cole, Desmond T. (b.1922)

Cole, Fay-Cooper (1881–1961)

Cole, Michael (b.1938)

Colebrooke, Henry Thomas (1765–1837)

Coleman, Algeron (1876–1939)

Coleman, James S. (b.1926)

Coleman, Julie (Margaret, b.1966)

Colenso, *bishop* John William (1814–1883)

Coler(us), Christopher (d.1604)

Coleridge, Herbert (1830–1861)

Coles, Elisha (c.1640–1680)

Coles, (James) Oakley (1845–1906)

Colet, John (*dean*, 1467–1519)

Colinet, Philemon (1833–1891)

Collado, Diego, O.P. (d.1638)S

Collas, John Peter (1911–1984)

Colli, Vincenzo, *see* (Il) Calmeta

Colliander, Börge (1909-1994)

Colliander, Peter (b.1953)K

Collier, John (1706–1786)

Collier, Trann Lamarr (1888–1947)

Collin d'Ambly (1759–1830)

Collin, Carl Sven Reinhold (1876–1944)

Collinder, Björn (1894–1983)S, E

Collinge, N(eville) E(dgar) ("Oscar", b.1921)

Collingwood, Robin George (1889–1943)

Collins, Henry Bascom (1899–19??)

Collins, Beverley S. (b.1938)

Collins, Randall (b.1941)

Collins, Rowland Lee (1934–1985)

Collins, William (1721–1759)

Collinson, William Edward (1889–1969)

Collis, Dermot Ronan Fitzgerald (1935–1998)

Collison, William Henry (1847–1922

Collitz, Hermann (1855–1935)S, E

Collitz, Klara (née Hechtenberg, 1863–1944)

Coluccini, Juan Bautista (1569–1641)

Collyer, John (d.1776)

Colmerauer, Alain Marie Albert (b.1941)

Colodny, Isidor Omar (d.1977)

Colombat, Bernard (b.1948)

Colonia, Dominique de (1660–1714)

Colson, Francis Henry (1857–1943)

Coluccini, Juan Bautista (1569–1641)

Columbus, Christopher (Cristóbal Colón, c.1451–1506)

Comanus (Gk. Kōmanós, c.150 B.C.)S

Combe, George (1788–1858)

Comber, Thomas (1575–1654)

Combrink, J.G.H. (d.1999)

Comenius (i.e., Jan Amos Komenský, 1592–1670)S, E

Commerlerán y Gómez, Francisco A. (1849–1919)

Commerson, Philibert (1727–1773)

Commines, Philippe de (1445–1511)

Comnena, Anna (alias Commene, Anne, 1083–1148)

Commire, Jean (1626–1702)

Compagnoni, Guiseppe (1754/55–1833)

Companys, Emmanuel (b.1927)

Compayré, Gabriel (fl.1886)

Comrie, Bernard (Sterling, b.1947)E

Comte, (Isidore) Auguste (Marie Xavier, 1798–1857)

Comtet, Roger (b.1940)

Conant, Carlos Everett (1870–1925)

Condillac, Étienne Bonnot de Mably de, abbé (1714–1780)S, E

Condon, Edward Uhler (1902–1974)

Condorcet, Marie Jean Antoine Nicolas de Caritat, marquis de (1743–1794)

Condren, Charles de (1588–1641)

Conev, Ben'o Stefanov (1863–1926)S

Confucius (Kongzi, 551–479 B.C.)

Conington, John (1825–1869)

Conkle, Ellsworth Prouty (1899–1994)

Conklin, Harold Colyer (b.1926)

Conolly, M. J. (alias Ó Coingeallaiġ, b.1943)

Conrad, Ernst (19th cent.?)

Conrad-Martius, Hedwig (1888–19??)

Conradi, Matthias (1745–1832)

Conrad, Rudi (b.1934)K

Conrart, Valentin (1603–1675)

Consentius (late 4th–early 5th cent. A.D.)
Considerant, Victor (1808–1893)
Constans, Léopold (1845–1916)
Constantin, Émile (John, 1888–1963)
Constantin, Robert (c.1530–1605)
Constantino, Ernest (b.1930)
Conte, Maria-Elisabeth (*née* Buse, 1935–1998)
Conti Rossini, Carlo (1872–1949)E
Contini, Gianfranco (1912–1990)
Contini-Morava, Ellen (b.1948)
Contreni, John J. (b.1944)
Contreras, Heles (b.1933)
Conway, Robert Seymour (1833–1933)
Cook, Albert Stanburrough (1853–1927)
Cook, James (1728–1779)
Cook, Walter A(nthony), S.J. (1922–1999)
Cook-Gumperz, Jenny (b. c.1935)
Cooley, Charles Horton (1864–1929)
Cooper, Christopher (c.1655–1698)S, E
Cooper, Frankin S(eaney, 1908–1999)
Cooper, Henry Ronald Jr. (b.1947)
Cooper, Leon N. (b.1930)
Cooper, Robert Lein (b.1931)
Cooper, Robin Hayes (b.1947)
Coopmans, Peter (b.1958)
Coornaert, Émile (1886–1980)
Coornhert, Dirck Volckertszoon (1522–1590)
Coote, Charles (1761–1835)
Coote, Edmund (fl.1596; d. *ante* 1620)S
Copceag, Dimitrie (1926–1994)

Copeland, James E. (b.1937)
Copernicus, Nicholas (1473–1543)
Copineau, *abbé* (fl.1750–1780)
Copleston, Frederick Charles, S.J. (1907–19??)
Copley, Gordon John (1914–1991)
Coquebert de Montbret, Eugène (1785–1849)
Corbett, Greville George (b.1947)
Corbett, Noel L(ynn, b.1938)
Corbinelli, Jacopo (1535–c.1590)
Cordemoy, Gérau(l)d de (1626–1684)E
Corder, S(tephen) Pit (1926–1990)
Cordes, Gerhard (1908–1985)S
Cordier, Henri (1849–1925)
Cordier, Mathurin de (1479–1564)
Córdoba, *Fray* Juan de, O.P. (*also* Córdova, 1501–1595)
Córdoba, *Fray* Pedro de, O.P. (1482–1521)
Corleva, Johanna (1698–1752)
Cornarius, Janus (1500–1588)
Corne, Chris (1942–1999)
Corneille, Pierre (1606–1684)
Corneille, Thomas (1625–1709)
Cornelio, Tommaso (1614–1684)
Corner, Julia (1798–1875)
Corney, Bolton G. (1851–1924)
Cornford, Francis Macdonald (1874–1943)
Cornellas, Clemente (1815–*post* 1882)
Cornips, Leonie (b.1960)
Cornu, Jules (1849–1919)
Cornu, Marcel (1909–2001)
Cornvallis, Caroline Frances (1786–1858)

Cowgill, Warren C(rawford, 1929–1985)S
Cowley, Arthur Ernest (1861–1931)
Coxito, Adelina Angélica Aragão Pinto (1941–1988)
Coyaud, Maurice (b.1934)
Coyer, Gabriel-François (1707–1782)
Crabb, David W. (b.1925)
Crabb, George (1778–1851)
Craddock, Jerry R. (b.1935)
Cram, David (Francis, b.1945)
Craig, Dennis (1929–2004)
Craigie, (Sir) William Alexander (1867–1957)S
Cramp, Rosemary (b.1929)
Crampon, abbé Augustin (1826–1894)
Crane, Diana (b.1933)
Cranmer, Thomas (Archbishop of Canterbury, 1489–1566)
Crates of Mallos (fl. mid-2nd cent. B.C.)S
Crathorn, William (or John, fl.1330)
Cratylus (mid-5th cent B.C.)S
Crawford, James Mack (1925–1989)S
Crawfurd, John (1783–1868)
Crazzolara, Josef (alias Giuseppe) Pascal (1884–1976)
Crecelius, Wilhelm (1828–1889)
Creizenach, Wilhelm (1851–1919)
Creed, Howard Hall (1908–1988)
Cremona, Joseph (Anthony, b.1922)
Crépin, André (Pierre René Louis, b.1928)
Crespo, Martin (19th cent.)
Creuzer, Georg Friedrich (1771–1858)

Crevier, Jean-Baptiste (1693–1765)
Creyke, William (15th cent.)
Criado de Val, Manuel (b.1917)
Crick, Francis Henry Compton (b.1916)
Crispin, Miles (12th cent. A.D.)
Cristofani, Mauro (c.1920–1998)
Croce, Benedetto (1866–1952)S, E
Crodelius, Marcus (fl.1540–1552)
Croiset van der Kop, A. C. (1859–1914)
Croke, Richard (1489?–1558)
Crollius, Oswald (1580–1609)
Crombie, Alexander (1762–1840)
Crome, Friedrich Wilhelm (1753–1833)
Cromwell, Oliver (1599–1658)
Cromwell, Thomas (1485–1540)
Cronia, Arturo (1896–1967)
Cronin, Grover J. (c.1890-c.1960)
Cronström, Anne-Marie (1923–1994)
Cros, Charles (1842–1888)
Cross, Ephraim (1893–1978)
Cross, Samuel Hazzard (1891–1946)
Crossland, Ronald Arthur (b.1920)
Crouzet, Paul (1873–1952)
Crow, Martin Michael (1901–1997)
Crowley, Terry (1953–2005)
Crowther, bishop Samuel Ajayi (alias Ajayi, 1806/1808–1891)E
Cruciger, Georg (alias Kreutzger, 1575–1637)
Cruden, Alexander (1700–1770)
Crusius, Martin(us) (1526–1607)
Cruttenden, Alan (b.1936)
Cruz, Frei Francisco de la, O.P. (d.1660)
Crystal, David (b.1941)
Csoma, Sándor Körösi (1784–1842)

Csipkes, Gyorgi (1628–1678)
Cua, Paulus (*alias* Huynh Tinh Cua, 1834–1907)
Cuadros y Valpuesto, Diego (1677–1746)S
Cubero, Fr. Fulgencio (1892–1950)
Čubinašvili, Davit (1814–1891)
Cucina, Carla (b.1960)
Cudworth, Ralph (1617–1688)
Cuervo, Rufino José (1844–1911)S
Cueva, Pedro, O.P. (d.1611)
Cuevas, José María Fausto de las, O.P. (fl.1824)
Cukerman, Isaak Iosofovič (1909–1998)
Culicover, Peter W(illiam, b.1945)
Culin, Stewart (1858–1929)
Culioli, Antoine (b.1924)E
Cullen, William (1710–1790)
Culler, Jonathan (Dwight, b.1944)
Cullingford, Richard E. (b.1946)
Culmannus, Leonhard (*alias* Kulmann, 1497/98–1562)
Culpeper, *Sir* Cheney (1601–1663)
Culpeper, Nicholas (1616–1654)
Cummings, Michael (b.1940)
Cummins, Jim (b.1949)
Cunha, Celso Ferreira da (1917–1989)
Cunradi, Johann Gottlieb (1757–1828)
Cuny, Albert (Louis Marie, 1869–1947)
Cuoco, Vincenzo (1770–1823)S
Cuoq, Jean-André (1821–1898)S
Čupr, Zemřel Karel (1919–1995)
Cuřín, František (1913–1988)
Curio, Caelus Secundus (1503–1569)
Curme, George Oliver (1860–1948)

Curreau de la Chambre, Marin (1594–1669)
Currie, Eva García (b.1912)
Currie, Haver Cecil (1908–1993)
Curry, Haskell B. (1900–1982)
Curti, Theodor (1848–1914)
Curtin, Jeremiah (1835–1906)
Curtius, Ernst (1814–1896)
Curtius, Ernst Robert (1886–1956)
Curtius, Georg (1820–1885)S, E
Cusanus, Nicholas, *see* Nicolaus of Cusa
Cushing, Frank Haldson (1857–1899)
Cushing, Harvey William (1869–1939)
Cust, Robert Needham (1821–1909)
Cuváminnáta Técikar (early 17th cent. A.D.)
Cuveiro Piño, Juan (1821–1906)
Cuvier, Georges (*recte*: Léopold Chrétien Frédéric Dagobert), *baron*, 1769–1832)
Cuvelier, J. (1869–1947)
Cuypers,Willem (1632–1702)
Cybulski, Wojciech (1808–1867)
Cyprian(us), Thascius Caelius (d.258 A.D.)
Cyrano de Bergerac, Sevinien de (1619–1655)
Cyril(lus), Saint (c.827–869 A.D.)
Cyzev'skyj, Dmytro Ivanovič (1896–1977)
Czambel, Samo (1856–1910)
Czapkiewicz, Andrzej (1924–1990)
Czarnecki, Tomasz (b.1944)K
Czech, Franz Hermann (*ante* 1818–*post* 1841)
Czekanowski, Jan (1882–1965)

D.

Daan, Jo (1910–2006))

Dabbs, Jack (Autrey, b.1914)

Dabène, Michel (b.1934)

Dabercusius, Matthias Marcus
(fl.1577)

Dąbrowska-Smektala, Elżbieta
Krystyna (1930–2000)

da Buti, Francesco (1324–1405)

D'Açarq, Jean-Pierre (c.1720–
c.1795)

Dacier, Anne Lefèvre (1647–1720)

Dacier, Bon-Joseph (1742–1833)

Dacus, Boethius, *see* Boethius of
Dacia

Dacus, Johannes, *see* John of Dacia

Dacus, Martinus, *see* Martin of Dacia

Dacus, Simon, *see* Simon of Dacia

Dadey, José, S.J. (1576–1659)

Daffner, Hugo (1882–1941)

Dafforne, Richard (c.1590–1660/70)

da Firenze, Angelo (fl.1755)

Dafydd Ddu (fl.1322)

Dagg, John Ladley (1794–1884)

Dagget, Windsor Pratt (1877–1958)S

Dagleish, Walter Scott (1834–1897)

D'Aguilar, Mosseh Rephael (*post*
1615–1679)

Dahl, Östen (b.1945)

Dahl, Otto Christian (1903–1995)

Dahl, Peter Edmund (c.1870–1930)

Dahl, Torsten (1897–1968)

Dahlerup, Verner (1859–1938)

Dahlmann, Friedrich Christoph
(1785–1860)

Dahlstedt, Karl-Hampus (1917–
1996)

Dahmen, Johann Wilhelm Anton
(1715–1773)

Dahmen, Wolfgang (b.1950)

Dahm Rinnan, Gyda (1922–1986)

Dai, Bingham (1899–19??)

Daka, Palokë (1925–1987)

Daines, Simon (fl.1640)

Dal, Ingerid (1895–1985)S

Dal', Vladimir Ivanovič (1801–1872)
S

Daladier, Anne (b.1952)

Dale, Francis (Richard, 18??–19??)

Dale, Johan Hendrik van (1828–
1872)

Dale, John Taylor (1905–1998)

Dale, Thomas (1797–1870)

Dalechamps, Jacques (1513–1588)

D'Alexis, Guillaume (1425–1486)

Dales, George F., Jr. (1928–1992)

Dalgado, Sebastião Rodolpho (1855–
1922)E

Dalgarno, George (1626–1687)S, E

Dalmas, Martine (b.1953)K

Dalmata, Hermannus (12th cent.)

Dal Pozzo, Ferdinando (1768–1843)

Dalton, Jack Parkes (1935–1981)

Dam, Roelf Jan (1896–1945)

Daman, Ernst (1904–*post* 1994)

Damascene, Saint John (c.673–777)

Dambe, Vallija (1912–1995)

Damberg, Pêtõr (1909–1987)

Damen, Wolfgang (b.1950)

Damiani, Encrico (1892–1953)

Damiron, Jean-Philibert (1794–1862)

Dammann, Ernst (1904–199?)

Damourette, Jacques (1873–1943)S

Dąmbska, Izydora (1904–1983)

Damsteeght, Boudewijn Cornelis
(b.1916)
Dana, James Dwight (1813–1895)
Danchev, Andrei (Dančev, Andrej,
1933–1996)
D'Ancona, Paolo (1878–19??)
D'Andrade, Roy G. (b. c.1935)
Daneš, Frantiček (b.1919)E
Danes, John (d.1639)
Danet, Pierre (c.1650–1709)
Dangeau, Louis Courcillon de, *abbé*
(1643–1723)S
Daňhelka, Jiří (1919–1993)
Daničić, Đura (father's surname
Popovič, 1825–1882)S
Daniel, Antoine, S.J. (1601–1648)
Daniel, Evan (1837–1904)
Daniel(l), Godfrey (fl.1634–1652)
Daniel(l), William (c.1580–1628)
Daniels, R. Balfour (1900–1987)
Danielsenus, Niels (Skovgaard,
1933–1987)
Danielsson, Olof August (1852–
1933)
Danilov, Georgij Konstantinovič
(1896–1937)
Danon-Boileau, Laurent (b.1946)
Dante Alighieri (1265–1321)S
Darbelnet, Jean (Louis, 1904–1990)
Dargan, Edwin Preston (1879–1940)
Darmesteter, Arsène (1846–1888)S
Darmesteter, James (1849–1894)
Darnell, George (1798–1857)
Darnell, Regna D(iebold, b.1943)
Darrigol, Jean Pierre (1790–1829)
Darski, Józef (b.1941)K
Daru, Pierre Antoine Noël Bruno,
comte (1767–1829)
Darwin, Charles (Robert, 1809–1882)

Darwin, Erasmus (1731–1802)
Darwin, George Howard (1845–
1912)
Darwin, William Erasmus (1839–
1914)
Dascal, Marcelo (b. c.1948)
Dasent, Charles Underwood
(1824/25–1895)
Dasent, (*Sir*) George Webbe (1817–
1896)
Das Gupta, Jyotirindra (b.1933)
Daškova, Ekaterina R. (1743–1810)
Dasypodius, Petrus (*alias* Peter
Hasenfratz *or* Hasenfuss, c.1490–
1559)S
Dathe, Johann August (1731–1791)
Dati, Agostino (1420–1478)
Dati, Carlo Roberto (1619–1676)
Daube, Louis-Jacques-Joseph (1763–
1847)
Daubert, Johannes (1877–1947)
Daukša, Kazimieras Kristupas
(1796–1824)
Dauksa, Mikalojus (1527/28–1613)
Daum, Christian (d.1687)
Daumas, François (1915–1984)
Daunou, Pierre Claude François
(1761–1840)
Dauses, August (b.1947)K
Dauzat, Albert (1877–1955)S, E
David b. Abraham, *see* al-Fāsī
David bar Paulos of Beth Rabban
(8th cent. A.D.)
David, *abbé* Bernard (1927–1998)
David, Christian (1590–1651)
David, J., S.J. (1647–1713)
David, Jan Baptist (1801–1866)
David, Jules (1783–1854)
David, Madeleine V. (d.1989)

Davidová, Dana (d.1998)
Davidson, Andrew Bruce (1831–1902)
Davidson, Donald (1917–2003)E
Davidson, *Colonel* John (1845–1917)
Davies, Alan (b.1931)
Davies, Anna Morpurgo, *see under* Morpurgo Davies, Anna
Davies, Donald Watts (b.1924)
Davies, Edward of Brecon (1756–1831)
Davies, Henry William (1834–1895)
Davies, *Dr.* John (c.1567–1644)S
Davies, John (1772–1855)
Daviet, Françoise (b.1955)K
Davis, Boyd H(arriet, b.1940)
Davis, John (1757–1854)
Davis, Joseph Lee (1906–1974)
Davis, *Sir* John Francis (1795–1890)
Davis, Norman (1913–1989)
Davis, William Jafferd (fl.1872–1877)
Davydov, Ivan Ivanovyč (1794–1863)
Dawkins, Richard M. (1871–1955)
Dawson, *Rev.* Benjamin (1729–1814)
Dawson, George M. (1849–1901)
Dawson, *Sir* John (1820–1899)
Dax, Gustave (1815–1893)
Dax, Marc (1770–1837)
Day, Dorothy (1897–1980)
Day, Gordon Malcolm (1911–1993)
Dayal, Veneeta (b.1956)E
Dean, Ruth Josephine (1902–2003)
Deanović, M. (1890–19??)
De Bal, Joseph (d.1856)
de Balmes, Abraham (Hebr. Avrāhām ben Mēᶜīr (c.1440–1523)S
De Breville, Roussel (1729–c.1793)
Debrie, René (1820–1889)

De Brosses, Charles, *see* Brosses, Charles de
Debrun, François-Joseph-Bénoni (1765–1845)
Debrunner(-Rudin), (Johann) Albert (1884–1958)
Debus, Friedhelm (b.1932)K
DeCamp, David (1927–1979)S
Dechert, Hans-Wilhelm (b.1929)K
Decimator, Henricus (*alias* Heinrich, c.1544–1615)
De Cosmi, Giovanni Agostino (1726–1810)S
Décsy, Gyula (b.1925)
Dee, John (1527–1608)
Deecke, Wilhelm (1831–1897)
Deese, James E(arle, b.1928)
De Felice, Emidio (1918–1993)
DeFrancis, John (b.1911)
Dégallier, Georges (1885–1973)
Degen, Carl Ferdinand (1766–1825)
Degenhardt, Rudolf (fl.1859–1891)
Dégerando, Joseph-Marie (*baron*, 1772–1842)
De Groot, Albert Willem (1892–1963)
Deguignes, Joseph (1721–1800)
Deiters, Carl (1839–1904)
Dejerine, Jules (1849–1917)
Dejna, Karol (b.1911)
Delafosse, Ernest François Maurice (1870–1926)
De la Mare, Albinia Catherine (1932–2001)
De la Mothe, G[iles?] (fl.1592)
De Laet, Jan (1593–1649)
De Laguna, Frederica ("Freddy"; full name: Frederica Annis Lopez de Leo de Laguna, 1906–2000)

De Laguna, Grace A(ndrus, 1878–1978)
Delany, Sheila (b.1945)
de la Vega, Garcilaso, *see* Vega, Garcilaso de la
Delacroix, Henri (Joachim, 1873–1937)
Delambre, Jean Baptiste Joseph (1749–1822)
Deland, Graydon Skerritt (1899–19??)
Delaplace, Guislain François (1557–1823)
Delattre, Pierre (Charles, 1903–1969)S, E
Delavenay, Émile (1905–2003)
Delboeuf, Joseph (1831–1896)
Delbouille, Maurice (1903–1984)
Delbrück, Berthold (Gustav Gottlieb, 1842–1922)S, E
Delbrück, Johann Friedrich Ferdinand (1772–1848)
Delbrück, Johann Friedrich Gottlieb (1768–1830)
Deleau, Nicolas (1797–1862)
Delesalle, Simone (b.1935)
Deleuze, Gilles (1925–1995)
Delgado, Manuel, O.S.A. (1731–1783)
Delgado León, Feliciano (1926–2004)
Delić, Mićo (1939–1992)
Delfico, Melchiorre (1744–1835)
Delicado, Francisco (c.1485–1535)
Delille, Jacques (1783–1813)
Delisle, Léopold-Victor (1826–1910)
Delitzsch, Friedrich (Konrad Gerhard, 1850–1922)
Delius, Nikolaus (1813–1888)

Della Bella, Ardelio, S.J. (1655–1737)
Della Corte, Francesco (1913–1991)
Della Luna, Niccolò (1410–*post* 1450)
Della Porta, Giambattista (1535?–1615)
Della Volpe, Galvano (1895–1968)S
Deloffre, Frédéric (b.1921)
De Lollis, Cesare (1863–1928)S
Deloria, Ella Cara (1889–1971)S
Delmenigo, Elijah (1460–1497)
De Maistre, Joseph (1754/55–1821)
De Man, Paul (1919–1983)
Demandre, A. (d.1808)
Demantius, (Johann) Christoph (1567–1643)
Demarest, de Saint-Sorlin, Jean (1596–1676)
Demartin, Adam (1930–1996)
De Mauro, Tullio (b.1932)E
Demaus, Robert (1829?–1874)
Demetrius, Chlorus (late 2nd or early 1st cent. B.C.)
Demetrius Chalkondyles (1424–1511)
Demetrius Laco (fl. 2nd cent. B.C.)
Demetrius of Phaleron (c.350 B.C.)
de Mille, Richard (b.1922)
Demina, Evgenija Ivanovna (b.1928)
Demiraj, Shaban (b.1919)
Dem'jankov, Valerij Zakievič (b.1948)
Democritus (460/457–mid-4th cent. B.C.)
De Morgan, Augustus (1806–1871)
Demosthenes (384–322 B.C.)
DeMott, Benjamin (b.1924)
Demoule, Jean (1915–1986)

De Moy, Charles Alexandre (1750–1834)

Demoz, Abraham (1935–1994)

Dempe, Hellmuth (1904–1990)K

Dempster, Germaine (d.1970)

Dempwolff, Otto (Heinrich August Louis, 1871–1938)

Denaisius, Peter (1560–1610)

Denes, Peter D. (1920–1976)

Denidel, A. (*fl.*1498)

Denina, Carlo (Giovanni Maria, 1731–1813)S

Denis, Ferdinand (1798–1890)

Denis, (Johann Nepomuk Cosmas) Michael, S.J. (1729–1800)

Dennis, John (1657–1734)

Denoeu, François (1898–1975)

Densusianu, Ovid (1873–1938)S

Den(t)zler, Johann Jakob (1622–1705)

Deny, Jean (1879–1963)

Denys, etc., *see under* Dionysius

De Palma, Armando (b.1937)

De Pauw, Cornelius (1739–1799)

Derbyshire, Desmond (b.1924)

Dérembourg, Hartwig (1844–1908)

Dérenbourg, Joseph (*orig.* Dernburg, 1811–1895)

Dèr Mouw, Johan Andreas (1853–1919)

Derdon, David (d.1664)

De Rijk, Lambertus Maria, S.J. (b.1924)

Derrida, Jacques (1930–2004)

Deržavin, Nikolaj Sergeevič (1877–1953)

Derwing, Bruce L. (b.1938)

Des Autels, Guillaume (1529–1581)

Desainliens, Claude (*alias* Ho(l)liband, c.1540–1597)

De Sanctis, Francesco (1817–1883)S

De Sanctis, Gaetano (1870–1957)

Desbordes, Françoise (1944–1998)

Descartes, René (Cartesius, 1596–1650)E

Deschamps, Claudio François (1745–1791)

Deschanel, Émile (1819–1904)

Desclés, Jean-Pierre (b.1943)

De Sélincourt, Basil (1875–1966)

Desgrouais (1703–1766)

Désirat, Claude (b.1930)

Desloges, Pierre (1742–*post* 1793)

Desmarais, François-Seraphin, *see* Regnier-Desmarais, F.-S.

Desmet, Piet (b.1965)

Desnickaja, Agnija Vasil'evna (1912–1992)K, E

Despauterius, Jo(h)annes (Jan Despauter, wrongly identified as Jan de Spauter or van Pauteren, c.1460–1520)

Desphande, Madhav M. (b.1946)

Desportes, Philippe (1546–1606)

Desroches, Jean (*alias* Jan Des Roches,1740–1787)

Dessalles, Jean Léon (1803–1878)

Destaing, (Léon) Edmond (1872–1940)

Destutt de Tracy, Antoine-César-Victor (1781–1864)

Destutt, *comte* de Tracy, Antoine-Louis-Claude (1754–1836)S

Detering, Klaus (b.1935)K

Detges, Ulrich (b.1958)

Deuerlein, Ernst (19th cent.?)

Deusen, Paul Jacob (1845–1919)

Deusingius, Antonius (1612–1666)
Deutschbein, Carl (fl.1875–1902)
Deutschbein, Max (Leo Ammon, 1876–1949)S
Deutschmann, Olaf (1912–1989)
Devarius, Matthaeus (c.1505–1581)
Devis, Ellin (1746–1820)
Devkin, Valentin Dmitrievič (b.1925)
De Vooys, Cornelius Gerrit Nicolaas (1873–1955)
Devoto, Giacomo (1897–1974)S, E
De Vries, Matthias (1820–1892)
D'Ewes, *Sir* Simonds (1602–1650)
Dewey, John (1859–1952)
De Witte, Aegidius (1649–1721)
De Worde, Wynkyn (d.1734)
Dhanapāla (10th cent.)S
D'Hayere, J. B. (18th cent.)
D'Hubelot de Morainville, Barthelemy (fl.1697)
Diakonoff (Djakonov), Igor' M., *see* D'jakonov, Igor Mixajlovič
Dias, Pedro, S.J. (1621–1700)
Diaz, Francesco (Dominican, 1606–1646)
Díaz del Castillo, Bernal (1492–1581)
Díaz Morante, Pedro (d.1636)
Díaz Rengifo, Juan, S.J. (1553–1615)
Diaz-Rubio y Carmera, Manuel Maria (pseud. El Misántropo, b. c.1850–*post* 1885)S
Dibbern, Nikolaus (1640–*post* 1692)
Dibbets, Geert Rutgerus Wilhelmus (b.1938)
Dibelius, Wilhelm (1876–1931)
Di Benedetto, Vincenzo (b. c.1915)
Di Breme, Ludovico (1780–1820)
Di Cesare, Donatella (b.1956)
Dickenmann, Ernst (1902–1985)

Dickins, Bruce (1889–1978)
Dickens, Patrick John (1953–1992)
Dickins, Bruce (1889–1978)
Diconson, Thomas (1590–*post* 1639)
Diderichsen, Paul (1905–1964)S
Diderot, Denis (1713–1784)E
Didymus ('Chalkenteros', late 1st cent. B.C.)S
Dieckmann, Walter (b.1933)K
Diefenbach, (Georg) Lorenz (Antn, 1806–1883)
Diego de la Encarnación, see Cisneros, Diego de
Diel, Florenz (Florentius, fl.1490–1509; d. *post* 1518)
Diels, Hermann (Alexander, 1848–1922)
Diels, Paul (1882–1963)S
Diensberg, Bernhard (b.1936)K
Dieth, Eugen (1893–1956)S
Diether, Jakob (*alias* Tabernaemontanus, Joacobus Theodorius, 1520/1530–1590)
Dietl, Georg Aloys (1752–1809)
Dietz, Klaus (b.1935)
Ditrich, Albrecht (1866–1908)
Dietrich, Franz Eduard Christoph (1810–1883)
Dietrich, Gerhard (1900–1985?)
Dietrich, Manfried (Leonhard Georg, b.1935)K
Dietrich, Rainer (b.1944)K
Dietrich, Wolf (b.1940)K
Dietze, Joachim (b.1931)
Diez, Friedrich (Christian, 1794–1876)S, E
Dieze, Johann Andreas (1729–1785)
Digby, (*Sir*) Kenelm (1603–1665)
Dignāga (481–540 A.D.)S

Dihigo, Juan Manuel (1866–1952)
Dijk, Johan Adriaan van (1830–1908)
Dijk, Teun (Adrianus) van (b.1943)
Dijksterhuis, Eduard Jan (1892–1965)
Dik, Simon Cornelis (1940–1995)
Dil, Anwar S. (b.1933)
Dilevski, Nikolaj Mixajlovič (1904–2001)
Dilich, Wilhelm (1571–1655)
Dillard, Joey Lee (b.1924)
Diller, Hans-Jürgen (b.1934)K
Diller, Karl (Conrad, b.1939)
Dillinger, Michael L. (*alias* Hyde, "Mike", b.1955)
Dillmann, Christian Friedrich August (1823–1894)S
Dillon, Myles (1900–1972)
Dilthey, Julius Friedrich Carl (1797–1857)
Dilthey, Wilhelm (1833–1911)
Dilworth, Thomas (d.1780)
Dimitrovski, Todor (1922–2000)
Dindic,Slavoljub (1935–2000)
Dinekov, Petăr (1910–1992)
Ding, Du (990–1053 A.D.)
Ding, Sheng-shu, *see* Ting, Sheng-shu
Dinges, Georg (*alias* Georgij Genrixvič, 1893–1933)
Dingler, Hugo (1881–1954)
Dingwall, William Orr (b.1934)
Dinis, *Dom* (1261–1325)
Dinneen, David Allen (b.1931)
Dinneen, Francis Patrick, S.J. ("Frank", 1923–1994)
Dinnsen, Daniel A. (b.1947)
D'Introno, Francesco (b.1942)

Diocles Magnes ('of Magnesia', 27 B.C.–14 A.D)S
Diodati, Giovanni (1576–1649)
Diodorus Siculus ('of Sicily', c.90–c.20 B.C.)
Diogenes Laertius (c.341–270 B.C.)
Diogenes of Oenoanda (c. 2nd cent. A.D.)
Diogenes the Babylonian (c.240–152 B.C.) S, E
Diomedes Grammaticus (fl.370–380 A.D.)S
Dionysia de Munchesny (13th cent.)
Dionysius (of) Halicarnass(e)us (55?–5? B.C.)S
Dionysius Thrax (c170–c.90 B.C.)S
Di Parma, (Michele) Leone (1776–1858)
Di Pietro, Robert Joseph (1932–1991)S
Dirac, Paul Adrien Maurice (1902–1994)
Dirr, Adolf (1867–1930)
Dirven, René (b.1930)
Dittmar, Norbert (b.1943)K
Dittrich, Ottmar (1865–1951)
Diver, William (Greenwald, 1921–1996)
Dixon, Hugh Neville (1861–1944)
Dixon, James Main (1856–1933)
Dixon, Robert M(alcolm) W(ard, "Bob", b.1939)
Dixon, Roland B(urridge, 1875–1934)
D'jakonov, Igor' Mixajlovič (1915–1999)
Djamo-Diacontă, Lucia (1916–1995)
Djupedal, Reidar (1921–1989)

Długosz, Jan (*alias* Longinus, 1415–1480)

Dłuska, Maria (1900–1992)

Dmitriev, Lev Aleksandrovič (1921–1993)

Dmitriev, Petr Andreevič (1928–1998)

Dmitrievskij, A. A. (1856–1929)

Dmochowski, Franciszek Krsawery (1762–1808)

Dobbie, Elliott van Kirk (1907–1970)

Dobie, James Frank (1888–1964)

Doblhofer, Ernst (b.1919)

Dobrev, Ivan K. (b.1938)

Dobritzhoffer, Martin, S.J. (1717–1791)

Dobromyslov, Vasilij Alekseevič (1892–1965)

Dobrovol'skij, Dmitrij (b.1953)K

Dobrovský, Josef (1753–1829)S, E

Dobruský, Václav (1858–1916)

Dobson, Eric John (1913–1984), E

Docen, Bernhard Joseph (1782–1828)

Dockstader, Frederick J. (b.1919)

Dod, John (1549–1645)

Dodart, Denis (1634–1707)

Dodd, Stuart Carter (1900–1975)

Dodd, Thomas Joseph (1907–1971)

Doddridge, Philip (1739–1786)

Dodge, Raymond (1871–1942)

Dodgson, John McNeal (1928–1990)

Dodoens, Rembert (Dodonaeus, 1517–1585)

Dodsley, Robert (1703–1764)

Dodsley, James (1724–1797)

Dögen, Matthias (*also* Mathys, 1605–1672)

Dögen, Wilhelm (1877–1967)

Döhne, Jacob Ludwig (1811–1879)

Döleke, Wilhelm Heinrich (late 18th–earely 19th cent.)

Dölger, Franz (1891–1968)

Döll, J(ohann?) Ch(ristian?, 1808–1885)

Doerfer, Gerhard (b.1920)K

Doergangk, Henricus (*alias* Heinrich, late 16th–early 17th cent.)S

Dogil, Grzegorz (b.1952)K

Dogramadžieva, Ekaterina (b.1933)

Dohna, Fabian von (1550–1621)

Doke, Clement Martyn (1893–1980)E

Dokulil, Milos (1912–2002)

Dolanský, Ladislav (1857–1910)

Dolben, John (Bishop of Rochester, later Archbishop of York, 1625–1686)

Dolce, Lodovico (1505–1568)S

Dolet, Estienne (c.1509–c.1546)

Doležal, Pavol (1700–1778)S

Dolgopol'skij, Aharon (Aron) Borisovič (b.1921)

Dollard, John (1900–1977)

Dolnik, Juraj (b.1931)

Dolobo, Milyj Gerasimovič (fl.1927)

Dolz, Johann Christian (1769–1843)

Domašnev, Anatolij Ivanovič (1927–2001)

Dombay, Franz Lorenz von (1756–1810)

Domenech, *abbé* Emmanuel Henri Dieudonné (1826–1886)

Doménech, Pedro, S.J. (d.1560)

Domergue, (François) Urbain (1745–1810)

Domi, Mahir (1915–2000)

Domingo de Santo Tomás, S.J. (1559–1630)

Domingo de Soto, *see* Soto, Domingo de

Domínguez, Ramón Joaquín (1811-1848)

Dominici, Giovanni (1356–1419)

Dominici, Marc (b.1948)

Donaldson, Ethelbert Talbot (1910–1987)

Donaldson, William (1811–1861)

Donath, Adolf (1919–1984)

Donatus, Aelius (mid-4th cent. A.D.)S

Donatus ortigraphus (anon. Irishman of 2nd half of the 7th cent. or author of text produced c.815?)S

Donders, Franz Cornelius (1818–1889)

Dondua, Karpez Darispanovič (1891–1951)

Donelaitis, Christian (1714–1780)

Doney, *abbé* Jean Marie (1794–1871)

Donner, Kai R. (d.1936)

Donner, Otto (1835–1909)

Dong, Zuobin (1895–1963)S

Doniol, Henry (= Jean Henri Antoine, 1818–1906)

Donovan, William Joseph (1883–1959)

Dony, Émile (1865–1944)

Donzé, Roland (André, b.1921)

Dordić, Petar (1904–1989)

Dorfmüller-Karpusa, Käthi (b.1935)K

Dorian, Nancy C(urrier, b.1936)E

Doritsch, Alexander (1887–1961)

Dorjiev, Avgan (1854–1938)

Dorn, Bernhardt Andreevič (1805–1881)

Dorn, Gerhard (fl.1570–1590)

Dornau, Caspar (1577–1632)

Dornblüth, Augustin (c.1680–1755/1768)

Dornseiff, Franz (1888–1960)S

Doroszewski, Witold (Jan, 1899–1976)

Dorotjaková, Viktória (d.1999)

Dorp, John (fl.1393–1405)

Dorp, Martin (1485–1525)

Dorph, Niels Vinding (1783–1858)

Dorsey, George Amos (1868–1931)

Dorsey, *Rev.* James Owen (1848–1895)S

Došen, Vid (1720–1778)

Dositheus (late 4th cent. A.D.)

Dosmüḥabet-ülï, Ḥalel (1883–1939)

Dossin, Georges (1896–1983)

Dostál, Antonín (1906–1997)

Dostert, Léon Émile (1904–1971)

Dotan, Aaron (b.1930)

Dottin, (Henri) Georges (1863–1928)

Douay(ex-Soublin), Françoise (b.1945)

Douceur, David (fl.1606)

Douchet, Jacques-Philippe-Augustin (c.1750–18??)

Douet, Jean (fl.1664)

Dougherty, Ray C(ordell, b.1940)

Douglas, Gavin, *bishop* of Dunkeld (1472–1522)

Douglas, Wilfrid (1917–2004)

Douglas, Mary (Tew]. b.1921)

Doujat, Jean (1609–1688)

Douwes Dekker, Eduard (*alias* Multatuli, 1820–1887)

Douza, Janus (1545–1609)

Dutz, Klaus D(ietrich?, 1953–2006)K
Du Vair, Guillaume (1556–1621)
Du Val, Paul-Marie (1912–1997)
Du Val, Pierre (1618–1683)
Duverney, Joseph-Guichard (1648–
  1730)
Duvivier, Charles-Pierre, *see* Girault-
  Duvivier, Charles-Pierre
Du Vivier, Gérard (fl.1560)
Du Wes (also: Du Guez), Gilles
  (c.1470–1553)
Dvřák, Emil (1925–1983)
Dwight, Benjamin Woodbridge
  (1816–1889)
Dwilewicz, Henryk (1929–1998)
Dwivedi, D(evi) S(hankar, b.1937)
Dworkin, Steven (b.1947)
Dybo, Vladimir Atononvič (fl.1962–
  1968)
Dybowski, Roman (1883–1945)
Dyche, Thomas (fl.1719–1735)S
Dyen, Isidore (b.1913)
Dyk, Walter (1899–1972)
Dyke, Daniel, the Elder (d.1614)
Dykerius, Joannes (c.1664–1733)
Dynamius (c.8th cent. A.D.)
Dyvik, Helge (b.1947)
Džamanjić, Rajmund, O.P. (c.1587–
  1597)
Džonov, Bojan (1918–1992)

E.

Earle, *Rev.* John (1824–1903)
Eastlake, Frank Warrington (1858–1905)
Eastman, Carol M. (1941–1997)
Easton, Morton William (1841–19??)
Eastwick, Edward B(ackhouse, 1814–1883)
Eb, Karl Wilhelm (1808–1840)
Ebbesen, Sten (b.1946)
Ebbinghaus, Ernst A. (1926–1995)
Ebbinghaus, Hermann (1850–1909)
Ebel, Hermann (Wilhelm, 1820–1875)
Ebeling, Christoph Daniel (1741–1817)
Eberhard, Johann August (1739–1809)S
Eberhardus Alemannus, *see* Evrard the German
Eberhardus Bethuniensis (Evrard de Béthume, d. c.1212)
Eberlein, Christian Gottlieb (*alias* Krystian Gottlieb, fl.1763)
Ebers, Georg Moritz (1837–1898)
Ebers, Johann (1742–1818)
Ebert, Adolf (1820–1890)
Ebert, Johann Arnold(1723–1795)
Ebert, Karen H. (b.1945)K
Ebert, Robert Peter (b.1944)K
Eble, Connie (b.1942)
Ebneter, Theodor (b.1923)K
Echard, Laurence (1670?–1730)
Echeberría, Juan de (1767–1845)
Echeverría, Esteban (1805–1851)

Echols, John M(inor, b.1913)
Eckart, Anselm, S.J. (1721–1809)
Eckermann, Karl Theodor (1779–1849)
Eckhart, Johannes (c.1260–1327)
Eckhar(d)t, Johann Georg von (Eccardus, 1664–1730)S
Eckma, Petrus (c.1744–1824)
Eckmann, János (1905–1971)
Eckstein, Friedrich August (1810–1885)
Eco, Umberto (b.1932)E
Edel, Elmar (1914–1997)
Edelman, Gerald Maurice (b.1929)
Edelman, Murray J. (b.1919)
Edelweiss, Frederico (1892–1976)
Edgerton, Franklin (1885–1967)S, E
Edgerton, Robert B. (b.1931)
Edgerton, William Franklin (1893–1970)S
Edgeworth, Maria (1767–1849)
Edgren, August Hjalmar (19th cent.)
Edison, Thomas (Alva, 1847–1931)
Edkins, Joseph (1823–1905)
Edmonds, George (1788–1868)
Edmonson, Munro S. (d.2002)
Edmont, Edmond (1849–1926)
Edmund, *Archbishop* of Canterbury (d.1242?)
Edmundson, Henry (1607–1659)
Edward, 'the Black Prince' (1330–1376)
Edward, *Lord* Zouche (1556?–1625)
Edward I, *King* of England (1239–1307)
Edward III, *King* of England (1312–1377)
Edwards, Anthony (Stockwell Garfield, b.1942)

Edwards, Ernest R. (1871–1948)
Edwards, John Robert (b.1947)
Edwards, *Rev.* Jonathan (1703–1753)
Edwards, *Rev.* Jonathan, Jr. (1745–1801)
Edwards, William (1724–1801)
Edwards, William Frederic (1777–1842)
Edzard , Dietz Otto (1930–2004)
Edzardi, Anton Philipp (1849–1882)
Eeden, Frederik Willem van (1860–1932)
Eekma, Petrus (c.1749–1824)
Egede, Hans (1698–1758)
Egede, Paul (1708–1789)
Egenolff, Johann Augustin (1683–1729)
Egenolff, Peter (1851–1901)
Egerod, Søren (Christian, 1923–1995)
Egerton, George (b.1941)
Eggan, Fred (1906–1991)
Eggeling, Julius (1841–1918)
Egger, Émile (1813–1885)
Egger, Victor (1848–1909)
Eggers, Hans (b.1907)
Egidius Candidus Pastor, pseud., *see* De Witte, Aegidius
Egli, Urs (b.1944)
Eguilaz y Yanguaz, Leopoldo (1829–1900)
Ehlers, Martin (1732–1800)
Ehlich, Konrad (b.1942)K
Ehn, Wolter (1931–1994)
Ehrenfels, Christian Maria, *Freiherr* von (1859–1932)
Ehrenreich, Paul (1855–1914)
Ehrensperger, Edward Charles (1895–1984)

Ehrismann, Otfried (b.1941)K
Ehrlich, Eugen (1832–1922)
Ehrman, Albert (1933–1981)
Ehrmann, Theophil Friedrich (1762–1811)
Eichhoff, Frédéric Gustave (1799–1875)
Eichhoff, Jürgen (b.1936)K
Eichholtz, Peter (d.1655)
Eichhorn, Johann Albrecht Friedrich (1779–1856)
Eichhorn, Johann Gottlieb (1752–1827)
Eichinger, Ludwig Maximilian (b.1950)K
Eichler, Albert (1879–1953)
Eichler, Ernst (b.1930)K
Eichler, Ernst (1954–1989)
Eichner, Heiner (b.1942)K
Eigminas, Kazimieras (1929–1996)
Eilers, Wilhelm (1906–1989)
Eijkman, Leonard Pieter Hendrik (1854–1937)
Eilers, Wilhelm (1906–1989)K
Eimas, Peter D. (b.1934)
Eimermacher, Karl (b.1938)K
Einenkel, Eugen (1853–1930)
Einhauser, Eveline (b.1960)K
Einion Offeiriad (*fl.*1322)
Eisenberg, Peter (b.1940)K
Eisenmeier, Josef (1871–1926)
Eismann, Wolfgang Ulrich (b.1942)K
Eisner, Sigmud (b.1920)
Eitrem (1872–1966)
Ejskjær, Inger (b.1926)
Ekblom, R. (1874–1959)
Ekwall, Eilert (1877–1965)

Eldad (ben Mahli) Ha-dani (9th cent. A.D.)
Elbert, Samuel Hoyt (1907–1997)
Elcock, William Dennis (1910–1960)
Elder, William (1864–1931)
Eleonor of Aquitaine (1122?–1204)
Elert, Claes-Christian (b.1923)
Elffers-van Ketel, E. L. C. ("Els", b.1946)
Elia, Silvio Edmundo (b.1913)
Eliade, Mircea (1907–1986)
Elias of Tirhan (d.1049)
Elias, Norbert (1897–1990)
Eliason, Norman Ellsworth (1907–1991)S
Eliasson, Stig (b.1937)
Eling, Paul(us Alphons Theresia Maria, b.1951)
Eliot, Charles William (1834–1926)
Eliot, John (1562–1593)
Eliot, *Rev.* John ('of Massachusetts', 1604–1690)S
Elis bar Shinaya (975–*post* 1049)
Elisto, Elmar (1901–1987)
Elizabeth I, *Queen* of England (1533–1603)
Elkin, Alphonsus P. (1891–1979)
Elkin, Frederick (b.1918)
Ellegård, Alvar (b.1919)
Ellen, Roy F. (b.1947)
Ellinger, Johann (*fl.*1902–1936)
Elliot, William (1792–1858)
Elliott, Aaron Marshall (1844–1910)
Elliott, Rev. Adam (fl.1845–1846)
Elliott, Ralph Warren Victor (*alias* Rudolf Ehrenberg, b.1920)
Ellis, Alexander John (*né* Sharpe, 1814–1890)S, E
Ellis, Edward Sylvester (1840–1916)

Ellis, Francis Whyte (c.1778–1819)E
Ellis, Jeffrey O. (b.1930?)
Ellis, John M. (b.1936)
Ellis, Tobias (*fl.*1670)
Ellis, Wayne (1915–1993)
Ellis, William (1794–1872)
Ellistone, John (d.1652)
Ells, Benjamin Franklin (1805–1874)
Elmendorf, William W. (1912–1997)
Elmqvist, Axel Louis (d.1949)
Elphinston, James (1721–1809)S, E
Els, Theo J(ohannes) M(aria) van (b.1938)
Elson, Benjamin F. (b.1921)
Elster, Ernst (1866–1940)
Elstob, Elizabeth (1683–1756)
Elstob, William (1673–1715)
Elwert, Wilhelm Theodor (1906–1997)K
Elyot, *Sir* Thomas (c.1490–1546)
Elze, (Friedrich) Karl (*or* Carl, 1821–1889)
Embleton, Sheila (Margaret, b.1954)
Emel'janov, A. E. (1879–1942)
Emeneau, Murray B(arnson, 1904–2005)E
England, Nora C. (b. c.1945)E
Emerson, George Barell (1797–1881)
Emerson, Oliver Farrar (1860–1927)
Emerson, Ralph Waldo (1803–1882)
Emilio, Paolo (= Aemilius, Paulus, fl.1544)
Emonds, Joseph (Embley, b.1940)
Emons, Rudolf (b.1945)K
Empedocles (c.490–c.430 B.C.)
Empson, William (1906–1984)
Emser, Hieronymus (fl.1523)
Encarnación, Juan de la, O.F.M. (18th cent.)

Encina, Francisco, O.S.A. (1715–1760)

Encina, Juan del (1468–1529?)

Encrevé, Pierre (b.1939)

Ende, Casparus van den (1614–1681/1695)

Endemann, Karl (Heinrich Julius, 1836–1919)

Endlicher, Stefan Ladislaus (*alias* István László, 1804–1849)

Endres, Rolf (b.1932)K

Endzelīns, Jānis (1873–1961)S

Engel, Johann Jacob (1741–1802)

Engel, Ulrich (b.1928)K

Engelberts Gerrits, Gerrit (1795–1881)

Engelien, August (1832–1903)

Engels, Friedrich (1820–1895)

Engler, Rudolf (1930–2002)K

Engwer, Theodor (1861–1944)

Enkvist, Nils Erik (b.1925)

Ennin (794–864 A.D.)

Enninger, Werner (b.1931)K

Enriques, Federigo (1871–1946)

Entick, John (1703?–1773)

Entrambosaguas, Joaquín de (1904–1995)

Enzinas, Fernando de (d.1523)

Épée, *abbé* de l', *see* under L'Épée

Epicurus ('of Samos', 341?–270/71 B.C.)S

Epifânio da Silva Dias, Augusto (1841–1916)

Episcopius (1583–1643)

Epling, Philip J. (b.1931)

Eppert, Franz (b.1934)K

Equicola, Mario (c.1470–1525)

Erades, Pieter A. (1898–1968)

Eramian, Gregory M(ichael, b.1942)

Erasmus, Desiderius ('of Rotterdam', 1467–1536)S

Eratosthenes of Kyrene (c.275–c.195 B.C.)

Erasun, José (1821–1894)

Erben, Johannes (b.1925)K

Erchanbertus of Freising (c.840–c.912 A.D.)S

Erdan, Alexandre (pseud. of Alexandre André Jacob, 1826–1878)

Erdélyi, István (1924–1973)

Erdmann, Axel (1843–1926)

Erdmann, Friedrich (1810–1893)

Erdmann, Karl Otto (1858–1931)

Erdmann, Peter (b.1941)K

Erdosy, George, Sr. (1928–1991)

Erelt, Mati (b.1941)

Erhardus Kna(a)b de Zwiefalten (14th cent. A.D.)

Erhart, Adolf (1926–2003)

Eric the Red (9th cent. A.D.)

Erickson, Frederick (b.1941)

Erickson, Jon (b.1937)

Erickson, Milton H. (1901–1980)

Ericson, Eston Everett (1890–1964)

Erikson, Erik (1902–19??)

Eringa, Sjoerd (1860–1945)

Eriugena (= Johannes Scotus, c.810–877)

Erlich, Victor (1914–still alive in 2004)

Erlinger, Hans Dieter (b.1937)K

Erman, Adolf (1854–1937)

Erman, Jean-Pierre Adolphe (1854–1937)

Ernault, Émile Jean Marie (1852–1938)

Erndtel, Christian Heinrich (d.1734)

F.

Faber, Andrzej (fl.1718–1733)

Faber, Basilius (*called* Soranus; *alias* Schmidt, 1520–1576)

Faber, Joseph (1786–*post* 1850)

Fabian, Johannes (b.1925?)

Fabo, Pedro (1883–1933)

Fabra, Pompeu (1868–1948)S

Fabre, Antonio (Fabrus, Antonius, fl.1626–1635)S

Fabre d'Olivet, Antoine (1768–1825)

Fabrés, Andrés (1734–1794)

Febri, Felix (1438/41–1502)

Fabri, Pierre (1460?–1520?)

Fabricius ab Aquapendente, Hieronymous (1533–1619)

Fabricius, Johann Albert (*pseud.* Veridicus Sincerus, 1668–1736)

Fabricius, Johann Andreas (1696–1769)

Fabricius, Johann Philipp (1711–1791)

Fabricius, Johann Seobald (d.1622)

Fabricius, *bishop* Otto (1744–1822)

Fabricius, Peter (d. *post*-1625)

Fabricius-Hansen, Cathrine (b.1942)K

Fabricius-Kovács, Ferenc (1919–1977)S

Fabri de Peiresc, Nicholas Claude (1580–1637)

Fabrini, Giovanni (1516–1580)

Fabritius, Hans (1608–1653)

Fabro, Pedro, S.J. (1506–1546)

Fabronius, Hermann (Mosemannus, 1570–1634)

Fabvre, Bonnaventure, S.J. (fl.1696).

Facciolati, Jacopo (1682–1769)S

Fähnrich, Heinz (b.1941)K

Faerno, Gabriello (d.1561)

Fäsch, Johann Rudolf (d.1762)

Fagan, Sarah M. B. (b.1955)K

Fagius, Paulus (1504–1549)

Fahlman, Scott E. (b.1948)

Fahrenkrüger, Johann Anton (1759–1816)

Faider, Paul (1886–1940)

Faidhebe, Louis Léon César (1818–1889)

Faidit, Gauclem (d.1220)

Faiguet de Villeneuve, Joachim (1703–1780)

Fahlman, Scott E. (b.1948)

Fairbanks, Gordon Hubert (1913–1984)

Fairbanks, Grant (1910–1964)S

Fairclough, Norman (b.1941)

Fairservice, Walter A., Jr. (1921–1994)

Faīrūzābādī, Muḥammad ben Yaᶜqūb al- (1329?–1415)

Fajks, Zygmunt (1905–1989)

Falc'hun, *canon* François (Marie, 1909–1991)E

Falconet, Camille (1671–1762)

Falk, Hjalmar (Sejersted, 1859–1928)S

Falk, Julia S(alebski, b.1941)

Falkenhahn, Viktor (1903–1987)

Falkmann, Christian Friedrich (1782–1844)

Fallet, Gedeon (1544–1615)

Fallot, (Joseph-Fréderic) Gustave (1807–1836)S
Fallside, Frank (1932–1993)
Faltz, Leonard (b.1940)
Famincyn, Andrej Sergeevič (1835–1918)
Fan, Jiang (1761–1831)
Fanselow, Gisbert (b.1959)
Fanshel, David (b.1923)
Fant, C(arl) Gunnar M(ichael, b.1919)E
Farabee, William Curtis (1865–1925)
Fārābī, Abū Naṣr Muḥammad ibn Muḥammad al- (257/870–339/950)S
Faraday, Michael (1791–1867)
Farber, Walter (b.1947)K
Faria, Ernesto de (1906–1962)
Faria, Gaspar, S.J. (d.1739)
Faria e Sousa, Manoel de (1590–1649)
Farina, Giulio (d.1947)
Faris, Ellsworth (1874–1953)
Faris, Robert E. Lee (1907–1998)
Fārisī, Abū ᶜAlī al-Ḥasan ibn Aḥmad al- (288/901-377/987)S
Farkas, Julius von (1894–1958)
Farmer, Paul (b.1959)
Farnaby, Thomas (1575–1647)
Farrā', Abū Zakariyyā' Yaḥyā ibn Ziyād al- (144/761–207/822)S
Farrar, Frederic William (1831–1903)
Fāsī, Dāwīd ben Avrāhām al- (alias Abū Sulaymān Dāwud ibn Ibrahīm al-Fasī, mid-10th cent. A.D.)S
Fasmer, Maksimilian Romanovič, see Vasmer, Max

Fasold, Ralph W(illiam August, b.1940)
Fassett, Frederick G., Jr. (1901–1991)
Fauchet, Claude (1530–1602)S
Fauconnier, Gilles (b.1944)
Faure, George (1910–1994)
Fauriel, Claude (also Foriel, 1772–1844)
Fausbøll, Michael Viggo (1821–1908)
Faust, George Patterson (b.1905)
Fava, Elisabetta (b.1947)
Favard, Jean (1902–1965)
Faversham, Simon de, see Simon of Faversham
Favre, Léopold (1817–1894)
Fawcett, Robin P. (b.1937)
Faye, Abraham de la (fl.1608–1631)
Faye, Jean-Pierre (b.1925)
Fazekas, Jenő (1906–1979)
Fearn, John (1768–1837)
Febrés, Andrés, S.J. (1731–1790)
Fecht, Gerhard (b.1922)K
Fedoseev, Petr Nikolaevič (1902–1990)
Fehr, Bernhard (1876–1938)
Fehrle, Eugen (1880–1957)
Feijó, João de Morais Madureira (also Feyjo, 1688–1741)
Feijoo y Montenegro, Benito Jerónimo (1676–1764)
Feilitzen, Hugo von (1854–1887)
Feinaigle, Gregor (alias Grégoire de, 1760–1819, not 1756–1820?)
Feist, Sigmund (1865–1943)
Felbinger, Jeremias (1616–c.1690)
Felin de São Pedro, padre Benito (1732–1801)

Flexner, Stuart Berg (1928–1990)S
Fliess, Wilhelm (1858–1928)
Flint, Abel (1765–1825)
Flom, George Tobias (1871–1960)
Flor, Christian (1792–1875)
Flora, Radu (1922–1989)
Flor, Fritz (fl.1936)
Florczak, Zofia (1912–1996)
Florenskij, Pavel Aleksandrovič
   (1882–1937)
Flores, Ildofonso Josep, O.F.M.
   (fl.1753; d.1772)
Flores Varela, Camilio (1949–1997)
Florido, Francesco (1511–1547)
Florinskij, V. M. (1834–1899)
Florinskij, Timofej Dmitri'evič
   (1854–1919)
Florinus, Henrik (Henricus, 1633–
   1705)
Florio, John (1553?–1625)
Florio, Michael Angelo (fl.1550)
Florovskij, Anton V. (1884–1968)
Florovskij, G. V. (1893–1979)
Flourens, Jean-Pierre Marie (1794–
   1867)
Flournoy, Theodore (1854–1920)
Fludd, Robert (1574–1637)
Flügel, Ewald (1863–1914)
Flügel, Felix (1820–1904)
Flügel, Gustav (1802–1870)
Flügel, Johann Gottfried (1788–18??)
Flydal, Leiv (1904–1983)S
Flynn, Suzanne Kennedy (b.1937)
Fodor, István (b.1920)
Fodor, Jerry A(lan, b.1935)E
Fodor, Köszöntő (b.19200
Fölsing, Johann Heinrich (1812–
   1894)

Förstemann, Ernst Wilhelm (1822–
   1906)S
Foerster, Heinz von (b.1911)
Förster, K(arl?) G. J. (fl.1851)
Förster, (Theodor Wilhelm) Max
   (1869–1954)S
Foerster, Otfrid (1873–1941
Förster, Wendelin (1844–1915)
Fogarasi, Miklós (1916–1992)
Fogazzaro, Antonio (1842–1911)
Fogel(ius), Martin (1634–1675)
Fogel, Robert William (b.1926)
Fogg, Peter Walkden (1765–1824)
Fohalle, René (1899–1984)
Foigny, Gabriel de (c.1650–1692)
Foisset, Joseph Théphile (1800–
   1873)
Foixa, Jofre de (13th cent. A.D.)
Fokker, Abraham Anthony (1862–
   1927)
Fokker, Adriaan Abraham (1810–
   1878)
Folejewski, Zbigniew (1910–1999)
Folena, Gianfranco (1920–1992)
Foley, James A(ddison, b.1938)
Foley, William A(uguste, b.1949)
Foligno, Cesare (1878–1963)
Folsom, Marvin (b.1929)K
Fónagy, Ivan (1920–2005)
Fonseca, José da (1788–1866)
Fonseca, Pedro José da (1734/37–
   1816)
Fonseca, Petrus (Pedro da, 1548–
   1594)
Fontaine, Jacques (b.1922)
Fontaine, Jean de la (1621–1695)
Fontaine, Pierre-François Léonard
   (1762–1853)

Fraula, Thomas-François-Joseph, *Comte* de (1729–1787)
Fraunce, Abraham (1587–1633)
Frauwallner, Erich (1898–1974)
Frayssinous, Denis-Antoine-Luc (Msg., *évèque* d'Hermopolis, 1765–1841)
Frazer, (*Sir*) James (George, 1854–1941)
Frček, Jan (1896–1942)
Frédégise (Fridugisus, d. c.834)S
Freedman, David Noel (1947–1982)
Freeland, Lucy Shepard ("Nancy", 1890–1972)
Frege, (Friedrich Ludwig) Gottlob (1848–1925)E
Frei, Henri (1899–1980)
Freidhof, Gerd (b.1942)K
Freidson, Eliot (Lazarus, b.1923)
Freigius, Johannes Thomas (*alias* Freige, 1543–1598)
Freire, Francisco de Brito (1623–1692)
Freire, Paulo (1921–1997)E
Freitag, Adam (1602–1664)
Freitag, A. (fl.1839–1846)
Frejdenberg, Ol'ga Mixailovna (1890–1955)
Frellesvig, Bjarke (b.1961)
Fren, Xristian Danilovič (1782–1851)
Frencelius, Abraham (*alias* Fren(t)zel, 1656–1740)
French, David (Plunkett, b.1925)
Frenssen, Gustav (1863–1945)
Fréret, Nicolas (1688–1749)
Fretheim, Thorstein (b.1942)
Freud, Sigmund (1856–1939)E
Freudenthal, Hans (b.1905)
Freund, Wilhelm (1806–1894)

Freycinet, Louis Claude Desaulses de (1779–1842)
Freydank, Dietrich (1928–1999)
Freyer, Hans (1887–1969)
Freyer, Hieronymus (1675–1747)
Freymond, Emile (1855–1918)
Freytag, Georg Wilhelm Friedrich (1788–1861)
Fricke, Gerhard (1901–19??)
Fried, Vilém (1915–1987)
Friederici, Georg (d.1947)
Friedrich, Henryk (1908–1944)
Friedrich, Johannes (1893–1972)S
Friedrich, Max (1856–1887)
Friedrich, Paul W. (b.1927)
Friedrich Wilhelm III, King of Prussia (1770–1840)
Friedrich Wilhelm IV, King of Prussia (1795–1861)
Friedwagner, Mathias (1861–1940)
Friend, Albert C. (1906–1985)
Fries, Charles Carpenter (1887–1967)S, E
Fries, Jakob Friedrich (1773–1843)
Fries, Norbert (b.1950)K
Fries, Peter Howard (b.1937)
Fries, Udo (b,1942)K
Friese, Jakob Bernhard (1769–1851)
Friesen, Otto von (d.1942)
Friis, Jens Andreas (1821–1896)S
Frings, Theodor (1886–1968)S, E
Frinta, Antonín (1884–1975)
Frisch, Johann Leonhard (1666–1743)S
Frischlin(us), (Philipp) Nic(k)odemus (1547–1590)
Frisius, Johannes (*alias* Fries, Hans, 1505–1565)S
Frisk, Hjalmar (1900–1984)

Fritsch, Gustav Theodor (1838–1927)

Fritz, Samuel, S.J. (1651–1734?)

Frobenius, Leo Viktor (1873–1938)

Froehde, Friedrich (1834–1895)

Froehde, Oskar (1868–1916)

Froissart, Jean (1337?–1410?)

Fromant, *abbé* Charles Paul (1714–1783)S

Froment, Jules (1878–1946)

Fromkin, Victoria Adelina (1923–2000)E

Fromm, Hans (b.1919)K

Frommann, Georg Karl (1814–1887)

Fromm-Reichman, Frieda (1889–1957)

Fromondus, Libertus (i.e., Libert Froidmont, 1587–1653)

Fron, Bathasar (fl.1564)

Frost, John (1800–1859)

Frumkina, Revekka Markovna (b.1931)

Fry, Dennis Butler (1907–1983)E

Frye, (Herman) Northrop (1912–1991)

Fu, Maoji (1911–1988)

Fu, Szenian (1896–1950)

Fubini, Mario (1900–1977)

Fucher (Focher), *Frei* Jean (d.1572)

Fuchs, Anna (1939–1992)K

Fuchs, August (1818–1847)

Fuchs, Catherine (b.1946)

Fuchsperger, Ortholphus (c.1490–*post* 1542)

Fudge, Eric (Charles, b.1933)

Fück, Johann (1894–1974)

Fürst, Julius (1805–1873)

Fuhrmann, Manfred (1925–2005)

Fuhrmann, Wilhelm (1919–1988)

Fujibayashi Fuzan (1781–1836)

Fujimura, Osamu (b.1927)

Fujioka, Katsuji (1872–1935)E

Fujitani, Nariakira (1738–1779)S, E

Fukushima, Kunihiko (b.1936)

Fulda, Friedrich Karl (1724–1788)S

Fulgentius (fl. late 5th–early 6th cent. A.D.)

Fulke, William (1538–1589)

Fuller, Nicholas (1587?–1653)

Fuller, Thomas (fl.1732)

Fulvio, Andrea (c.1470–1527)

Fumi, Fausto Gherardo (1840–1915)

Funk, Isaac Kaufman (1839–1912)

Funke, Emil (1873–1923)

Funke, Otto (Viktor Conrad Wilhelm, 1885–1973)

Funkhaenel, Karl Hermann (1808–1874)

Furdal, Antoni (b.1928)

Furetière, Antoine (1619–1688)S

Furfey, Paul Hanly (1896–1992)

Furiqis, Petras A. (1878–1936)

Furnivall, Frederick James (1825–1910)

Furtmar(us), Wolfgang (first half of 16th cent.)

Fus(ius), Adam (d.1648)

Fusella, Luigi (1914–1992)

Futaky, István (b.1926)K

G.

Gaaf, Willem van de (1867–1937)

Gaatone, David (b.1932)

Gabain, Annemarie von (1901–1993)K

Gabbema, Simon Abbes (1628–1688)

Gabelentz, (Hans) Georg (Conon) von der (1840–1893)S, E

Gabelentz, Hans Conon von der (1807–1874)S

Gabka, Kurt (b.1924)K

Gabrielson, Arvid (b.1889?)

Gadamer, Hans-Georg (1900–2002)E

Gaden, Nicolas Jules Henri (1867–1939)

Gadžieva, Ninel' Zejnalovna (1926–1992)

Gaecés, *Frei* Julián, O.P. (1457–1542)

Gärtner, Wilhelm (1811–1875)

Gätje, Helmut (1927–1986)

Gätschenberger, Richard (1865–1936)

Gaffney, Wilbur G. (1906–1986)

Gagé, Jean (1902–19??)

Gage, Thomas (1603?–1656)

Gagne, Étienne Paulin (1808–1876)

Gahiz (d.868)

Gaidoz, Henri (1842–1932)

Gaiffe, Félix (1874–1934)

Gaifman, Chaim (1920–1973)

Gaillard, Gabriel-Henri (1726–1806)

Gaimar, Geoffrey (fl.1140)

Gaj, Ljudevit (1809–1872)

Gajdarzhi, Garril A. (1938–1998)

Gal, Susan (b.1949)

Gała, Slawomir (b.1945)

Gălăbov, Konstantin (1892–1980)

Galanti, Giuseppe Maria (1743–1806)

Galas, Piotr (1888–19??)

Galazzi, Enrica (b.1951)

Gáldi, László (1910–1974)S

Galdo Guzmán, *Frei* Diego de, O.S.A. (1569–1612)

Gale, Theophilus (1628–1678)

Galeani Napione (di Cocconato), Giovan(ni) Francesco (1748–1830)S

Galen(us 'of Pergamon'; Lat. Claudio Galenus, c.130–201 A.D.)S

Gálffy, Mózses (1915–1988)

Galiani, Ferdinando (1728–1787)S

Galichet,Georges (1904-1992)

Galileo, Galilei (1564–1642)

Galindo Romeo, Mateo, S.J. (1610–1667)

Galinsky, Hans (1909–1991)

Galí y Claret, Bartomeu (1850–1902)

Galichet, Georges (1904–1992)

Galkina-Fedoruk, Evdokija Mixajlovna (1898–1965)

Gal'perin, Il'ja Romanovič (1905–1974)

Gall, Franz (Joseph, 1758–1828)

Gallais, Jean-Pierre (1756–1820)

Galland, Antoine (1646–1715)

Galland, Lionel (b.1920)

Gallardo, Bartolomé José (1776–1852)

Gallatin, (Abraham Alfonse) Albert (1761–1849)S
Gallaudet, Thomas Hopkins (1787–1851)
Gallavotti, Carlo (1909–1992)
Galle, Henryk (1872–1948)
Gallé, Johan Hendrik (1847–1908)
Gallego, Juan Nicosio (1777–1853)
Gallegos, Francisco, O.P. (fl.1676)
Gallet, Félix (fl.1800)
Galli, Celestino (1804–1869)
Gallis, Arne (1908–1997))
Galmace, Antonio (fl.1740–1748)
Galton, (Sir) Francis (1822–1911)
Galton, Herbert (alias Goldstaub, b.1917)K
Galvarriato, Eulalia (1904–1997)
Galyas, Kroly (1936-1990)
Gambarara, Daniele (b.1948)
Gamillscheg, Ernst (1887–1971)S
Gamkrelidze (Gamq'reliӡe), Tamaz V(alerianovič, "Thomas", b.1929)
Gamsaxurdia, Zviad (1939–1993)
Ganander, Hendric (Ganandrus, Henricus, d.1752)
Ganander, Hendrik (1757–1819)
Ganander, Kristfrid Henriens (also Christfrid, 1741–1790)
Gândavo, Pêro de Magalhães (d. post 1579)S
Gangler, Jean-François (1788–1856)
Ganim, John M. (b.1945)
Garner, Alan (b.1934)
Ganschow, Gerhard (b.1923)K
Gansfort, Wessel (c.1420–1489)
Gansiniec, Ryszard (1888–1958)
Gante, Frei Pedro de, O.F.M. (ante 1520–1572)
Gantter, Ludwig (fl.1848–1867)

Garaj, Ján (1907–1987)
Garat, Dominique-Joseph (comte, 1749–1833)
Garbbe, Richard Karl von (1857–1927)
Garcés, Gregorio, S.J. (1733–1805)
Garcés, Frei Julián, O.P. (1457–1542)
Garci-Pérez de Vargas, Joseph (fl.1799)
García, Erica C. (b.1934)
García, Fray Gregorio (1560?–1627)
García, Manuel Patricio (1805-1906)
García Ayuso, Francisco (1835–1897)
García Bacca, Juan David (1901–1992)
García Blanco, Antonio María (1800–1890)
García Calvo, Augustín (b.1926)
García de Arboleya, José (d.1876)
García de Diego, Vicente (1878–1978)
García de la Huerta, Vicente (1734–1787)
García de Olarte, Tomás, S.J. (alias García de Vargas, Juan, 18th cent.)
García de Palacio, Diego (16th cent.)
García del Río, Juan (1794–1856)
García de Santa María, Gonzalo (1447–1521)
García de Vargas, Juan, S.J. (1652–post 1711)
García Icazbalceta, Joaquín (1825–1894)
García-Lomas, Adriana (1891–1972)
García Marquez, Gabriel José (b.1928)
Garcin, Eugène André (1830–1909)

Ġawharī, Abū Naṣr Ismāʿīl ibn
Ḥammād al- (d.393/1003)S
Gayoso, Benito Martínez Gómez, *see*
Gómez Gayoso, Benito Martínez
Gayton, Anna (1899–1977)
Gaza, Theodorus (1430–1476)
Gazdar, Gerald (James Michael,
b.1950)
Gazier, Louis Auguste (1844–1922)
Ġazzālī, Abū Ḥāmid Muḥammad al-
(c.1058–1111)
Gburek, Hubert (b.1940)
Geach, Peter (Thomas, b.1916)E
Gebauer, Jan (1838–1907)S
Gebwiler, Hieronymus (fl.1513)
Geckeler, Horst (b.1935)K
Geddes, Alexander (1737–1802)
Geddes, James, Jr. (1858–1948)
Gedeon, Rudolf (1938–2001)
Gedike, Friedrich (1754–1803)
Gedney, William J(ohn, b.1915)
Geel, Jacobus (1789–1862)
G(h)eel. Joris (*alias* Adriaan
Willems, 1617–1652)
Geertz, Clifford (b.1926)
Gegenbaur, Carl (1826–1903)
Gehlen, Arnold (1872–1970)
Gehlen, Arnold (1904–1976)
Geier, Manfred (b.1943)K
Geiger, Lazarus (1829–1870)
Geiger, Ludwig Wilhelm (1856–
1943)
Geijer, Herman (d.1941)
Geijer, Per Adolf (1841–1919)
Geisler, Heinrich (fl.1493)
Geitler, Leopold (1847–1885)
Gelb, Adhemar (Maximilian Maurice,
1887–1936)
Gelb, Ignace Jay (1907–1985)S, E

Geldner, Karl Friedrich (1853–1929)
Geleji Katona, István (1589–1649)
Gelenius, Sigismund (1497–1554)
Gelli, Giovanni Battista (1498–
1563)S
Gellius, Aulus (c.123–c.165 A.D.)S
Gellner, Ernest André (b.1925)
Gembloux, Pierquin de, pseud., *see*
Claude, Charles
Gemistos, Georgios ("Plethon",
1355/60–1452)
Gemona, *Father* Basilio de (1648–
1704)
Gendron, Jean-Denis (b.1925)
Genebrardus (Genebrard), Gilbert
(c.1537-1597)
Génestet, Petrus Augustus de (1829–
1861)
Genette, Gérard (b.1930)
Genetz, Arvid (Oscar Gustav; Fin-
nish: Arvi Jönnes, 1848–1915)S
Génin, Francis (1803–1856)S
Genko, A. N. (1896–1941)
Gennadios Scholarios (1405–1472)
Genovesi, Antonio (1712–1779)S
Gensini, Stefano (b.1953)
Gentile da Cingoli (fl.1295; d. *ante*
1334)
Gentile, Giovanni (1875–1944)S
Gentilhomme, Yves (b.1920)
Gentilis de Cingulo (1551–1611)S
Genung, John Franklin (1850–1919)
Geoffrey o Vinsauf (fl. late 12th
cent.)S
Georgacas, Demetrius John (1908–
1990)
George of Brussels (d.1510)
George of Trebizond (Georgius
Trapezuntias, 1395–1484)

Georges, Karl Ernst (1896–1959?)
Georgi, Antonio (Augustinian friar, fl.1762)
Georgius Choiroboiscus (mid 9th-cent. A.D.)
Georgius Lecapenus (fl. c.1297–1311)
Georgiev, Stan'o (b.1929)
Georgiev, Vladimir (Ivanov, 1908–1986)S, E
Georgopoulos, Carol (b.1943)
Georgov, Ivan A. (1862–1936)
Gérando, Joseph-Marie de, *see* Degérando, J. M.
Gérard, Charles (1814–1877)
Gerasimov, Vladimir Ivanovič (b.1948)
Gerber, Gustav (1820–1901)
Gerbier, *Sir* Balthazar (c.1591–1667)
Gercke, A. (1860–1922)
Gerdy, Pierre-Nicolas (1797–1856)
Gerdžikov, Georgi (1940–2002)
Gergely, Jean (1911–1996)
Gerhardt, Carl Immanuel (1816–1899)
Gericke, Johann Friedrich Carl (1798–1857)
Gerig, John Lawrence (1878–1957)
Gering, Hugo (1847–1925)
Germanus, Dominicus, O.F.M. (1588–1670)
Gerner, Henrik (*alias* Henrich Thomaesøn, 1629–1700)
Gerov, Boris (1903–1991)
Gerov, Najden (1823–1900)
Gerritsen, Marinel (b.1949)
Gerson, John (1365–1429)
Gerstman, Louis J. (1930–1992)S

Gerth, Friedrich Bernhard (1844–1911)
Gerth, Hans H. (1908–1979)
Gertz, Martin Clarentius (1844–1929)
Gerulis, Jurgis (1888–1945)
Géruzez, Jean-Baptiste François (1764–1830)
Gervase of Malkley (Lat. Gervasius de Saltu Lacteo, b. c.1185)S
Gervase of Tilbury (fl.1211)
Gervinus, Georg Gottfried (1805–1871)
Geschwind, Norman (1926–1984)E
Gesemann, G. (1888–1948)
Gesenius, (Friedrich Heinrich) Wilhelm (1785–1842)S, E
Gesenius, Friedrich Wilhelm (1825–1888)
Gesner, Chr(istian?) F(riedrich? (c.1748)
Ges(s)ner(us), Conrad (von, 1516–1565)S
Gesner, Johann Matthias (1691–1761)
Gessinger, Joachim (b.1945)
Gessler, J(e)an (1878–1952)
Geulincx, Arnold (1623–1670)
Gevirtz, Stanley (1929–1988)
Gezelius, Johannes Georgii (*alias* Göransson, 1615–*post* 1664)
Gherardini, Giovanni (1778–1861)S
Gheorgov, Ivan (1862–1936)
Ghilini, Girolamo (1589–1675)
Ghijsen, Hendrika Catharina Maria (1884–1976)
Ghigi, Mariano (d.1762)
Giacalone Ramat, Anna (b.1937)
Giadraitis, Merkelis (c.1536–1609)

Giambullari, Pier Francesco (1495–1555)S

Giammarco, Ernesto (1916–1987)

Giard, Luce (b. c.1950)

Gibbens, Nicholas (fl.1601)

Gibbon, Edward (1737–1794)

Gibbs, George (1815–1873)

Gibbs, Josiah Willard (1790–1861)

Gibert, Balthasar (1662–1741)

Gibson, Edmund (1669–1748)

Gibson, John (1849–1919)

Gibson, *Chief* John A. (1849–1912)

Gibson, Margaret (d.1996)

Gibson, Simeon (1889–1943)

Gibbs, Jack P. (b.1927)

Giddings, Franklin (Henry, 1855–1931)

Gidel, Charles (1827–1900)

Giedratis, Juazapas Arnulfas (1757–1838)

Giegerich, Heinz J. (b. c.1945)

Gierach, Erich (1881–1941)

Giese, Albert (1803–1834)

Giese, Wilhelm (1895–1990)

Gifford, Edward Winslow (1887–1959)

Gigli, Girolano (1660–1722)

Gigli, Mariano (1782– *post* 1819)

Gikatilla, Joseph (1247–1305)

Gil, Alberto (b.1952)

Gil, Juana (b.1955)

Gil, Fr. Thomas (1898–1943)

Gil de Zamora, Juan (fl.1280)

Gilbert de la Porré, *see* Gilbert of Poitiers

Gilbert de la Porrée (c.1070–1154)

Gilbert of Poitiers (1085/90–1154)S

Gilbert, Humphrey (1539?–1583)

Gilbert, Martin (fl.1563)

Gilbert, William (1597?–1640)

Gilberti, *Fray* Maturino, O.F.M. (1498–1585)

Gilbertson, Albert Nicolay (1885–19??)

Gilchrist, James (1783–1835)

Gilchrist, John Borthwick (1759–1841)

Gildemeister, Johannes Gustav (1812–1890)

Gildersleeve, Basil Lanneau (1831–1924)

Gildon, Charles (1565–1624)

Giles of Rome (c.1243/47–1316)S

Giles, Herbert Allen (1845–1935)

Giles, *Rev.* John Allen (1804–1884)

Giles, Peter (1860–1935)

Gilhausen, Isaac (Gilhusius, d. *post* 1597)

Gili (y) Gaya, Samuel (in Catalan: Gili i Gaya, 1892–1976)S

Gilij, Filipo Salvatore, S.J. (1721–1789)

Gil(l), Alexander (1567–1635)S

Gilles de Rome (1243–1316)

Gilles, Nicole (d.1503)

Gilliéron, Jules (Louis, 1854–1926)S, E

Gilman, Daniel Coit (1831–1908)

Gilman, Albert (1923–1989)

Gilman, Sander L(awrence, b.1944)

Gilmore, Joseph Henry (1834–1918)

Gilson, Étienne Henri (1884–1978)

Gimbutas, Marija (1921–1994)

Gimon, Tōjō, *see* Tōjō Gimon

Gimson, A(lfred) C(harles, 1917–1985)E

Gindin, Leonid Aleksandrovič (1928–1994)

Gingras, Jules Fabieu (1829–1884)
Ginguené, Pierre Louis (1748–1816)
Ginneken, Jacobus Joannes Antonius
  van, S.J. ("Jacques", 1877–1945)S
Ginsberg, Harold Louis (b.1903)
Gioberti, Vincenzo (1801–1852)S
Gioia, Melchiorre (1767–1829)
Giordani, Pietro (1774–1848)S
Giordini, Giambattista (1818–1906)
Giorgi, Alessandra (b.1957)
Giorgini, Giambattista (1818–1906)S
Giovanni Balbi, see John of Genua,
  Johannes Balbus
Giovanni del Virgilio (fl.1319–
  1327)S
Giphanius, Hubertus (1534–1604)
Gipper, Helmut (1919–2005)K
Gippert, Jost (b.1956)K
Giral del Pino, Hipólito San José
  (fl.1763–1777)
Giraldus Cambrensis (1146?–1220?)
Girard, Antoine-Gervais (1752–1822)
Girard, Charles François (1811–
  1875)
Girard, abbé Gabriel (1677–1748)S
Girard, le père Jean-Baptiste
  Grégoire (1765–1850)
Girard de Rialle, Julien (1841–1904)
Girard de Rialle, Nathanaël (1841–
  1907)
Girault-Duvivier, Charles-Pierre
  (1765–1832)S
Girbert, Johann (1603–1671)
Ġirğī Zaidān, see Zaydān, Ġurğī
Gislason, Konrað (or Konrád, 1808–
  1891)
Giuffredi, Argistero (1535?–1593)
Givón, Talmy ("Thomas", b.1936)E
Gizel', Innokentij (c.1600–1683)

Gladkij, Aleksej Vsevolodovič
  (b.1928)
Gladwin, Hugh (b.1941)
Gladwin, Thomas (b.1946)
Glässer, Edgar (1880?–1945)
Glaire, abbé Jean-Baptiste (1798–
  1879)
Glanvill, Joseph (1636–1680)
Glarean(us), Heinrich (1488–1563)
Glasenapp, Otto Max Helmuth von
  (1891–1963)
Glaser, Edward (orig.: Eduard, 1918–
  1972)
Glaser, Elvira (b.1954)K
Glasersfeld, Ernst von (b.1917)
Glasheen, Adaline (1920–1993)
Glassner, Jean-Jacques (b.1944)
Glauber, Johann Rudolf (1604?–
  1668)
Glavičić, Branimir (b.1926)
Glazer, Sidney (b.1911)
Gleason, Henry Allen, Jr. ("Al",
  1917–2007)
Gleason, Jean Berko (b.1935?)
Gleditsch, Johann Ludwig (fl.1694–
  1717)
Glemona, Basilio Brollo de (alias de
  Gemona, di Glemona, a Glemona,
  de Cremona, 1648–1704)
Gleßgen, Martin-Dietrich (b.1963)
Glinz, Hans (b.1913)K, E
Glisson, Francis (1597–1677)
Gloger, Zygmunt (1845–1910)
Glover, Trienne (b.1948)
Glück, Christian Wilhelm (1810–
  1866)
Glück, Helmut (b.1949)K
Glunz, Hans (1907–1944)

Glykys (Glycis), Johannes (c.1260–1320)
Gnaphaeus (Fullonius), Guillelmus (1493–1220?)
Gneuss, Helmut (Walter Georg, b.1927)K
Gniadek, Stanisław (1909–1991)
Gnipho, (Marcus) Antonius (early 1st cent. B.C.)
Goad, John (1616–1689)
Gobert, Napoléon, *baron* (1807–1833)
Gobineau, Joseph Arthur, *comte* de (1816–1882)
Goclenius, Rudolf (d.1628)
Godailh, Jean Gaspard Julin (1764–1840)
Godard, Jean (1564–1630)
Goddard, (R. H.) Ives (b.1941)
Goddard, Jonathan (1617?–1675)
Goddard, Pliny Earle (1869–1928)S
Godden, Malcolm Reginald (b.1945)
Goddes de Liancourt, Caliste Auguste de (1805–*post* 1874)
Gode, Alexander (1906–1970)
Godefroid, Henri (d.1942)
Godefroy, Frédéric-Eugène (1826–1897)S
Godefroy-Demombynes, Laurent Joseph Maurice (1862–1957)
Godel, Robert (1902–1984)S
Godescalc of Orbais (Gottschalk, c.808–867)
Godfrey of Fontaines (c.1250–1306/1309)
Godinka, Anton (1864–1946)
Godra, Michael (1801–18??)
Godwin (d.1053)
Godwin, Francis (1562–1633)

Godwin, William (1756–1836)
Goebel, Julius (1857–1931)
Goebl, Hans (b.1943)K
Göbl, László, *see* Gáldi, László
Gödel, Kurt (1906–1978)
Goeje, Cornelius H. de (18??–19??)
Goeje, Michaël Jan de (1836–1909)
Goelzer, Henri Jules Ernest (1853–1929)
Goens, Rijklof Michaël van (1748–1810)
Görlach, Manfred (b.1937)K
Görres, Ernst Moritz Guido (1805–1852)
Göseken(s), Heinrich (1612–1681)
Goethe, Johann Wolfgang (von, 1749–1832)
Götlind, Johann Alfred (d.1939?)
Goettling, Carl Wilhelm (1793–1869)
Goetz, Hermann (1898–1976)
Goetze, Albrecht (1897–1971)S
Götze, Alfred (August Woldemar, 1876–1946)S
Götzinger, Max(imilian) Wilhelm (1799–1856)S
Goffman, Erving (1922–1982)E
Gogolewski, Stanislaw (b.1939)
Goidànich, Pier Gabriele (1806–1953)S
Goitain, Solomon Dov (Fritz, 1900–*post* 1980)
Gołab, Zbigniew (1923–1994)
Golanov, Ivan Grigor'evič (1890–1967)
Goldberg, Baer Dov Ben Alexander (1800–1884)
Goldenweiser, Alexander A. (1880–1940)
Goldfarb, Charles F. (fl.1969–2002)

Goldsbury, John (1795–1890)
Goldschmidt, Paul (1850–1877)
Goldschmidt, Siegfried (1844–1884)
Goldschmidt, Victor (1853–1933)
Goldschmidt, Walter R. (b.1913)
Goldsmith, Emanuel S. (b.1935)
Goldsmith, Francis (c.1605–1655)
Goldsmith, John A. (b.1951)
Goldsmith, Oliver (1728–1774)
Goldstein, Kurt (1878–1965)
Goldstücker, Theodor (1821–1872)
Goldziher, Ignaz (1850–1921)
Gołębiowska, Teresa (b.1939)
Golescu, Iordache (1768–1848)
Golius, Jacobus (1596–1667)
Golius, Theophilus (1528–1600)
Golla, Victor (Karl, b.1939)
Gollancz, (*Sir*) Israel (1864–1930)
Golling, Joseph (1848–*post* 1904)
Golopenţia-Eretescu, Sanda (b.1940)
Golosovker, Jakov Èmmanuilovič
    (1890–1967)
Golter, Wolfgang (1863–1945)
Goltz, Friedrich Leopold (1834–
    1902)
Golwalkar, Madhev Sadashiv (1906–
    1973)
Gombocz, Zoltán (1877–1935)S
Gomes de Matos, Francisco (b.1933)
Gómez (de) Hermosilla, José
    Mamerto (1771–1837/38?)S
Gómez Aguado, Enrique (b.1940)
Gómez de Enterría, Angel (fl.1845)
Gómez de Salazar, Fernando
    (d.1879)
Gómez Gayoso, Benito Martínez
    (c.1710–1787)S
Gomperz, Heinrich (1873–1943)
Gomperz, Theodor (1832–1912)

Gonçalves, *Padre* Joaquim (Alfonso,
    17881–1834)
Gonçalves Viana, Aniceto dos Reis
    (1840–1914)S
Gonda, Jan (1905–1991)
Gonon, Marguerite (1914–1996)
González, Bernardino, O.F.M.
    (c.1665–1735)
González, Diego Pablo, S.J. (1690–
    1758)
Gonzáles, Luis, O.P. (fl.1652)
González, Tomás, S.J. (1592/93–
    1659)
González Arnao Vicente (1766–
    1845)
González Dávila, Gil (1578–1658)
González de Dios, Juan (fl.1724)
González de la Calle, 1879–1966)
Gonzáles de Santa Cruz, Roque, S.J.
    (d.1628)
Gonzáles Holguín, Diego, S.J.
    (1552–1618)
González i Hernández, Ireneo (1842–
    1918).
González Manrique, Juan (fl.1674–
    1683)
González (de) Valdés, Juan Antonio
    (c.1750–*post* 1791)S
Goodchild, John George (1844–
    1906)
Goode, Phillip (1951–1999)
Goodenough, Ward H(unt, b.1919)
Goodenow, Smith Bartlett (1817–
    1889)
Goodglass, Harold (1920–2002)
Goodison, Ronald Allan Cameron
    (b.1921)
Goodman, Godfrey (1583–1656)
Goodman, Morris (b.1933)

Greenfield, Stanley Brian (1922–1987)

Greenfield, William (1799–1831)

Greenough, James Bradstreet (1833–1901)

Greenwood, James (d.1737)

Greet, (William) Cabell (1901–1972)S

Gregg, Robert John (1911–1998)

Grégoire, Antoine (1871–1955)

Grégoire, Ernest (1828–*post* 1872)

Grégoire, *abbé* Henri Baptiste (1750–1831)

Grégoire, Henri (1881–1964)

Gregorio de Valencia (16th cent. A.D.)

Gregorius, St., *bishop* of Tours (*alias* Gregory the Great , 538/39–594)

Gregorius, Abba (c.1610–1659)

Gregor(ius) of Corinth (d.1058)

Gregor(ius) of Rimini (Gregor Ariminensis, c.1300–1358)

Gregorski, Adam (1906–1993)

Gregory of Nazianz (329/30–c.390 A.D.)

Gregory of Nyssa (c.335–*post* 394 A.D.)

Gregory of Utrecht (707–776 A.D.)

Gregory, Michael (b.1935)

Greibach, Sheila (b.1939)

Greiffenhahn, Johann Elias (1687–1749)

Greimas, Algirdas Julien (1917–1992)

Grein, Christian Wilhelm Michael (1825–1877)S

Greitemann, Nico(laus, 1903–1990)

Grek, Maksim (1475?–1556)

Grellmann, Heinrich Moritz Gottlieb (1756–1804)

Grenier, Albert Jules Eugène (1878–1961)

Grenzstein, Ado (1849–1916)

Greppin, John A(ird) C(outts, b.1937)

Grets(ch)er (*also* Gretser), Jacob, S.J. (1562–1625)

Gretsch, Mechthild (b.1945)

Gretter, Kaspar (1st half of 16th cent.)

Greusser, Joannes (2nd half of 15th cent.)

Grevenbroek, Johannes Gulielmus de (1644–c.1725)

Grevisse, Maurice (1895–1986)S

Grew, Nehemiah (1641–1712)

Grey, *Sir* George (1812–1898)

Grey, Nicholas (1590?–1660)

Greyerz, Otto von (1863–1940)

Grice, H(erbert) P(aul, 1913–1988)E

Grickat, Irena (b.1922)

Griera, Antoine (1887–1973)

Grierson, *Sir* George (Abraham, 1851–1941)S, E

Griesbach, Heinz (b.1918)K

Griesinger, Heinrich (d.1511)

Grieve, Robert (b.1944)

Griffith, Belver C. (b.1931)

Griffiths, Bill (b.1948)

Grigoriev, Vassilij Vassil'evič (1816–1881)

Grigorovič, Viktor Ivanovič (1815–1876)

Grijns, Cornelis Dirk (1924–1999)

Grimarest, Jean Leonor de Gallois (*alias* Juan Enrique Le Gallois de, 1659–1713)

Grimaud, Aimé (1789–1866)
Grimes, Joseph E(vans, b.1928)
Grimes, Ruth Elaine (b.1949)
Grimke, Thomas Smith (1786–1834)
Grimm, Jacob (Ludwig Karl, 1785–1863)S, E
Grimm, Melchior, *baron* de (1723–1807)
Grimm, Wilhelm (Karl, 1786–1859)
Grimme, Hubert (1864–1942)
Grimmelshausen, Hans Jakob Christoffel von (1621?–1676)
Grimshaw, Allen D. (b.1929)
Grinaveckis, Uladas (1925–1995)
Grinaveckienė, Elena (1928–1999)
Grinda, Klaus R. (b.1933)
Gringore, Pierre (1475?–1538?)
Griselini, Franz (1717–1783)
Grize, Jean-Blaise (b.1922)
Grob, Johannes (1643–1697)
Grochowski, Maciej (b.1948)
Grocyn, William (1446?–1519)
Gröber, (Max) Gustav (1844–1911)S
Groening, Michael (1714–1778)
Grognet, Allene Guss (b.1938)
Grønbech, Vilhelm (1873–1948)
Gronovius, Jacobus (1645–1716)
Gronovius, Johann Friedrich (1611–1671)
Groot, Albert Willem de (1892–1963)S
Groot, Dirk de (1825–1895)
Grootaers, Ludovic(us, 1885–1956)
Grootaers, Willem A. (1911–1999)
Grose, Francis (1731–1791)
Gross, Maurice (1934–2001)E
Große, Rudolf (b.1924)K
Grossberg, Stephen (b.1939)
Grosse, Siegfried (b.1924)K

Grosseteste, Robert, *see* Robert Grosseteste
Grot, Jakov Karlovič (1812–1893)S
Grote, George (1794–1871)
Grotefend, (Friedrich) August (Ludwig Adolf, 1798–1836)
Grotefend, Georg Friedrich (1775–1853)S
Grotefend, Karl Ludwig (1807–1874)
Grotius, Hugo (*alias* de Groot, 1583–1645)
Groussier, Marie-Line (b.1935)
Grout, *Rev.* Lewis (1815–1905)
Grube, Bernhard Adam (1715–1808)
Grube, Wilhelm (1855–1908)
Gruber, Jacob (b.1921)
Gruber, Jeffrey Steven (b.1940)
Gruchamowa, Monika (1922–2001)
Grünbaum, Anton Abraham (1885–1932)
Grünenthal, O. (1880–c.1942)
Grüning, Andreas (1756–1822)
Grünwedel, Albert (1856–1935)
Grüßbeutel, Jacob (fl.1531)
Grützner, Paul (1847–1919)
Grugnoli, Giuliano (2nd half of 20th cent.)
Grundström, Harald (1885–1960)
Grundtvig, Nikolai Fredrik Severin (1783–1872)
Grundy, Lynne Mary (b.1935)
Grunig, Blanche-Noëlle (b.1939)
Grun(t)zel, Joseph (1866–1934)
Gruppe, Otto Friedrich (1804–1876)
Gruszczyński, Włodzimierz (b.1953)
Gruska, Apollon Apollonovič (1869–1929)
Grucza, Franciszek (b.1937)K

Grzebieniowski, Tadeusz (1894–1973)
Grzegorczykowa, Renata (b.1931)
Grzeszczuk, Stanisław (b.1934)
Gsell, René (1921–2000)
Gu, Yanwu (1613–1682)
Guadagnoli, Philippus, O.F.M. (1596–1656)
Guadalajara, Tomás de, S.J. (1645–1729)
Gua de Malves, *abbé* Jean Paul de (1712–1786)
Guadix, Diego (d.1615)
Gualdo, Diego de (16th cent.?)
Gualterus of Alliacus (Gauthier d'Ailly)
Gualterus Burlaeus, *see* Walter Burley
Gualtperius, Otho (1546–1624)
Guarini, Guarino (*alias* Guarinus Veronensis, 1374–1460)S
Guarino Veronese, *see* Guarini, Guarino
Guarnerio(-Guarino), Pier Enea (1854–1919)
Guaschis/Guastis, Ludovicus de (fl.1400–1450)
Guattari, Félix (1930–1993)
Guazzo, Stefano (1530–1593)S
Guberina, Petar (1913–2005)
Gučinskaja, Nina Olegovna (d.2001)
Gudeman, Alfred (1862–1942)
Gudrius, Johann (fl.1659)
Gudschinsky, Sarah C(aroline, 1919–1975)S
Güldemann, Moritz (1855–1918)
Gülich, Elisabeth (b.1937)
Günter, Hans Richard Gerhard (1898–19??)

Güntert, Hermann (Georg Konrad, 1886–1948)
Günther, Erika (1957–1994)
Günther, Hans Friedrich Karl ('Rasse-Günther', 1891–1968)
Günther, James (1806–1879
Günther, Ruffus (fl.1528)
Günther, Werner (1898–19??)
Gueintz, Christian (1592–1650)S
Guer, Charles, *see* Guerlin de Guer, Charles
Guérard, Benjamin (1797–1854)
Guérin de la Grasserie, Raoul, *see* La Grasserie, Raoul Guérin de
Guerlin de Guer, Charles (1871–1948)
Guerra Navarro, Francisco (1909–1961)
Gürtler, Johann Daniel (1776–1846)
Guessard, François (1814–1882)
Guest, Edwin (1800–1880)
Guerios, Rosario Farani Mansur (1907–1987)
Guerrier de Dumast, *baron* (1796–1883)
Gürtler, Nicolaus (1654–1711)
Guess, George (*alias* Sikwaja, c.1770–1843)
Guessard, Francis (1814–1883)
Guest, Edwin (1800–1880)
Güterbock, Bruno G(ustav?, 1858–1940)
Güterbock, Hans Gustav (1908–2000)
Gueth, Anton Walter Florus (*alias* Nyanatiloka, 1878–1957)
Gützlaff, Karl (1803–1851)
Guevara, Antonio de (1480?–1545?)
Guex, François (1861–*post* 1890)

H.

Haack, Wilhelm (1706–1754)
Haag, Friedrich (1846–1914)
Haag, Karl (1860–1946)
Haak, Theodor (1605–1690)
Haarmann, Harald (b.1946)K
Haas, Josef/ph (1863–1929)
Haas, Mary R(osamond, 1910–1996)E
Haas, William (1912–1997?)
Haase, (Heinrich Gottlob) Friedrich (Christian, 1808–1867)
Haatela, Sampo (1908–1993)
Haavio, M. (1899–1973)
Habdelić, Juraj, S.J. (1609–1678)
Habel, Muriel, *see* Vasconcellos, Muriel
Habermann, Johann, *see* Avenarius, Johannes
Habermas, Jürgen (b.1929)E
Habicht, Maximilian (1775–1839)
Habichthorst, Andreas Daniel (1634–1704)
Habrecht, Isaac (1589–1633)
Hachette, Louis (1800–1864)
Hacker, Paul (1913–1979)
Hackerman, Norman (b.1912)
Haden, Ernest F. (1904–1993)
Hadgraft, Nicholas (1955–2004)
Hadley, George (1685–1768)
Hadley, *Captain* George (d.1798)
Hadley, Hiram (1833–1922)
Hadrianus Junius, *see* Junius, Hadrianus

Hadrovics, László (1910–1997)
Haeckel, Ernst (Heinrich Philipp August, 1834–1919)
Hægstad, Marius (1850–1927)S
Haenicke, Gunta (b.1939)
Härd, John Evert (b.1932)K
Haeringen, Coenraad Bernardus van (1892–1983)
Haessler, Louise (1866–*post* 1946)
Häusermann, Hans Walter (1902–1973)
Häusler, Frank (b.1930)K
Haff, Marianne Hobæk (b.1949)
Hagedorn, William (b.1936)
Hagège, Claude (b.1936)
Hagen, Anton(ius Maria, b.1936)
Hagen, Friedrich Heinrich von der (1780–1856)
Hagen, Hermann (1844–1898)
Hagen, Sivert Nielsen (1872–c.1960)
Hager, Joseph (1757–1819)
Hagio, Barnino (fl.1680)
Hagstrom, Warren O. (b.1930)
Hahn, Carl Hugo (1818–1895)
Hahn, E(mma) Adelaide (1893–1967)S, E
Hahn, Hans (1879–1934)
Hahn, Karl August (1807–1857)
Haider, Hubert (b.1953)K
Haighton, Alfred A. (1897–1943)
Haile, *Father* Berard, O.F.M. (1874–1961)
Hainhofer, Hieronymus (1611–1683)
Haislund, Niels (1900–1969)
Haiman, John (Michael, b.1946)
Hajdu, Peter (b.1923)
Haji, Raja Ali (1809-1872)
Hajdú, Péter (1923–2002)
Hajicová, Eva (b.1935)

Hakluyt, Richard (1552–1616)
Hakulinen, Lauri (1899–1985)S
Hakpŏn, *see* Pak Sūngbin
Halaf al-Aḥmar, Abū Muḥriz ibn
  Ḥayyān (d. c.180/796)S
Halász, Ignác (1855–1901)
Halbertsma, Joast (*or* Justus) Hiddes
  (1789–1869)
Halcón, Manuel (1900–1989)
Hald, Kristian (1904–1885)S
Haldeman, Samuel Stehman (1812–
  1880)
Hale, Edward Everett (1822–1909)
Hale, Horatio Emmons (1817–
  1897)S
Hale, Kenneth L. ("Ken", 1934–
  2001)E
Hale, (*Sir*) Matthew (1609–1676)
Hale, Salma (1781–1866)
Hale, William Gardner (1849–1928)
Halévy, Joseph (1827–1917)
Halévy, Léon (1802–1883)
Haley, Jay (b.1923)
Halhed, Nathaniel Brassey (1751–
  1830)
Halil, Abū ᶜAbd ar-Raḥmān ibn
  Aḥmad al- Farāhīdī (100/718–
  170/786)S
Halīl, ibn Aḥmad , *see* Khalīl Ibn
  Aḥmad al-
Halkowski, Timothy (b.1959)
Hall, Alfred (1853–1918)
Hall, Edward T. (b.1914)
Hall, Edmund (1620?–1686)
Hall, Fitzedward (1825–1901)
Hall, John Richard Clark (1855–
  1931)
Hall, Pauline Cook (b.1913)

Hall, Robert A(nderson), Jr. (1911–
  1997)E
Hall, Samuel Dwight (1795–1877)
Hallager, Laurents (177–1825)
Hallam, Thomas (1819–1895)
Hallan, Nils (1926–1997)
Hallap, Vamen (1928–1987)
Hallbauer, Friedrich Andreas (1692–
  1750)
Halldórsson, Halldór (1911–2000)
Halle, Morris (b.1923)E
Haller, (Victor) Albrecht von (1708–
  1777)
Haller, Jiří (1896–1971)
Halley, Edmund (1656–1742)
Halliday, M(ichael) A(lexander)
  K(irkwood, b.1925)E
Hallig, Rudolf (1902–1964)
Halliwell, James Orchard (1820–
  1889)
Hallowell, A. Irving (1892–1974)
Halberstma, Joast (*or* Justus) Hiddes
  (1789–1869)
Halma, François (1653–1722).
Halpern, Abraham Meyer (1914–
  1985)S
Haloun, Gustav (d.1951)
Halsema, Diderik Frederik Johan van
  (1736–1784)
Hamaker, Hendrik Arent (1789–
  1835)S
Hambis, Louis (1906–1978)
Hamann, Johann Georg (1730–1788)
Hamel, Anton Gerard van (1842–
  1907)
Hamel, Anton Gerardus van (d.1945)
Hamer, Richard (b.1935)
Hamilton, Alexander (1762–1824)
Hamilton, Gavin (d.1907)

Hamilton, James (1769–1829)
Hamilton, William (1788–1856)
Hamilton, William (1811–1891)S
Hamlin, Frank Rodney (1935–2000)
Hamm, Frank Richard (1920–1973)
Hamm, Josip (1905–1986)S
Hammel, Eugene A. (b.1930)
Hammarström, Göran (b.1925?)
Hammerich, L(ouis) L(eonor, 1892–1975)S
Hammer-Purgstall, Joseph *Freiherr* von (1774–1856)
Hammershaimb, Erling (1904–1994)
Hammershaimb, Venceslaus Ulricus (1819–1909)S
Hamp, Eric P(ratt, b.1920)E
Hardenberg, Friedrich, *Freiherr* von ("Novalis", 1772-1801)
Hampl, (Zemřel) Zdeněk (1929–1986)
Hamy, Ernest-Théodore (1842–1908)
Han, Mieko S. (b.1929)
ha-Nagid, Samuel (*alias* Ismail ibn Nagrel'a, 933–1055/56)
Hančilová, Miluse (1928–1987)
Hancov, Vsevolod M. (1892–1979)
Handke, Kwiryna (b.1932)
Hanley, Miles (Lawrence, 1893–1954)S
Hanna, Ralph, III (b.1942)
Hannemann, Karl (1813–1898)
Hanoteau, Louis Joseph Adolphe Charles Constance (1814–1897)
Hanse, Joseph (1902–1992)
Hansen, Aage (1894–1983)S
Hansen, Adolf (1850–1908)
Hansen, Klaus (b.1934)K
Hanssen, Federico (*alias* Friedrich, 1857–1919)

Hanus, (Ignác) Jan (1812–1869)
Hanusz, Jan (1858–1887)
Hanxleden, Johann Ernst (1681–1732)
Hanzeli, Victor E(gon, 1925–1991)
Haraïri, Soliman al- (1824–1877)
Harbsmeier, Christoph (b.1938?)
Hardeland, August (1814–1891)
Hardenberg, Karl August (1750–1822)
Harder, Hans-Bernd (1934–1996)
Harduin, Alexandre Xavier (1718–1785)
Hardy, Claude (fl.1620–1678)
Hardy, Edmund (1852–1904)
Hare, Richard Mervyn (b.1919)
Hargus, Sharon Louise (b.1958)
Hariot, Thomas, *see* Thomas Harriot
Harīrī, al-Qasim ben cAlī al- (1054–1122?)
Harkavy, Abraham Elijah (1835–1919)
Harkavy, Alexander (1863–1939)
Harl, Wolfgang von (1907–1943)
Harless, Emil (1820–1862)
Harlez (de Deulin), *Mgr.* Charles Joseph de (1832–1899)
Harlow, Christopher Geoffrey (b.1924)
Harlow, Stephen J. (b.1943)
Harman, Gilbert Helms (b.1938)
Harms, Robert Thomas (b.1932)
Harnack, Adolf von (1851–1930)
Harnisch, Rüdiger (b.1955)K
Harnisch, Wilhelm (1784–1864)
Harper, Kenneth Eugene (b.1918)
Harper, William Rainey (1856–1906)
Harries, Lyndon P(ritchard, b.1909)

Harrington, John Peabody (1884–1961)S, E
Harriot, Thomas (1560–1621)S
Harris, Alice C. (b.1945?)
Harris, Brian (Maurice, b.1926)
Harris, Georges (c.1830–post 1869)
Harris, James (1709–1780)S, E
Harris, James W. (b.1932)
Harris, Katherine S. (b.1925)
Harris, Marvin (b.1927)
Harris, P. H. (1896–1992)
Harris, Rachel Joan (b.1946)
Harris, Randy Allen (b.1956)
Harris, Roy (b.1931)
Harris, Zellig Sabbettai (1909–1992)S, E
Harrison, Charles (d.1926)
Harrison, Ralph (1748–1810)
Harrison, Rev. Matthew (1792?–1862)
Harsdörffer, Georg Philipp (1607–1658)S
Hart, C.W.M. (1905–1976)
Hart, Herbert Lionel Adolphus (1907–19??)
Hart, John (c.1501–1574)S, E
Hart, John Seeley (1810–1877)
Hartel, Wilhelm Ritter von (1839–1907)
Hartknoch, Johann Friedrich (1740–1789)
Hartl, Eduard (earlier 20th cent.)
Hartley, David (1705–1757)
Hartlib, Samuel (c.1608–1662)
Hartman, Jacobus Johannes (1851–1924)
Hartman, James Walter (b.1939)
Hartmann, August (1846–1917)

Hartmann, (Robert Karl) Eduard von (1842–1906)
Hartmann, Hans (1909–post 1997)
Hartmann, John (1568–1631)
Hartmann, Martin (1851–1918)
Hartmann, Nicolai (1882–1952)
Hartmann, Peter (1923–1984)
Hartmann, Reinhard Rudolf Karl (b.1938)K
Hartmann, Richard (1901–post 1961)
Hartt, Charles Frederik (1840–1878)
Hartung, Wolfdietrich (b.1933)K
Hartzenbusch, Juan Eugenio (1806-1880)
Hārūn ibn al-Faraǧ, Abū (alias Aharōn ben Jehōšūa, first half of 11th cent.)S
Harvey, Gabriel (1550?–1631?)
Harvey, Thomas Wadleigh (1821?–1892)
Harvey, William (1578–1657)
Harwood, F. W. (fl.1955–1960)
Hasan, Ruqaiya (b.1931)
Hasdeu, Bogdan Petriceìcu (1838–1907)S
Hase, Charles-Benoît (alias Carl Benedict, 1780–1864)
Hashimoto, Shinkichi (1882–1945)S
Hasink, Michel (b.1923)Haskins, Charles Homer (1870–1937)
Haskins, David Greene (1818–1896)
Haspelmath, Martin (b.1963)K
Hass, Wilbur A(dolf, b.1941?)
Hasselgård, Hilde (b.1963)
Hasselbrink, Gustav (1900–1982)
Hassen, Martinus (1677–1750)
Hassia, Henri de (alias Heinrich von Langenstein, c.1300–1397)
Haßler, Dietrich (1803–1873)

Ḥayyūǧ, Yēhūdāh ben Dāwīd (*alias*
     Abū Zakariyyā Yaḥyā ibn Dā'ūd,
     c.945–c.1000)S, E
Hazaël-Massieux, Guy (1936–
     1993)S
Hazai, George (b.1932)
Hazen, Marshman William (1845–
     1911)
Hazlitt, William (1778–1830)
Head, Henry (1861–1940)
Head, Richard (c.1637–c.1686)
Headland, Thomas N. ("Tom",
     b.1935)
Healey, Antonette di Paolo (b.1945)
Hearst, Phoebe Apperson (1842–
     1918)
Heath, Daniel (b.1960?)
Heath, Peter (b.1949)
Heath, Shirley Brice (b. c.1930)
Heath, Terrence (b.1936)
Heath, Thomas (fl.1837)
Hécaen, Henri (b.1912)
Hecht, Hans (1876–1946)
Hecht, Ilse (1907–1975?)
Hecht, Max (1857–1940?)
Hecker, Johann Julius (1707–1768)
Heckewelder, John Gottlieb
     Ern(e)st(us) (1743–1823)
Heemskerk, Theodorus (1852–1932)
Heepe, Martin (1887–1961)
Heerdegen, (Eugen Gottfried)
     Ferdinand (1845–1930)
Heeroma, Klaas Hanzen (1909–
     1972)
Heffner, Roe-Merrill Secrist (1892–
     1981)S
Hegel, (Georg Wilhelm) Friedrich
     (1770–1831)

Hegendorf(fer), Christoph (1500–
     1540)
Heger, Klaus (1927–1993)K
Hegerová, Katarina (d.2001)
Hegius, Alexander (1433–1498)
Hehn, Victor (1813–1890)
Heiberg, Ludwig (1760–1818)
Heiberg, Johan Ludwig (1791–1860)
Heiberg, Johan Ludwig (1854–1928)
Heidegger, Martin (1889–1976)E
Heiden, Sebald, *see* Heyden, Sebald
Heidenreich, David Elias (1638–
     1688)
Heidolph, Karl Erich (1932–1998)K
Heiermeier, Annliese (1913–1985)
Heike, Georg (b.1933)
Heike, Monogatari (c.1131–1191)
Heilig, Otto (1865–*post* 1905)
Heilmann, Luigi (1911–1988)S
Heimann, Betty (1888–1961)
Heimeric(us) de Campo (Dutch:
     Heymericus van de Velde, 1395–
     1460)S
Heimsoeth, Heinz (1886–1975)
Heine, Bernd (b.1939)K, E
Heinekamp, Albert (1933–1991)
Heinicke, Samuel (1727–1790)
Heinimann, Siegfried (1917–1996)K
Heinrich, Guillaume-Alfred (1829–
     1887)
Heinrichmann, Jacob (1482–1561)
Heinrichs, Heinrich Matthias (1911–
     1983)
Heinroth, Johann Christian August
     (1773–1843)
Heinse, (Johann Jakob) Wilhelm
     (1746–1803)
Heinsius, Daniel (1580–1655)
Heinsius, Jacobus (1872–1947)

Heinsius, Nicolaas (1620–1681)
Heinsius, Theodor Otto Friedrich (1770–1849)
Heinz, Adam (1914–1984)S
Heinz, John M. (b.1933)
Heinz, Sabine (b.1963)
Heinzel, Richard (1835–1905)
Helias, Peter, *see* Peter Helias
Helber, Sebastian (v.1530–*post* 1598)
Helbig, Gerhard (b.1929)K
Helciová-Koslová, Karla (1905–1996)
Helgason, Jón (1899–1986)
Heliade-Rădulescu, Ion (19th cent.)
Heliodorus (6th cent. A.D.)
Hellan, Lars (b.1945)
Helland, Hans Petter (b.1961)
Heller, Ludwig (1866–1945)
Hellinga, Wytze Gs. (1908–1985)
Hellquist, Elof (1864–1933)S
Hellwag, Christoph Friedrich (1754–1835)
Hellwig, Christopher (1581–1617)
Helm, Karl (c.1860–c.1940)
Helmer, Olaf (1910–??)
Helmholtz, Hermann (Ludwig Ferdinand) von (1821–1894)E
Helmont, Franciscus Mercurius van (1614–1699)
Helmont, Johann(es) Baptista (1579–1644)
Helmsdörder, Georg (fl.1854)
Helsztyński, Stanisław (1891–1986)
Helten, Willem H. van (1740–1831)
Helten, Willem Lodewijk van (1849–1917)
Heltveit, Trygve (1913–1985)
Helvétius, Claude Adrien (1715–1771)

Helvétius, *Madame* (= Anne-Cathérine Helvetius de Ligneville d'Autricourt, 1722–1800)
Helwich, Christophor (1581–1617)
Helvigius, Andreas (*alias* Helwig, d.1643)
Helwig, Christoph (1581–1617)
Hemacandra Sūri, Jain (1089–1172)S
Hemmer, Johann Jacob (1733–1790)
Hémon, Roparz (*alias* Louis Némo, 1900–1978)E
Hempel, Carl Gustav (1905–1997)
Hempel, Friedrich Ferdinand (*pseud.* Peregrinus Syntax, 1778–1836)
Hempl, Georg Friedrich (fl.1693)
Hempl, George (1859–1921)S
Hemsterhuis, Tiberius (1685–1766)S
Hencken, Hugh O'Neil (1902–*post* 1955)
Henderson, Eugénie Jane Andrina (1914–1989)E
Hendricks, William Oliver (b.1939)
Hendriksen, Hans Frederik (1913–1989)
Hendrup, Svend (1936–1997)
Hengeveld, Kees (b.1957)
Henisch, Georg, genant von Bartfeld (1549–1618)
Henley, John ("Orator", 1692–1756)
Henley, Nancy E. (b.1934)
Henne, Helmut (b.1935?)
Henning, Baltazar Gottlob (1742–1808)
Henning, Rudolf (1852–1930)
Henrichmann, Jakob (1499–1561)
Henricus Aristippus (fl.1150–1165)
Henricy, Casimir (1819–1892)
Henriksen, Carol (b.1944)

Heyne, Mori(t)z (1837–1906)S
Heyse, Johann Christian August
  (1764–1829)S, E
Heyse, Karl Wilhelm Ludwig (1797–
  1855)S
Heyse, Gustav Ferdinand (1809–
  1883)
Heyse, Theodor Friedrich (1803–
  1864)
Heytesbury, William, *see* William
  Heytesbury
Heywood, Peter (1773–1831)
Hezel, Johann Friedrich (1754–1829)
Hibiya, Junko (b.1959)
Hickes, George, bishop of Worcester
  (1642–1715)
Hickey, Raymond (b.1954)
Hidalgo, Juan (pseud. of Cristóbal de
  Chaves, d.1602)
Hieronymus (*alias* Sophronius
  Eusebius, 331/340–420 A.D.)
Hieronymus of St. Mark (fl.1507)
Hiersche, Rolf (1924–1996)K
Higden, Ranulf (1299?–1364?)
Higgins, John (1545?–1602)
Higginson, Edward (1807–1880)
Hilbert, David (1862–1943)
Hildebrand, Alfred (1853–1927)
Hildebrand, Dietrich (1889–19??)
Hildebrand, Rudolf (1824–1894)S
Hildebrand-Nilshorn, Martin
  (b.1943)
Hildemar (*c.*819 A.D.)
Hilderic (= Ilderico, *abbot* of Monte
  Cassino, 9th cent. A.D.)
Hildreth, Ezekiel (1784–1856)
Hildum, Donald C. (b.1930)
Hilferding, Alexander (= Gil'ferding,
  Aleksandr Fedorovič, 1831–1872)

Hill, Abraham (1635–1721)
Hill, Archibald A(nderson, 1902–
  1992)S, E
Hill, Jane H(assler, b.1939)E
Hill, Peter C(hristopher, b.1934?)
Hill, Thomas Wright (1763–1851)
Hill, Trevor (c.1922–2005)
Hill, William (1619–1667)
Hill, William (1806–1881)
Hill-Tout, Charles (1858–1944)
Hille, Karl Gustav von (1590?–1647)
Hillebrand, Josef (1788–1871)
Hille, Karl Gustav von (c.1590–
  c.1647)
Hillenius, Francis (b.1613)
Hilmarsson, Jörundur (1946–1992)
Hilner, Johannes (*ante* 1581–1610)
Hilprecht, Hermann (1859–1925)
Hilspach(ius), Michael (d.1570)
Hilty, Gerold (b.1927)K
Himly, Karl (1836–1904)
Hincks, Edward (1792–1866)
Hinderling, Robert (b.1935)K
Hinds, John (1943–1994)
Hindsdale, Burke Aaron (1837–
  1900)
Hinkel, Johann Carl (1817–1894)
Hinnebusch, Thomas (b.1939)
Hinsley, Curtis (b.1945)
Hintikka, Jaakko (b.1929)E
Hintze, Fritz (1915–1993)
Hinz, Walther (1906–1992)
Hipp, Helga (1934–1996)
Hippeau, Célestin (1803–1877)
Hippocrates of Kos (c.460–c.377)S
Hirata Atsutane (1776–1843)
Hirayama, Teruo (b.1909)E
Hirsch, Ernst (1904–1984)

Hirschberg, Lydia (b. c.1920)
Hirt, Herman (Alfred, 1865–1936)S, E
Hirtle, Walter (Heal, b.1927)
Hirschfelder, Wilhelm (1829–*post* 1881)
Hirzel, Ludwig (Heinrich Caspar, 1838–1897)
Hirzel, Salomon (1804–1877)
Hišām, Ibn, *see* Ibn Hišām
Hispanus, Petrus, *see* Peter of Spain
Hißmann, Michael (1752–1784)
Hitschmann, Edward E. (1871–1957)
Hittmair, Rudolf (1889–1940)
Hitzig, Eduard (1838–1907)
Hixson, Jerome Canady (b.1901)
Hiż, Henry (b.1917)
Hjärne, Urban (*also* Hiärne, 1541–1724)
Hjelmslev, Louis (Trolle, 1899–1965)S, E
Hjelmqvist, Th(omas?) (1864–1936)
Hjort, Grethe (*alias* Greta Hort, 1903–1967)
Hjort, Peder (1793–1871)
Hladká, Elička (1916–1998)
Hlavsa, Odešel Zdeněk (1926–1998)
Hoad, Terence Frederick (b.1946)
Hobbes, Thomas (1588–1679)S
Hoby, Thomas (1524–1585)
Hoccleve, Thomas (1370?–1450?)
Hochegger, Franz (1815–1875)
Hock, Hans-Henrich (b.1938)
Hock, Wolfgang (b.1959)
Hockett, Charles F(rancis,1916–2000)E
Hodann, Johann Friedrich (17th cent. scribe of Leibniz's)

Hodge, Clifton F. (1859–1949)
Hodge, Carleton T(aylor, 1917–1998)
Hodge, Frederick Webb (1864–1956)
Hodges, Richard (fl.1634–1649)
Hodgkin, John (1766–1845)
Hodgson, Brian Houghton (1800–1894)
Hodgson, William Ballantyne (1815–1880)
Hodler, Hector (1887–1920)
Hodson, Thomas Callan (1871–1953)
Hodura, Kvido (1877–*post* 1949)
Hoebeke, Marcel (1918–1989)
Hoefer, (Karl Gustav) Albert (1812–1883)
Höfler, Manfred (1937–1995)K
Höfler, Otto (1901–1987)S
Höfner, Maria (1900–1992)
Hoegel, Johann Baptist (fl.1862–1877)
Högström, Pehr (1714–1784)
Hoekstra, Albert ten Broecke, *see* Broecke Hoekstra, Albert ten
Hoekstra, Theunis Arie ("Teun", 1953–1998)
Hoel, Kåre (1922–1989)
Hölderlin, Friedrich (1770–1843)
Hölzer, Victor (1873?–19??)
Hoene-Wronski, Josef Maria (1776–1853)
Hoenigswald, Henry M(ax, 1915–2003)
Hönigswald, Richard (1875–1947)
Hoepfner, Ernst (1836–1915)
Hörmann, Hans (1924–1983)

Hörnle, (August Friedrich) Rudolf (1841–1918)
Hoffmann (von Fallersleben), (August) Heinrich (1798–1874)
Hoffmann, Johann Joseph (1805–1878)S
Hoffmann, Karl (b.1915)
Hoffmann, Margaret (d.2000)
Hoffmann, S[amuel] F[riedrich] W[ilhelm] (1803–1872)
Hoffmann-Krayer, Eduard (1864–1936)
Hoffmeister, Karl (1796–1844)
Hoffory, Julius (1855–1897)
Hofman, Johann Baptist (1886–1954)S
Hofman, Rijcklof (Henri Frans, b.1958)
Hofman Peerlkamp, Petrus (1786–1965)
Hofmann, Andreas Joseph (1752–1849)
Hofmann, Erich (1895–1982)
Hofmann, Konrad (1819–1890)
Hofmann, Thomas Ronald ("Ron", 1937–1994)
Hofstadter, Douglas R(ichard, b.1945)
Hofstetter, Walter (b.1939)
Hogan, Robert F. (b.1927)
Hogben, Lancelot Thomas (1895–1975)
Hogg, Richard Milne (1944–2007)
Hogg, William (17th cent.)
Hohenheim, Theophrast von, see Paracelsius
Hoijer, Harry (1904–1976)S, E

Holbach, Paul Henri Thiery (= Paul Heinrich Dietrich), baron d' (1723–1789)
Holbrook, Alfred (1815–1909)
Holbrook, Richard Thayer (1870–1934)
Holder, William (1616–1698)S, E
Holenstein, Elmar (b.1937)K
Holkot, Robert (c.1290–1349)E
Holland, Dorothy (b.1924)
Holland, Georg Jonathan (1742–1784)
Holland, Wilhelm Ludwig (1822–1891)
Hollman, Georg (d.1873)
Hollý, Ján (1848–??)
Hollyband (or Holiband), Claudius, see Sainliens, Claude de
Hollyman, K. J. (1922–198?)
Holm, Oskar William ("Bill", b.1925)
Holm, Thomas Campanius (c.1670–1702)
Holmer, Nils M. (1904–1994)
Holmes, George Frederick (1820–1897)
Holmes, James Stratton (1924–1986)
Holmes, Janet (b.1947)E
Holmes, Urban Tigner, Jr. (1900–1972)
Holmes, William Henry (1846–1933)
Holovac'kyj, Jakov (1814–1880)
Holst, Clara (1868–1935)
Holsten, Robert (1862–1954)
Holt, Jens (1904–1973)
Holthausen, Ferdinand (1860–1956)S
Holthusius, Ioannes (fl.1567–1582)
Holthusen, Johannes (1924–1985)

Holtsmark, Anne (Elisabeth, 1896–1974)S, E
Holtus, günter (b.1946)
Holtz, Louis (Leo, b.1937[1929?])
Holyoake, George Jacob (1817–1906)
Holyoke, Francis (1567–1653)
Holtzmann, Adolf (1810–1870)
Homa, Edward (1932–2000)
Homans, George Caspar (1910–1990)E
Homburger, Lilias (1880–1969)
Home, Herbert (Lord Kames, 1696–1782)
Homer (8th cent. B.C.)
Hommel, Fritz (1854–1936)
Homorodean, Mircea (1927–1989)
Honeyman, Alexander Mackie (1907–1988)
Hong Kimun (1903–c.1989)S
Honikman, Beatrice (1905–1997)
Hood Roberts, A. (b.1928)
Hooft, Pieter Corneliszon (1581–1647)
Hoogeveen, Henricus (1712–1791)
Hoogstraten, David van (1658–1724)
Hoogvliet, Jan Marius (1860–1924)
Hooke, Robert (1635–1703)
Hooker, Thomas (1586–1647)
Hoole, Charles (1610–1667)
Hoops, Johannes (1865–1949)
Hoops, Reinald (d.1944)
Hooton, Ernest A. (1887–1954)
Hopkins, Edward Washburn (1857–1932)S
Hopkins, Gerard Manley (1844–1889)
Hopper, Paul J(ohn, b.1939)
Hopper, Robert (1945–1998)

Hora, Karel (1904–1996)
Horace (Quintus Horatius Flaccus, 65–8 B.C.)S
Horacek, Blanka (1913–2001)E
Horálek, Karel (1908–1992)
Horbač, Oleksa (Germ. Horbatsch, Olexa, 1918–1997)
Hordé, Tristan (b.1938)
Horden, *Rev.* John (1828–1893)
Horecký, Ján (b. 1920)E
Horger, Antal (d.1947)
Horkheimer, Max (1895–1973)
Horman, William (d.1535)
Horn, Georges (1620–1670)
Horn, Paul (1863–1908)
Horn, Stefan F. (1900–1996)
Horn, Wilhelm (1876–1952)S
Hornby, Albert Sidney (1898–1978)E
Horne, Colin J. (1912–1999)
Horne, *Col.* Kibbey Minton (b.1924)
Horne Tooke, John, *see* Tooke, John Horne
Horneffer, Ernst (1871–1954)
Hornero, Calixto (Escolapio, 1742–1797)
Hórnik, Michał (1833–1894)
Hornkens, Henricus (d.1600)
Hornung, Boris, *see* Gornung, B. V.
Hornung, Maria (*née* Jechl, b.1920)K, E
Hornung, Herwig (1921–1987)
Hornung, Johann (1660–1715)
Horsch, Paul (1925–1971)
Horstmann, Carl (1847–19??)
Horvát, István (1784–1846)
Hosák, Ladislav (1898–1972)
Hoskyns, *Sir* John (1634–1705)
Hosoe, Itsuki (1884–1947)

Hospers, Johannes Hendrik (1921–1993)
Hotham, Charles (1615?–1672?)
Hotham, Durand (1617?–1691)
Hotman, François (1524–1590)
Hottinger, Johann Heinrich (fl.1661)
Hotzenköcherle, Rudolf (1903–1976)S
Houaiss, Antonio (b.1915)
Houbigant, Charles (1686–1783)
Houis, Maurice (1923–1990)
Householder, Fred W(alter, 1913–1994)E
Houtman, Frederick de (1571–1627)
Hovda, Per (1908–1997)
Hovdhaugen, Even (b.1941)
Hovelacque, Abel (1843–1896)S
Hovland, Carl Iver (1912–1961)E
Howard, Alan (b.1934)
Howard, Henry, *Earl* of Surrey (1517–1547)
Howard, Luke (1772–1864)
Howell, James (1594?–1666)
Howell, Mortimer Sloper (1844–1925)
Howell, Peter (b.1947)
Howell, Wilbur Samuel (1904–1949?)
Howerton, Paul William (b.1916)
Howren, Robert Ray (1929–1997)
Howse, Joseph (early 19th cent.)
Hoybye, Poul (1903–1989)
Høysgaard, Jens Pedersen (1698–1773)S
Hrabanus (Magnentius) Maurus (780?–856)
Hrabec, Stefan (1912–1972)
Hrdina, Karel (d.1948?)

Hrinčenko, Borys Dmytrovyč (1863–1910)S
Hrdlicka, Ales (1869–1943)
Hrístea, Theodor (b.1930)
Hrozný, Bedřich (*alias* Friedrich, 1879–1952)
Hrycjutenko, Ivan Jefremovyć (1914–1995)
Hsü Shen (c.58–147 A.D.)E
Hu, Shih (1891–1962)
Hualde, José Ignacio (b.1958)
Huama Poma de Ayala, Felipe (1526–1604)
Huang, Xiaming (2nd half of 20th cent.)
Huarte de San Juan, Juan (c.1532–1592)
Hubbel, Allan F. (1914–1976)
Huber, Konrad (b.1916)K
Huber, Victor Aimé (1800–1869)
Hubert, Anthonis de (1583–*post* 1664)
Hubert, Henri (1872–1927)
Hubschmid, Johannes (1916–1995)K
Huchon, René Louis (1872–1940)
Huck, Geoffrey J. (b.1944)
Hude, Karl von der (1860–1936)
Huddleston, Rodney Desmond (b.1937)
Hudson, Anne Mary (b.1938)
Hudson, Richard A(nthony, b.1939)
Hueber, Christoph (fl.1477)
Hübner, Arthur (1885–1937)
Hübner, August Nathanael (1689–1725/27)
Hübner, Johann (1668–1731)
Hübner, Emil (1834–1901)
Hübner, Joseph A. (1811–1892)
Hübner, Walter (1884–1970)

Hübschmann, (Johann) Heinrich (1848–1908)
Hügel, Fr. Francis (1902–1991)Love, James R. B. (1889–1947)
Hüllen, Werner (Ernst, b.1927)K
Hültenschmidt, Erika (b.1945)
Hüttl-Folter, Gerta (1923–2000)
Hülzer-Vogt, Heike (b.1961)K
Huerta, Alonso de (d.1640)
Huet, Pierre-Daniel (1630–1721)
Huet, François (1814–1869)
Hüttner, John Christian (1766–1847)
Huffman, Alan (b.1948)
Hugh of St Victor (1090–1141)S
Hughes, David Edward (1831–1900)
Hughes, Everett Cherrington (1897–1983)
Hughes, Ewerett S. (1885–1957)
Hughlings Jackson, John, *see* Jackson, John Hughlings
Hugo de St. Victor (*alias* Santo Victore, 1090–1141)
Hugo, *le père* Herman(nus, 1588–1629)
Hugues de St. Cher (c.1190–1263)
Huguet, Edmond (1863–1948)
Hugutio Pisanus (= Hugutio de Pisa), *see* Uguccione da Pisa
Huillard-Bréholles, Jean-Louis (1817–1871)
Huitziméngar, Antonio (c.1549–1562)
Huizinga, Johan (1872–1945)
Hujer, Oldřch (1880–1942)
Hulbert, James Root (1884–1969)S
Hull, Clark Leonard (1884–1952)
Huloet, Richard (fl.1552)
Hulsius, Levinus (? *alias* Lieven van Hulst, c.1546–1606)S

Hulsker, Johannes Lucas Maria ("Jos", b.1954)
Hulstaert, Gustaaf (1900–1990)
Hultman, Oskar Fredrik (1862–1929)S
Hultzén, Lee Sisson (1896–1968)S
Hultzsch, Eugen Julius Theodor (1857–1927)
Humbertus de Romains (fl.1274)
Humboldt, (Friedrich Heinrich) Alexander, *Freiherr* von (1769–1859)
Humboldt, (Friedrich) Wilhelm (Christian Karl Ferdinand), *Freiherr* von (1767–1835)S, E
Hume, Alexander (c.1560–c.1617)
Hume, David (1711–1776)
Humec'ka, Lukija Ljukanivna (1901–1988)S
Hummelstedt, Eskil (1906–1986)
Humperdinck, Gustav (1823–1902)
Humphreys, Humphrey (1648–1712)
Hundeiker, Wilhelm Theodor (1786–1828)
Hund(t), Magnus (1449–1519)
Hundsnurscher, Franz (b.1935)K
Huneker, James G. (1859–1921)
Hunfalvy, Pál (1810–1891)
Hunger, Wolfgang (1507–1555)S
Hunnius, Klauš (b.1933)K
Hunold, Christian Friedrich (*alias* Menantes, 1681–1721)
Hunt, George (1854–1933)
Hunt, James (1833–1869)
Hunt, Richard William (1908–1979)
Hunt, Thomas (1611–1683)
Hunter, *Rev.* John (1849–1917)
Huntsman, Jeffrey F(orrest, b.1942)
Hupel, August Wilhelm (1737–1829)

I.

Ibbeken, Hermann Ludolph (*pseud.*
William Thompson, 1740–1808)
Ibn Abīsḥāq, ibn Zayd ᶜAbdallāh Abū
Baḥr (29/650 *or* 39/659–117/735
or 127/745)S
Ibn Āǧurrum, Abū ᶜAbdallāh
Muḥammad ibn Muḥammad as-
Sanhāǧī (672/1273–723/1323)S
Ibn al-ᶜAla', Abū ᶜAmur (690–771)
Ibn al-Anbārī, Abū Bakr Muḥammad
ibn al-Qāsim (271/885–328/940)S
Ibn al-Anbārī, Abū l-Barakāt Kamāl
ad-Dīn ᶜAbd ar-Raḥmān ibn
Muḥammad (513/1119–
577/1119)S
Ibn ᶜAqil, Baha' ad-Dīn ᶜAbdallāh
ibn ᶜAbd ar-Raḥmān (694/1294–
769/1367)S
Ibn Balᶜam, Yēhudah ben Sēmu'ēl
(*alias* Abū Zakariyyā Yaḥyā, mid-
11th cent.)S
Ibn Barūn, Abū Ibrāhīm Isḥaq ibn
Yūsuf ibn Benveniste (mid-11th
cent.)S
Ibn Durayd, Abū Bakr Muḥammad
ibn al-Hasan (223/838–321/933)S
Ibn Durustawayhī, Abū Muḥammad
ᶜAbdallāh Ibn Gaᶜfar (d.347/958)
Ibn ᶜEzra, Avrāhām ben Mē'īr (Arab
name: Abū Isḥāq, 1089–1165)S, E
Ibn Fāris, Abū l-Ḥusayn Aḥmad
(d.395/1004)S

Ibn Gabriol, Solomon ben Judah
(c.1021–c.1058)
Ibn Ǧanāḥ, (*Rabbi*) Yonāh (Arab
name: Abū l-Walīd Marwān, c.990–
c.1050) S, E
Ibn Ǧiḳaṭilla, Mošeh ben Šĕmuᶜēl ha-
Kōhēn (2nd half of 11th cent.)S
Ibn Ǧiḳaṭilla, Yiẓḥāq (10th cent.)S
Ibn Ǧinnī, Abū l-Fatḥ ᶜUtmān
(c.330/942 or c.320/932–
392/1002)E
Ibn al-Ḥaǧib, Ǧamāl ad-Dīn Abū
ᶜAmr ᶜUtmān ibn ᶜUmar (b. *post*
510/1174–646/1249)S
Ibn Ḥālawayhi, Abū ᶜAbdallāh al-
Ḥusayn ibn Aḥmad (d.370/980)
Ibn Haldūn (d.1382)
Ibn Hišām, Ǧamāl ad-Dīn Abū
Muḥammad ᶜAbdallāh ibn Yūsuf
(708/1310–761/1360)S
Ibn-Hazm (994–c.1050)
Ibn Kaspi, Joseph (1279–1340)
Ibn Kaysān, Abū l-Ḥasan ibn Aḥmad
(d.299/912 or 320/932)S
Ibn Labraṭ, Dūnāš (*alias* al-Abrad,
Hebrew name: Adōnīm ha-Lēwī,
c.920–c.980)S
Ibn Maḍā', Abū l-ᶜAbbās Aḥmad ibn
ᶜAbd ar-Rahmān al-Qurṭubī (1120–
1196)S, E
Ibn Mālik, Ǧamāl ad-Dīn Abū
ᶜAbdallāh Muḥammad ibn
ᶜAbdallāh (600/1203–672/1274)S
Ibn Manẓūr (*also* Ibn Mukarram),
Abū l-Faḍl Muḥammad ibn
Mukarram (630/1232–711/1311)S
Ibn Marūth Sikhem, Abū Isḥāq Ibra-
hīm b. Farag (first half of 12th
cent.)

J.

Jaberg, Karl (1877–1959)S, E
Jablonski, Daniel Ernst (1660–1741)
Jablonski, Paul Ernst (1693–1757)
Jablonskis, Jonas (pseud. Jonas Rygiškų, 1860–1930)S
Jaccard, Henri (1844–19??)
Jachnow, Helmut (b.1939)K
Jacimirskij, Aleksandr Ivanovič (1873–1925)
Jackendoff, Ray S(aul, b.1945)E
Jackson, Abraham Valentine Williams (1862–1937)S
Jackson, Don D. (1920–1968)
Jackson, Helen (Maria) Hunt (1830–1885)
Jackson, Jean (b.1943)
Jackson, Kenneth H. (1909–1991)
Jackson, John Hughlings (1835–1911)
Jackson, Kenneth Hurlstone (1909–1991)
Jacob of Edessa (d.708 A.D.)
Jacob of Tagrit (*alias* Severus bar Shakjko, d.1286)
Jacob, Alexandre André (pseud. Alexandre Erdan, 1826–1878)
Jacob, André (b.1921)
Jacob, Brüder (1785–1863)
Jacob, Daniel (b.1957)
Jacob, Georg (1862–1957)
Jacob, Henry (b.1909)
Jacob, Judith M. (b.1923)
Jacobi, Christian (fl.1626–1660?)
Jacobi, Friedrich Heinrich (1743–1819)
Jacobi, Hermann (Georg, 1850–1937)
Jacobi, Johann Georg (1740–1814)
Jacobi, Wilhelm Alexander Theodor (1816–1848)
Jacobs, Friedrich (1764–1847)
Jacobs, Joachim (b.1948)
Jacobs, Melville (1902–1971)
Jacobs, Roderick A(rnold, b.1934)
Jacobsen, Elisabeth ("Lis", 1882–1961)S, E
Jacobsen, Jacob Peter (1869–1918)
Jacobsen, Johan Adrian (1853–1947)
Jacobsen, Thorklid (b.1904)
Jacobsen, William H(ornton), Jr. (b.1931)
Jacobsohn, Hermann (1879–1933)S
Jacobson, Rodolfo (b. c.1935)
Jacobson, Sven (b.1922)
Jacobus Clericus of Venice (fl.1128)
Jacobus de Placentia (fl.1340–1347)S
Jacotot, Joseph (1770–1840)
Jacquement, Frédéric François Venceslas (1757–1836)
Jacquet, Eugène (Vincent-) Stanislas (1811–1838)
Jäck, Heinrich Joachim (1777–1847)
Jäger, Andreas (c.1660–1730)
Jäger, Gert (b.1935)K
Jäger, Siegfried (b.1937)K
Jäger, Werner (1888–1961)
Jaeggli, Osvaldo A. (1953–1990)
Jährig, Johann (d.1795)
Jagemann, Christian Joseph (1735–1804)

Jesenius, Johann (1745–1829)
Jespersen, (Jens) Otto (Harry, 1860–1943)S, E
Jesup, Morris K. (1830–1908)
Jesus, Rafael de (1614–1693)
Jeudi, Colette (b.1936)
Jevons, William Stanley (1835–1882)
Jewel, John (1522–1571; since 1559: Bishop of Salisbury)
Jewell, *Rev.* Frederick Swartz (1821–1903)
Jílek-Oberpfalcer, František (1890–1973)
Jimbo (Jinbou), Kaku (1883–1965)
Jimbô, Kiichi (1912–1991)
Jiménez, Francisco (1436–1517)
Jiménez, Francisco, O.P. (1666–1730)
Jiménez Arias, Diego, O.P. (1490–1579?)
Jiménez de Cisneros, *Cardinal* Francisco (1436–1517)
Jiménez de la Espada, Marcos (1831–1898)
Jiménez Patón, Bartolomé (1569–1640)S
Jiráček, Jiři (b.1924)
Jirát, Vojtěch (1902–1945)
Jirecek, Constantin (1854–1918)
Jireček, Josef (1825–1888)
Jiriczek, Otto (1867–1941)
Joannes Gasconius Bilibilitanus
Joas, Hans (b.1948)
Job, Michael (b.1948)K
Jocher, Adam Benedykt (1791–1860)
Jochmann, Carl Gustav (1789–1830)
Jodogne, Omer (1908–1996)
Joël, Judith (1927–1996)
Jönnes, Arvi, *see* Genetz, Arvid

Jörgen, Tams (1924–1987)
Jogues, Isaac, S.J. (1607–1646)
Johann von Sachsen (*alias* Philalethes, 1801–1873)
Johannes Buridanus, *see* John Buridan
Johannes Dacus, *see* John of Dacia
Johannes Aurifaber (fl.1330)
Johannes Balbus or de Balbis, *see* John of Balbi
Johannes de Adorf (fl.1491)
Johannes de Nova Domo (d.1418)S
Johannes de Rus (fl. c.1250)
Johannes Gersonius (1363–1429)S
Johannes Glogoviensis (*alias* von Glogau, d.1507)
Johannes Januensis, *see* John of Balbi
Johannes Pagus (Fr. Jean le Page, fl.1125–1140)S
Johannes Scottus (c.810–877 A.D.)
Johannisson, Ture (1903–1990)
Johanson, Lars (b.1936)K
Johansson, Karl Ferdinand (1860–1926)
Johansson, Stig (b.1939)
John Barton (fl.1400–1410)S
John Buridan (c.1295–*post* 1358)S
John Chrysoston (347–407 A.D.)
John Duns Scotus ("Doctor subtilis", c.1266–1307)S
John Leylond (fl.1401; d.1428)S
John of Balbi (Giovanni Balbi, *also* John of Genoa, d.1286)
John of Cornwall (fl.1344)S
John of Dacia (fl.1280)
John of Damascus (Damascenus, c.650/70–754 A.D.)

Jordan of Saxony (d.1221)S
Jordan, Jan Petr (*also* Piotr, 1818–1891)
Jordan, Johann Christoph von (fl.1745)
Jordan, Karl Richard (1877–1925)
Jordan, Leo (orig.: Leopold Hermann, 1874–1940)
Jordan, Peter (d.1552)
Jordanes (fl.530 A.D.)
Jorden, Eleanor Harz (b. c.1920)
Joret, (Pierre Louis) Charles (Richard, 1839–1914)
Jørgensen, Jørgen (1899–1970)S
Joscelyn, John (1529–1603)
Joseph, Brian D(aniel, b.1951)
Joseph, John E(arl, b.1956)
Josse, Agustin Louis (1763–1841)
Josselson, Harry Hirsch (1906–1971)
Josselyn, Freeman Marshall, Jr. (1866–1916)
Josserand, Kathryn (1942–2007)
Jost, Isaak Marcus (1793–1860)
Jostes, Franz (1858–1925)
Jouannet, Francis (1948–1989)
Joubert, Joseph (1640–1719)
Joubert, Laurent (1529–1583)
Jouenneaux, Guy (Guido Juvanalis, c.1460–1505)
Jouffroy, Théodore (1796–1842)
Joüon, Paul (1871–1940)
Jourdain de Saxe (Pseudo-, 13th cent.)
Jouvancy, Joseph (1643–1719)
Jouvency, *le père* Joseph de (*fl.*1692–1725)
Jovellanos, Gaspar Melchior de (1744–1811)S

Jović, Dušan (1921–1996)
Ju, Jiunsheng (1788–1858)
Juchem, Johann Georg (1939–2003)
Jucker, Andreas H. (b.1957)K
Jud, Jakob (1882–1952)S,E
Jud, Leo (1482–1542)
Judas, Auguste Célestin (1805–1873)
Judycka, Irmina (1920–2000)
Jünger, Ernst (1901–2002)
Juhász, János (1925–1989)
Juilland, Alphonse (1922–2000)
Julian of Toledo (Julianus Toletanus, 642?–690 A.D.)S
Julien, (Aignan-) Stanislas (1797–1873)
Julien, Gustave Jacques Henri (1870–1936)
Jullian, Camille Louis (1859–1933)
Jullien, Bernard (1798–1881)
Juncker, Georg Adam (1720–1805)
Jung, Carl Gustav (1875–1961)
Jung, Joachim (1587–1657)
Junge, Joachim (1587–1677)
Jung, Michael (1743–1826)
Junggrammatiker (= Neogrammarians, dominant, c.1875–c.1920)
Jungmann, Johann Georg (1720–1808)
Jungmann, Josef (Jakub, 1773–1847)S
Jungner, Hugo (d.1940?)
Jungraithmayr, Herrmann (b.1931)K
Junius, Franciscus (the Younger, 1591–1677)E
Junius, (H)adrianus (*alias* Adriaans de Jonghe(n), 1511–1575)
Junker, Heinrich (1889–1970)
Jurasova, Irina I. (1953–1997)
Juret, Abel-Claude (1872–c.1950)

K.

Kabasanov, Stajko Konstantinov
(1906–1997)
Kabelka, Jonas (1914–1986)
Kabis, Johannes (1853–1919)
Kabjalka, Jonas, *see* Kabelka, Jonas
Kabrda, Josef (1906–1968)
Kaccayāna (7th/8th cent. A.D.)S
Kachru, Braj B(ehari, b.1932)
Kačić, Miro (1946–2001)
Kačić-Miošić, Andrija, O.F.M.
(1704–1760)
Kacenovskij, Mixail Trofimovič
(1775–1842)
Kacnel'son, Solomon Davidovič
(1907–1985)
Kaczmarek, Leon (1911–1996)
Kaczmarek, Ludger (b.1953)
Kadushin, Charles (b.1932)
Kaeding, Friedrich Wilhelm (1843–
19??)
Kaecher, Ernst Friedrich (1789–
1855)
Kähler-Meyer, Emmi (b.1903)
Kährig, Aimo (1942–1991)
Källskogs, Margareta (1941–1994)
Kärgi, Adolf (1849–1923)
Käsmann, Hans (b.1923)
Kagan, Moisej Samojlovič (1921–
2006)
Kahane, Henry (1902–1992)
Kahane, Renée (*née* Toole, b.1907)
Kahle, Bernhard Hermann (1861–
1910)

Kahle, Paul (1875–1964)
Kahlert, Karl August Timotheus
(1807–1864)
Kaibel, Georg (1849–1901)
Kaindl, Johann (fl.1815)
Kainz, Friedrich (1897–1977)
Kaiser, Karl (d. c1940)
Kaiser, Louise (1891–1973)
Kaiser, (Oskar) Rolf (1909–1979)
Kaiser, Stefan (b.1946)
Kaisov, Ivan Andreevič (1893–1978)
Kaldewaj, Jelle (b.1954)
Kalenič, Vatroslav (1930–1981)
Kalepky, Theodor (1862–1932)
Kalff, Gerrit (1856–1923)
Kalina, Antoni (1846–1906)
Kalima (originally: Landgren), Jalo
Lahja (1884–1952)S
Kallenberg, Hermann (1845–*post*
1906)
Kalleris, Giannis (1901–1992)
Kallimachos of Kyrene (c.310–c.240
B.C.)
Kálmán, Béla (1913–1997)
Kallstenius, Gottfried (1873–1942)
Kálmán, Béla (1913–1997?)
Kalmár, György (1726–*post* 1781)
Kaltschnidt, Jacob Heinrich (1800–
1873)
Kaltz, Barbara (b.1946)
Kålund, (Peter Erasmus) Kristian
(1844–1919)
Kaluza, Max (1856–1921)
Kalynovyč, M. Ja. (1888–1949)
Kamei, Takashi (b.1912)E
Kamińska, Halina Jadwiga (1927–
2002)
Kamińska, Maria (b.1930)
Kamlah, Friedrich (1905–1976)

Kate, Jan Jacob Lodewijk ten (1819–1889)

Kate, Lambert (Hermanszoon) ten (1674–1731)S, E

Katičić, Radoslav (b.1930)

Katona, Lucia (b.1956)

Katre, Sumitra Mangesh (1906–1998)E

Katsumata, Senkichiro (1872–1959)

Kātyāyana (3rd cent. B.C.)S, E

Katz, David S. (1884–1953)

Katz, Dovid (b.1956)

Katz, Hartmut (1943–1996)K

Katz, Jerrold Jacob (1932–2002)E

Kauffmann, Friedrich (fl.1890)

Kaufman, Terrence (Scott, b.1937)

Kaulen, Franz Philipp (1827–1907)

Kaulfers, Walter V. (1904–1990)

Kaulfuss, Jan (*alias* Johann) Samuel (1780–1832)

Kautzsch, Emil (Friedrich, 1841–1910)

Kavanagh, Morgan Peter (c.1800–1874)

Kavelin, Konstantin Dmitrievič (1818–1885)

Kavtaradze, Ivane (1920–1985)

Kawamoto, Shigeo (1913–1983)E

Kay, Alan C. (b1940)

Kay, Christian Janet (b.1940)

Kay, Martin (b.1935)E

Kay, Paul (b.1934)

Kaye, Alan S(tewart, 1944–2007)

Kayne, Richard S(tanley, b.1944)

Kaysenberg, Johann Geiler von (1445–1510)

Kayser, Wolfgang (Johannes, 1906–1960)

Kazaku, Boris, *see* Cazacu, Boris

Kazama, Kiyozō (b.1928)E

Kazazis, Kostas (d.2002)

Kazimirski-Biberstein, A. von (1808–1887)

Kazinczy, Ferenc (1759–1831)

Kazlauskas, Jonas (1930–1970)S

Keane, Augustus Henry (1833–1912)

Keating, William Hypolitus (1799–1840)

Keckermann, Bartholomaeus (1571–1609)

Keckman, Carl N. (fl.1812–1838)

Keem, Hella (1915–1997)

Keenan, Edward L. (b.1937)

Keeney, Barnaby C. (1914–1986)

Keesing, Roger Martin (1935–1993)S

Kehr, Carl (1830–1885)

Kehr, Georg Jakob (1692–1740)

Kehrein, Joseph (1808–1876)S

Keichu, Monk (1640–1701)

Keil, (Gottfried Theodor) Heinrich (1822–1894)

Keith, Arthur Berriedale (1879–1964)

Kelkar, Ashok R. (b.1929)

Kelke, William Henry Hastings (1839–*post* 1885)

Kelle, Johann Nepomuk von (1829–1909)

Keller, Adelbert von (1812–1883)

Keller, Albert Galloway (1874–1956)

Keller, Gerard (1829–1899)

Keller, Hans-Erich (1922–1999)

Keller, May Lansfield (1877–1964)

Keller, Otto? (1889–1945)

Keller, Rudi (*alias* Rudolf, b.1942)K

Keller, Wolfgang (1873–1943)

Kellner, Hermann Camillo (1839–1916)

Kettunen, Lauri Einari (1885–1963)S
Key, Mary Ritchie (1924–2003)
Key, Thomas Hewitt (1799–1875)
Keyfitz, Nathan (b.1913)
Keynes, Simon Douglas (b.1952)
Keyser, Jan Pieter de (1818–1878)
Keyser, Samuel Jay (b.1935)
Keyser, Sijbrand (1904–1989)
Khalīl, ibn Aḥmad, al- (d.791)
Khan, Masd Husain (b.1919)
Kho, Songmo (1947–1993)
Khubchandani, Lachman M. (b.1932)
Kibbee, Douglas A(lan, b.1949)
Kibler, William W. (b.1942)
Kibrik, Aleksandr Evgen'evič
    (b.1939)
Kibrik, Andrej Aleksandrovicč
    (b.1963)
Kida, Jan (b.1931)
Kidder, Alfred V. (1885–1963)
Kiddle, Lawrence Bayard (1907–
    1991)
Kiefer, Ferenc (b.1931)K
Kiel, Cornelis van, see Kiliaan,
    Cornelis van
Kielar, Barbara Z. (b.1930)
Kielhorn, (Lorenz) Franz (1840–
    1908)
Kienle, Richard von (1908–19??)
Kiekegaard, Søren (1813–1855)
Kielski, Bolesłan Felicjan (1879–
    1965)
Kiely, Benedict (b.1919)
Kieser, Otto (1921–1983)
Kihlbom, Asta (1892–1984)
Kihm, Alain (b.1946)
Kikuzawa, Sueo (1900–1985)
Kilbury, James S. (b.1946)K

Kiliaan, Corneli(u)s van (alias [van]
    Kiel, 1530–1607)S, E
Killean, Carolyn G. (b.1936)
Kilpinen, Volmari (alias Wolmar
    Styrbjörn Schöldt, 1810–1893)
Kilvington, Richard, see Richard
    Kilvington
Kilwardby, Robert, see Robert
    Kilwardby
Kimball, John P. (1941–1977)
Kimball, Solon T(oothaker, b.1909)
Kimḥi, David (Dāwīd ben Yōsēf,
    "Radak", c.1160–1235?)S, E
Kimḥi, Joseph b. Isaak (Yōsēf ben
    Yiẓhaq, c.1105–c.1170)S
Kimḥi, Moshe (Mōšēh ben Yōsēf, d.
    c.1190)S
Kim Tubong (1889–post 1958)S
Kim Yun'gyŏn (alias Han'gyŏl,
    1894–1969)S
Kinberg, Naphtali (1948–1997)
Kindaichi, Haruhikio (b.1913)
Kindaichi, Kyôsuke (1882–1971)S, E
Kinder, Philip (1597–post1665)
Kindermann, Balthasar (1636–1706)
King, Gilbert William (b.1914)
King, Harold V(osburgh, b.1917)
King, Larry D(awain, b.1949)
King, Robert D(esmond, b.1936)
Kingdon, Roger (1891–1984)
Kingsbury, Stewart A. (1923–1994)
Kingsley, Norman William (1829–
    1913)
Kinkade, M(arvin) Dale (1933–2004)
Kinkel, Gottfried (1815–1882)
Kinker, Johannes (1764–1845)
Kinloch, Alexander Murray (1923–
    1993)
Kinner, Cyprian (fl.1650)

Kock, (Karl) Axel (Lichnowsky,
1851–1935)S
Kock, Ernst Albin (1864–1943)S
Kočubinskij, Aleksander A. (1845–
1907)
Kodučova, V. I. (1919–1996)
Kodzasov, Sandro Vasil'evič
(b.1938)
Kodzu, Harushige (1908–1973)E
Köfferl, Simon (d.1585)
Kögel, (Georg) Rudolf (1855–1899)
Köhler, Oswin (1911–1996)K
Köhler, Otto (1827–1913)
Köhler, Reinhard (b.1951)
Köhler, Reinhold (1830–1892)
Köhler, Wolfgang (1898–1967)
Kökeritz, (Karl August) Helge
(1902–1964)S
Koekkoek, Byron J. (b.1924)K
Kölbing, Eugen (1846–1899)
Koeler, Georg David (1758–1818)
Koelle, *Rev.* Sigismund Wilhelm
(1823–1902)E
Kölliker, Rudolf Albert von (1817–
1905)
Kölver, Bernhard (1938–2001)
Koen, Gisbert (1736–1767)
König, Ekkehard (b.1941)K
König, Georg Matthias (1616–1699)
König, Rudolph (1832–1901)
Königseer, Christof Michael (1723–
1786)
Könnye, Nándor (1850–1912)
Köppen, Peter von (*alias* Petr
Ivanovič Keppen, 1793–1864)
Körner, Christian Gottfried (1756–
1831)
Koerner, E[rnst] F[rideryk] K[onrad]
("Konrad"; b.1939)K, E

Körner, Georg (1717–1772)
Körner, Josef (1888–1950)
Körner, Karl-Hermann (1941–
1996)K
Kőrösi Csoma, Sándor (1784–1842)
Körting, Gustav (1845–1913)
Köster, Henrich Martin Gottfried
(1734–1862)
Köster, Jens Peter (b.1942)K
Köster-Thoma, Soia A. (1945–
2001)Koestler, Arthur (1905–1983)
Kövesi, Madga (1910–1992)
Koffka, Kurt (1886–1941)
Kohn, Christian Wilhelm (1829–??)
Kohn, János (1941–1999)
Kohnstamm, Oscar (1871–1917)
Kohonen, Teuvo (b.1934)
Kohrt, Manfred (b.1947)K
Koivulehto, Jorma (b.1934)K
Koizumi, Tamotsu (b.1926)
Kók, Alardus Lodewijk ("Allert"
1616–1653 or: 1614–1649)
Kokla, Paul (b.1929)
Kokovcov, Pavel Konstantinovič
(1861–1942)
Kolb, Herbert (1924–1991)
Kolberg, Oskar (1815–1890)
Kolbinger, Abraham (1549–1622?)
Kolbuszewski, Stanisław Franciszuk
(1933–1986)
Koldewey, Karl Friedrich Ernst
(1839–*post* 1886)
Kolding (Colding), Poul Jensen
(1581–1640)
Kolehmainen, John Ilmari (b.1910)
Kollár, Jan (*or* Johann, 1793–1852)
Kølle, Christian (1737–1814)
Kollewijn, Roeland Anthonie (1857–
1942)

Koller, Werner (b.1942)K
Kollmer, Michael (1917–2001)
Kołmaczewski, Leonard (Leonard
Zenonovič Kolmačevskij, 1850–
1889)
Kontzi, Reinhold (b.1924)K
Kolojažnyj, Andrit Stepanovyč
(1904–1992)
Kolomijeć, Vera Tytivna (1922–
1993)
Kolosov, M(itrofan) A(lekseevič,
1839–1891)
Kolross, Johannes (c.1487–
1558/1560)
Kolsrud, Sigurd (188–1957)
Komárek, Miroslav (b.1924)
Komáromi Csipkés, György (1628–
1678)
Komenský, Jan Amos *see* Comenius
Komlev, Nikolaj Georgievič (1924–
1999)
Komorowska, Hanna (b.1940?)
Kondrat'ev, Vladimir G. (1939–
1998)
Kondrašov, Nikolaj Andreevič
(1919–1995)
Koneczna, Halina (1899–1961)
Koneski, Blaže (1921–1993)
Konfederáková, Galina (1940–1994)
Kong Guangsen (1752–1786)
Kono, Rokuro (1912–1998)E
Kononov, Andrej Nikola'evič (1906–
1986)
Konopielko, Bronisław (1944–1997)
Konov, Sten (d.1948)
Konrad, Gustav (b.1911)
Konrad, Nikolaj I. (1891–1970)
Konrath, Matthias (1843–1925)

Konstantinos, Porphyrogenetos (*reg.*
912–959)
Kooij, Jan (1940–2004)
Kooper, Erik Simon (b.1942)
Koopman, Hilda (b.1953)
Kopaliński, Władysław (b.1907)
Kopec, Gary (1952–1998)
Kopczyński, Onufry (baptized
Andrzej, 1735–1817)S
Kopeckij, Leontief Vasil'evič (1894–
1976)
Kopeckij, Leontij V. (1894–1976)
Kopelev, Lev Zinov'evič (1912–
1997)
Kopertowska, Danuta (b.1935)
Kopečný, František (1909–1990)
Kopievskij, Il'ja Fedorovič (c.1650–
1701)
Kopitar, Jernej (Bartholomäus, 1780–
1844)S
Koppers, Wilhelm (1886–1961)
Koppmann, Karl (1839–1905)
Korbut, Gabriel (1862–1934)
Koreň, Jozef (1887–1969)
Kořenský, Jan (b.1938)
Korff, Hermann August (1882–1963)
Korhammer, Michael (b.1941)
Korhonen, Jarmo (Atero, b.1946)
Korhonen, Mikko (1936–1991)
Korínek, Josef Miloslav (1899–1945)
Korlén, Gustav (b.1915)K
Korn, Karl (1908–1991)
Kornaszewski, Marek (1930–1998)
Korolev, A. A. (1944–1999)
Korošec, Tomo (b.1938)
Korš, Fedor Evegen'evič (1843–
1915)
Korubin, Blagoja (1921–1995)
Korsakas, Kostas (1909–1986)

Kronasser, Heinz (1913–1968)
Kronvaids, Atis (1837–1875)
Kropp, George Philip (1872–1934)
Krüger, Fritz (1889–1974)
Krüger, Georg Theodor August (1793–1873)
Krüger, Gustav (1859–1922)
Krueger, John R. (b.1927)
Krüger, Karl Wilhelm (1796–1874)
Kruijsen, Joep (b.1943)
Kruijt, Albertus Christiaan (1869–1949)
Kruisinga, Etsko (1875–1944)S, E
Krumbacher, Karl (1856–1909)
Kruopas, Jonas (1908–1975)
Krusenstern, Adam Johan (von, *alias* Ivan Fedorovič Kruzenstern, 1770–1846)
Kruszewski, Mikołaj (Habdank; in Russian: Nikolaj Vjačeslavovič Kruševskij, 1851–1887)S, E
Kruyskamp, Cornelis Helenus Adrianus (1911–1990)
Kruyt, A.C., *see* Kruijt, Albertus Christiaan
Krylov, Ivan Andreevič (1769–1844)
Krylov, Sergej Aleksandrovič (b.1938)
Kryms'kyj, Agafangel (Axatanhel) Efimovič (1871–1942)
Kryński, Adam Antoni (1844–1932)
Krzeszowski, Tomasz P. (b.1939)
Kuba, Ludvík (b.1928)
Kubczak, Hartmut (b.1941)K
Kubouchi, Tadao (b.1939)
Kucala, Marian (b.1927)
Kučera, Henry (b.1925)
Kudaev, Pavel Stepanovič (1926–1887)

Kudang, *see* Sŏngmu
Kudělka, Milan (b.1922)
Kudrajavcev, Mixail Vasil'evič (1949–1995)
Kudzinowski, Czesław (1908–1988)
Kücher, Walther (1877–1953)
Külpe, Oswald (1862–1915)
Kühn, Herbert (fl.1932)
Kühne, Friedrich Theodor (1758–1834)
Kühnel, (Wilhelm Ernst) Paul (1848–1924)
Kühner, Raphael (1802–1878)S
Kühnert, Franz (1852–1918)
Külpe, Oswald (1862–1915)E
Kümmel, Hans Martin (1937–1986)
Kuen, Heinrich (1899–1989)S
Künnap, Ago (b.1931)
Kürschner, Wilfried (b.1945)K
Küster, Ludolf (1670–1716)
Kugler, Paul (b.1935)
Kuhlnann, Quirinus (1650?–1689)
Kuhn, (Franz Felix) Adalbert (1812–1881)S
Kuhn, Ernst (Wilhelm Adalbert, 1846–1920)
Kuhn, Hans (1899–1988)
Kuhn, Hugo (1909–1978)
Kuhn, Sherman M(cAllister, 1907–1991)
Kuhn, Thomas S(amuel, 1922–1996)
Kuiper, Franciscus Bernardus Jacobus (1907–2003)E
Kuiper, Gerrit (1904–1973)
Kuipers, Aert Hendrik (b.1919)
Kukenheim, Louis (1905-1972)
Kulagina, Olga Sergeevna (b.1932)
Kul'bakin, Stepan Mixajlovič (1873–1924)

L.

Laanest, Arvo (b.1931)

Laas, Ernst (1837–1885)

La Barre, Weston (b.1911)

Labat, Jean-Bptiste (1663–1738)

Labbé, Philippe (1607–1667)

La Boétie, Etienne de (1530–1563)

Labonia, Daniel Alberto (b.1959)

Laborde, Jean-Baptiste Vincent (1830–1903)

Laboulaye, Édouard (1811–1883)

Labouret, Henri (1878–1959)

Labov, William (b.1927)E

Labrousse, Pierre (b.1939)

La Bruyère, Jean de (1645–1696)

Lacabane, Jean-Léon (1798–1884)

Laca, Henrik (1909–1991)

La Calle, Antonio de (1843–1889)

Lacan, Jacques (Marie Émile, 1901–1981)E

LaCapra, Dominik (b.1939)

Lacaze, Marie Jean Lucien (1860–1955)

Lacepède, Etienne de (1756–1825)

Lacerda, Armando de (1902–19??)

La Chambre, Marin Cureu de (1594–1669)

Lachmann, Karl (Konrad, 1793–1851)

Laclotte, Fauste (fl.1902)

Lacombe, François (1729–1795)

Lacombe, Georges (1879–1947)

La Condamine, Charles-Marie de (1701–1669)

Lacoutz de Levizac, *abbé* Jean-Pont-Victor (1753–1813)

Lacretelle, Jean Charles Dominique ('le jeune', 1766–1855)

Lacretelle, Pierre Louis ('l'aîné', 1704–1780)

La Croze, Maturin Veyssière de, *see* Veyssière de la Croze, Maturin

Lacueva, Francisco (c.1795–*post* 1832)S

La Curne de Sainte-Palaye, Jean-Baptiste de (1697–1781)

Lacy, Phillip Howard de (b.1913)

Laçzak, Józef (1926–1989)

Ladd, William P. (1870–1941)

Ladefoged, Peter (Nielsen, 1925–2006)E

Lado, Robert (1915–1995)E

Ladvocat, *abbé* Jean-Baptiste ("le Vosgien", 1709–1765)

Laet, Jan de, *see* De Laet, Jan

Lafargue, Paul (1842–1911)

Lafaye, Pierre-Benjamin Lafaist, *dit* (1809–1867)S

Lafiteau, *père* Joseph-François, S.J. (1681–1746)

La Flesche, Francis (1857–1932)S

La Flotte, […] de (fl.1765–1774)

Lafon, René (1899–*post* 1975)

Lagane, René (b.1922)

La Grasserie, Raoul (Robert Marie-Guérin) de (1839–1914)S

La Grue, Thomas (d.1673)

Laguna, Andrés (1494/94–1559/60)

Laguna, Frederica de (1906–2004?)

Laguna, Grace Mead Andrus de (1878–1978)

Lagunas, *Fray* Juan Bautista (Bravo) de, O.F.M. (fl.1539–1574, d.1604)

Lascaris, Constantine (1433–1501)
Lascaris, Jean (*alias* Laskaris, Janus, c1445-c1534)E
Las Casas, *Fray* Bartolomé de (1494–1566)
Las Casas, Christóbal de (fl.1570; d.1576)
Lasch, Agathe (1879–1942)S, E
Lashley, Karl S(pence, 1890–1958)
Lasnik, Howard (b.1945)
Lass, Roger (b.1937)
Lassen, Christian (1800–1876)S
Lasso, El Licendiado (fl.1550)
Lasteyrie du Saillant, Charles–Philibert, *comte* de (1759–1849)
Lastra, Yolanda (b.1932)
Laswell, Harold Dwight (1902-1978)E
Latacz, Joahim (b.1934)E
Latham, Robert Gordon (1812–1888)
Latimer, Hugh (*c.*1485–1555)
Latini, Brunetto (c.1220–c.1294)S
La Touche (Latouche), *abbé* Auguste (1783–1878)
La Touche, Pierre (also: Nicolas) de (d.1730)
Lattes, Elia (1843–1925)
Lattmann, Julius (1818–1898)
Laud, *Archbishop* William (1573–1645)
Laudan, Larry (b.1941)
Laufer, Berthold (1874–1934)
Laugel, Auguste (1830–1914
Launay, Pipoulain de (d.1767)
Laur, Eugen (1825–18??)
Lauremberg, Johann (1590–1658)
Laurence, *Dean* Nowell (c.1514–1576)
Laurent, Pierre (1882–c.1945)

Laurent, Stephen (*alias* Étienne, 1909–2001)
Laurian, August Trebonin (1810–1881)
Laurie, Simon Somerville (1829–1909)
Lausberg, Heinrich (1912–1992)K,S
Lautensach, Otto (1852–*post* 1911)
Lauterbeck, Georg (d.1578)
Lauzon, Matthew J(ustin, b.1972)
Lavagnini, Bruno (1898–1992)
Lavandera, Beatriz (d.1998)
Lavater, Johann Caspar (1741–1801)
Lavater, Johann Konrad (1609–*post* 1659)
Laveaux, Jean-Charles Thibault de (also: La Veaux, 1749–1827)
Laver, John (David Michael Henry, b.1938)
Laves, Gerhardt (1906–1992)
La Villemarqué, Théodore Claude Hersat de, *vicomte* (1815–1895)
La Villegille, Paul-Arthur Nouail de (1803–1876)
Lavoisier, Antoine Laurent de (1740–1796)
Lavondès, Henri (b.1926)
Lavrat, Louis (1827–1893)
Lavrovskij, Petr (1827–1886)
Law, Vivien (Anne, 1954–2002)
Lawler, Traugott Francis (b.1937)
Lawrence, John (1850–1916)
Lawrence, William Witherle (1876–1958)
Layamon (c.1190)
Laycock, Donald C. (1936–1988)
Lazard, Gilbert (Léon Jean, b.1920)
Lázaro, Juan, O.F.M. (d.1650)

Lituanus, Michalo (*alias* Mykolas Lietuvis *alias* Vaclovas Mikolajevičius *alias* Wencesław Mikołajewicz, c.1490-c.1560)
Litzmann, Berthold (1857–1926)
Liu, E. (1857–1909)S
Liu, Fu (1891–1934)
Liu Xie (c.500 A.D.)
Liver, Ricarda (b.1941)K
Livet, Charles Louis (1828–1896)
Livingston, William (1723–1790)
Livius Andronicus (fl.272–250 B.C.)
Livshits (Livšic), Vladimir Aronovič (b.1926?)
Livy (Titus Livius, 59 B.C.–17 A.D.)
Lixačev, Dmitrij Sergeevič (1906–1999)
Ljackij, Evgenij (also: Èvčen) Aleksandrovič (1868–1942)
Ljapunov, Aleksej Andreevič (1911–1973)
Ljapunov, Boris Mixajlovič (1862–1943)
Ljubarskij, Jakov Nikolaevič (1929–2003)
Ljudskanov, Aleksandar Konstantinov (1926–1976)
Llorente, Antonio (1922–1998)
Lloyd, Hannibal Evans (1771–1847)
Lloyd, Paul M. (b.1929)
Lloyd, Richard J(ohn, 1846–1906)
Lloyd, William (1627–1717)
Lloyd James, Arthur (1884–19??)
Llull, Ramón, *see* Lullus, Raimundus
Lo, Ch'ang P'ei (1899–1958)
Lobo, Francisco Rodrigues (1580?–1622)
Lobscheid, Wilhelm (fl.1848–1869)
Lo Cascio, Vincenzo (b.1935)

Lochner, Johann Hieronymus (the Elder; pseud. Chlorenus Germanus, 1700–1769)
Lochner von Hüttenbach, Fritz *Freiherr* (b.1930)K
Locke, John (1632–1704)S, E
Locke, Patricia (1928–2001)
Locke, William Nash (1909–c.1980)
Lockhart, Leonora (1906–19??)
Lockwood, David Glen (1940–2007)
Lodewyckx, Augustin (1876–1964)
Lod(o)wick (Lodowyck), Francis (1619–1694)S,E
Lødrup, Helge (b.1952)
Lods, Adolphe (1867–1948)
Lods, Jeanne (c.1909–*post* 1984)
Loebe, (August) Julius (1805–1900)
Löffler, Heinrich (b.1938)K
Löfstedt, Bengt (d.2004)
Löhneyss, Georg Engelhardt (von, 1552–1622?)
Lönnrot, Elias (1802–1884)
Lőrincze, Lajos (1915–1993)
Lőrinczy, Éva B. (19290–2002)
Lötzsch, Ronald (b.1931)
Löw, Immanuel (d. *ante* 1947)
Löwe, Richard (1863–19??)
Loey, Adolphe (Clement Henri) van (1905–1987)
Logau, Friedrich von (1604–1655)
Logeman, Hendrik (1862–1936)
Logeman, Willem Sijbrand (1850–1933)
Loglio, Guido (fl.1545)
Lohmann, Johannes (1899–1982?)
Loja, Jan Vejumovič (*alias* Jānis Viļuma, 1896–1969)
Lombard, Alf (1902–1996)
Lombardo, Natal, S.J. (1648–1704)

Lotheissen, Ferdinand (1833–1887)

Lotman, Jurij Mixajlovič (1922–1993)

Lott, Julius (fl.1890)

Lottner, Carl (Friedrich, 1834–1873)

Lotz, John (*alias* János, 1913–1973)S

Lotze, (Rudolf) Hermann (1817–1881)

Loughridege, Robert McGill (1809–1900)S

Loukotka, Čestmír (d.1966)

Lourenço, Brás, S.J. (c.1525–1605)

Lounsbury, Floyd G(len, 1914–1998)E

Lounsbury, Thomas Raynesford (1838–1915)

Lovas, Gizella R. (1916–1992)

Love, James R. B. (1889–1947)

Loveday, Leo (b.1955)

Lovejoy, Arthur O(ncken, 1873–1962)

Low, Seth (1850–1916)

Lowe, Solomon (d.1750)

Lowell, James Russel (1819–1891)

Lowie (orig. Löwe), Robert H(arry, 1883–1957)S

Lowman, Guy Sumner, Jr. (1909–1941)S

Lowth, Robert (Bishop of London, 1710–1787)S, E

Loyola, Ignácio de, S.J. (1491–1556)

Loyola, Martín Ignacio de, O.F.M. (d.1606)

Lozano, Pedro (1697–1753)

Łoziński, Josef (1807–1889)

Lozovan, Eugen (1929–1997)

Lu Fa-yen (*alias* Lu Ci, fl.5811–601 A.D.) E

Lubaś, Władysław (b.1932)

Lubbe, H. F. A. van der, O.F.M. (1911–1991)

Luc, Jean André de (1727–1817)

Lucae, Karl (1833–1888)

Lucanus, Marcus Annæus (39–65 A.D.)

Lucas, Angela Mary b.1945)

Luce, Clare Boothe, *see* under Boothe Luce, Clare

Luce, Gordon H. (mid-20th cent.)

Lucero, Juan, S.J. (fl.1661)

Lucian(us, 'of Samosata', c.125–c.192 A.D.)

Lucidi, Mario (1913–1961)S

Lucius, Ludwig (c.1600)

Lucretius (Titus Lucretius Carius, c.96–55 B.C.)

Lucy, John A(rthur, b.1949)

Lüders, Else, *née* Peipers (1880–1945)

Lüders, Heinrich (1869–1943)

Ludewig, Hermann (fl.1858)

Ludolf, Heinrich Wilhelm (1655–1710)

Ludolf, Hiob (*alias* Job Leutholf, 1624–1704)

Ludolphus de Lucho (de Hildesheim, 13th cent. A.D.)

Ludovicus, Laurentinus (1536–1594)

Ludvíkovský, Jaroslav (1895–1984)

Ludwig, Alfred (1832–1911)

Ludwig, Christian (1660–1728)

Ludwig, Karl (1815–1895)

Ludwig, Laurentinus, *see* Ludovicus, Laurentinus

Ludwig, Otto (b.1931)K

Lüdecke, Henry (1889–1962)

Lüdtke, Helmut (b.1926)K

Lüdtke, Jens (b.1941)K
Lühr, Rosemarie (b.1946)K
Luelsdorff, Philipp Allan (b.1941)
Lu Fayan (*alias* Lu Ci, fl.581–601)S
Lugo, Bernardo de, O.P. (fl.1617)
Lugowski, Clemens (d.1942)
Luhmann, Niklas (1929–1998)E
Luhrman, Gerard Johannes ("Hans",
    1934–2004)
Luhtala, (Kaija) Anneli (b.1956)
Luick, Karl (1865–1935)S, E
Luijks, Carla (1958–2001)
Lukas, Johannes (1901–1980)E
Lukasiewicz, Jan (1878–1956)
Lukens, Herman T. (1865–1949)
Lukjanow, Ariadne W. (b.1948?)
Lukoff, Fred (1920–2000)
Lullus, Raimundus (Llull, Ramón,
    1235–1315)E
Lulofs, Barthold Henrik (1787–1849)
Luna, Fabricio (d.1559)S
Luna, Juan de (c.1580–c.1630)S
Lund, Sophie (d.1947)
Lundahl, Ivar (1894–1985)
Lundell, Johan August (1851–1940)S
Lundeby, Einar (b.1914)
Lunt, Horace G(ray, b.1918)
Luó, Chángpéi (1899–1958)S
Luo, Zhebyu (1866–1940)S
Lupulus, Sigismundus (*alias* Wölflin,
    Siegmund, 1542–1551)
Luquiens, F. B. (1875–1940)
Lurija, Aleksandr Romanovič (1902–
    1977)E
Lusitano, Amato (1511–1568)
Luther, Martin (1483–1546)E
Lutosławski, Wincenty (1863–1954)
Lutterer, Ivan (b.1918)
Lutz, Cora E. (b.1906)

Lu(t)z, Joseph Anton (1731–1799)
Lutzeier, Peter Rolf (b.1948)K
Luynes, Louis Charles d'Albert, *duc
    de* (1620–1690)
Luzac, Johan (1746–1807)
Luzzato, Filosseno (*or* Philoxène,
    1829–1854)
Luzzato, Samuel David (1800–
    1865)E
Lyberis, Anatanas (1909–1996)
Lydgate, John (1370?–1451?)
Lye, Edward (1694–1767)
Lye, Thomas (1621–1684)
Lyell, (*Sir*) Charles (1797–1875)
Lyle, John (1769–1825)
Lye, Thomas (1621–1684)
Lynch, Irina Borisova-Morosova
    (b.1921)
Lyngby, Kristen Jensen (1829–1871)
Lyon, Otto (1853–1912)
Lyons, (*Sir*) John (b.1932)E
Lysjanskyi, Jurij (1773–1837)
Lysons, Samuel (1806–1877)
Lytinen, Steven L. (2nd half of 20th
    cent.)
Lytkin, Vasilij Il'ič (1895–1981)
Lytle, Eldon G(rey, b.1936)
Lytkin, Vasilij I. (1895–1981)
Lyttleton, George (1709–1773)
Lyttleton, Lucy Caroline *see*
    Cavendish, Lucy

M.

Ma, Jianzhong (1845–1900)S, E

Maaler, Josua (*alias* Maler, Mahler, Pictorius, 1529–1599)S

Maas, Utz (b.1942)K

Mabillon, Jean (1632–1707)

Mably, Gabriel Bonnot de (1709–1785)

Ma^carrï, Abū-^cAlā al- (d.1058)

Mac Airt, Seán (1918–1959)

Mač'avariani, Givi (1927–1968)

MacCabe, John Alexander (1842–1902)

Macaulay, Ronald K. S. (b.1927)

Macaulay, Thomas Babington (1800–1859)

Macbeth, Madge (1878–1965)

MacCurdy, George Grant (1863–1947)

Macdonald, Agnes Margaret (1901–19??)

MacDonnell, Arthur Anthony (1854–1930)

Macé, Jean, O.Carm. (pseud. Père Léon de Saint-Jean, sieur du Tertre; 1600–1681)

Macedo Soares, Antonio Joaquim de (fl.1874–1890)

Macek, Josef (1922–1991)

Mac Eoin, Gearóid (b.1929)

Máčelović-van den Broecke, Emmy (b.1921)

Macfarlane, Alexander (1851–1913)

MacFarlan(e), Robert (1734–1804)

MacGowan, John (d.1922)

Mac Gréagóir, Aoidhmín (1884–1950)

Macmillan, Duncan (1914-1993)

Mac Neill, John(alias Eoin, 1867–1945)

Mach, Ernst (1838–1916)

Macha, Jürgen (b.1949)K

Machač, Jaro (1928–1990)

Machan, Tim William (b.1956)

Mach'avariani, Givi (1927–1968)

Machek, Václav (1894–1965)S

Machiavelli, Niccolò (1469–1527)S

Machoni de Cerdeña, Antonio, S.J. (1671–1753)

Machovec-Cerne, Jasna (d.1996)

Macht, Konrad (b.1938)K

Maciejewski, Jerzy (1923–1992)

MacIntyre, John (fl.1879–1915)

Mackensen, Lutz (1901–1994)

MacKenzie, Colin (1753?–1829)

MacKenzie, *Sir* George (of Rosehaugh, 1636–1691)

Mack, Johann Martin (1715–1784)

Mackenzie, D. Neil (b.1926)

Mackert, Michael (b.1958)

Mackin, Ronald A. (1916–1992)

Mackintosh, *Sir* James (1765–1832)

Macklovitch, Elliott (b.1948)

MacKnight, James (1721–1800)

MacLaury, Robert E. (1944–2004)

Maclean, Edward (fl.1840)

MacLeod, Norman (b.1940)

MacMahon, Michael K(enneth) C(owan, b.1943)

MacMillan, Cyrus (1880–1953)

Macmillan, Duncan (b.1914)

MacMillan, Michael (1863–1925)

Macpherson, James (1736–1796)

Mançano, Melchior de, O.P. (fl.1620)

Mancelius, Georg (*alias* Manzel, 1593–1654)

Mančev, Krasimir (1938–1997)

Manchester, Martin L. (b.1950?)

Mancinelli, Antonio (1452–1506)

Mańczak, Witold (b.1924)K

Mańczyk, Augustyn (b.1946)K

Mandelbaum, David G(oodman, 1911–1987)

Mandelbaum, Maurice (b.1908)

Mandelbrot, Benoît (b.1924)

Mandeville, Bernard de (1670–1733)

Mandeville, François (1878–1952)

Mándoky Kongur, István (1944–1992)

Mañer, Salvador José (*alias* José Lorenzo de Arenas, M. Le-Margne, 1676–1751)

Manessi, Gabriel (1923–1997)

Manetti, Giovanni (b.1949)

Manget, Jacques (Louis, b.1784)

Manget, Johann Jacob (1652–1742)

Mangold, Max (b.1922)K

Mann, Stuart Edward (1905–c.1986)

Mann, William C. ("Bill", d.2004)

Mannewitz, Cornelia (b.1955)K

Mannhardt, Johann Wilhelm Emanuel (1831–1880)

Mannheim, Karl (1893–1947)

Manni, Domenico Maria (1690–1788)S

Manning, Peter K. (b.1940)

Manning, Owen (1721–1801)

Mannoury, Gerrit (1867–1956)

Mannyng de Brunne, Robert (fl.1288–1338)

Manrique C(astañeda), Leonardo (b.1934)

Manrique, Gómez (1413–1491)

Manrique, Jorge (1440–1479)

Manseau, Joseph Amable (1837–1887)

Mansion, Josef (1877–1937)

Mantegazza, Paolo (fl.1873)

Manthey, Fred (b.1939)K

Manuel Moschopoulos (c.1265–1316)

Manuel y Rodríguez, Miguel de (18th cent.)

Manupella, Giacinto (1901–1990)

Manuzio, Aldo (Aldus Pius Manutius Romanus, "the Elder", 1449–1515)

Manuzio, Aldo (*alias* Manutius, Aldus, the Younger, 1547–1597)

Manuzio, Paolo (1511–1574)

Manzini, Maria Rita (b.1956)

Manzoni, Alessandro (1785–1873)S

Mao Zhedong (1893–1976)

Maquieira, Marina (b.1960)

Marantz, Alec (b.1959)

Marazzini, Claudio (b.1949)

Marbais, Michel de, *see* Michel de Marbais

Marbán, Pedro, S.J. (1647–1713)

Marbe, Karl (1869–1953)

Marçais, William (1874–1956)

Marčec, Snježana (1963–2001)

Marcel, Claude Victor André (1793–1876)

Marcellesi, Jean-Baptiste (b.1930)

Marcellus, Nonius (4th cent. A.D.)

Marcet, Jane Haldimand (1769–1858)

March, Francis Andrew (1825–1911)S
March, George Perkins (1801–1882)
March, Sadie (c.1890–19??)
Marchand, Hans (1907–1978)S
Marchand, James W(oodrow, b.1926)
Marchese, Maria Pia (b.1947)
Marci, Juan Marco (1595–1667)
Marckwardt, Albert Henry ("Al", 1903–1975)S
Marcq, Philippe (b.1922)K
Marčuk, Jurij Nikolaevič (b.1932)
Marden, Charles Carroll (1867–1932)
Marek, Antonín (1785–1877)
Mareš, František Václav (1922–1994)
Marest, Pierre Gabriel, S.J. (1662–1714)
Maretič, Tomislav (1854–1938)S
Marey, Étienne Jules (1830–1904)
Margalit, Avishai (b.1939)
Margalits, Edéről (1847–1940)
Margarit i Pau, Joan (Cardinal Bishop of Gerona, c.1415–1484)
Marggraf, Georg (1610–1644)
Mariana, Juan de, S.J. (1535–1624)
Marie, Pierre (1853–1940)
Mariès, Louis (1876–1958)
Mariette, Auguse-Édouard (1821–1881)
Marín, Juan Martínez (b.1945)
Marin, Pierre (1667–1718)
Marin, Louis (1931–1992)
Marinelli, Curcio (16th cent.)
Mariner, Sebastián (1923–1988)
Mariner, William (1791–1853)
Marinescu, Mihail (1927–1995)
Marin, Pierre (c.1667–c.1719)

Marini, Marco (1541–1593)
Maritain, Jacques (1882–1973)
Marius Victorinus (late 4th cent. A.D.)
Mark, Julius von (1890–1959)
Markey, Thomas L(loyd, b.1940)
Markov, Andrej Andre'evič (1856–1922)
Marković, Miroslav (1919–2001)
Markus, Manfred (b.1941)K
Markwort, Johann Christian (1778–1866)
Marmier, Xavier (1809–1892)
Marmontel, Jean-François (1723–1799)
Marno, Ernst (1844–1883)
Maro Grammaticus, *see* Virgilius Maro
Marot, Clément (1495?–1544)
Marouzeau, Jules (Émile, 1878–1964)
Marperger, Paul Jakob (1656–1730)
Marquand, John P. (1893–1960)
Marquardt, Hertha (1897–1965)
Marquette, Jacques, S.J. (1637–1666)
Marqués, Buanventura, O.F.M. (d.1822)
Marquis, Donald G. (1908–1973)
Marquis, Pierre (fl.1609)
Marr, David (1945–1980)
Marr, James (*alias* Jakov Petrovič, 1779–1874)
Marr, Nikolaj Jakovlevič (in Georgian: Marr, Nik'o, 1865–1934)S, E
Marré, Eugène Aristide (1823–1918)
Marrou, Henri-Irénée (b.1904)
Marsafī Ḥusayn ibn Aḥmad al- (1810/15?–1890?)S

Marty, (Martin) Anton (Maurus, 1847–1914)E
Marty-Laveaux, Charles (1823–1901)
Martyr, Peter (*alias* d'Anghiera, Pietro Martire, 1457–1526)
Marulus, Marcus (*alias* Marko Marulić, 1450–1524)
Márvány, János (b.1921)K
Marx, Karl (Heinrich, 1818–1883)
Marx-Moyse, Janine (b.1937)K
Mary-Lafon, Jean Bernard Lafin, *dit* (1812–1884)
Marynisssen, Clem (1922–1996)
Mas, Diego (fl.1621)
Más y Sanz, Sinibaldo de (1809–1868)
Masařík, Zdeněk (b.1928)K
Masaryk, Tomás G(arrigue, 1850–1937)
Masdeu, Juan Francisco (1776–1854)
Masica, Colin (b.1931)
Masing, Ferdinand (c.1845–1915?)
Masing, Leonhard (1845–c.1930)
Masing, Uku (1909–1985)
Maslov, Jurij Sergeevič (1914–1990)
Mason, Charles Peter (1820–1900)
Mason, C(harles) Thomas, III (b.1954)
Mason, George (*fl.*1622)
Mason, John (1706–1763)
Mason, John Alden (1885–1967)
Mason, Max (1877–1961)
Mason, Otis Tufton (1838–1908)
Maspero, (*Sir*) Gaston Camille Charles (1846–1916)
Maspero, Henri (1883–1945)
Masqueray, Émile (1843–1894)
Massé, Ennemond, S.J. (1574–1646)

Massé, Étienne Michel (1778–*post* 1848)
Massebieau, Louis (1840–1904)
Massenbach, *Freiin* Gertrud Dorothea von (1883–1975)
Massia, Pietro (d.1945)
Massias, Nicolas, *baron* (1764–1848)
Massignon, Louis (1883–1962)
Massim, Ioan C. (1825–1877)
Massmann, Hans Ferdinand (1797–1874)
Masson, Olivier (1922–1997)
Masson, Peter (b.1945)
Massono, F. (fl.1730)
Master Guido (12th cent. A.D.)
Master Nicholas (12th cent. A.D.)
Masterman, Margaret (Braithwaite, 1910–1986)E
Mastrelli, Carlo Alberto (b.1924)
Mastrelli, Giulia Anzilotti (1927–1999)
Masui, Michio (1914–1992)
Mata y Araujo, Luis (fl.1832)
Máté, Jakab (1926–2001)
Matejčík, Ján (1933–1997)
Matejka, Ladislav (b.1919)
Mater, Erich (b.1924)K
Mates, Benson (b.1919)
Matešić, Josip (b.1926)
Mathesius, Vilém (1882–1945)S, E
Mather, Cotton (1663–1728)
Mather, Richard (1596–1664)
Matheus da Gubbio, *see* Matthew of Gubbio
Matheus Vindocinensis, *see* Matthew of Vendôme
Mathevet, *Rev.* Jean-Claude, S.S. (1717–1781.)

Mathews, Mitford McLeod, Sr. (1891–1985)S
Mathews, Peter H(ugoe, b.1934)
Mathews, Robert Hamilton (1841–1918)
Mathiassen, Terje (1938–1999)
Mathieu, Abel (c.1500–*post* 1560)
Mathiot, Madeleine (b.1927)
Matič, Tomo (1874–1968)
Matilal, Bimal Krishna (1935–1991)
Matisoff, James A(lan, b.1937)
Matoré, Georges (1908–1998)E
Matos (Guerra), Gregório de (1633–1692)
Matos, Francisco de, S.J. (1636–1720)
Matos, *Frei* Eusébio de Soledade (1629–1692)
Matov, Xristo (1872–1922)
Matov, Dimitir A. (1864–1896)
Matras, Christian (1900–1988)S
Matras, Daniel (1597–1689)
Matsuda, Takami (b.1958)
Matsumoto, Katsumi (b.1929)E
Matsunami, Tamostu (1924–1995)
Matsushita, Daizaburô (1878–1935)S
Mattā ibn Yūnnus (d.328/940)
Matthäi, August Heinrich (1769–1835)
Mattheier, Klaus J. (b.1941)K
Matthes, Heinrich Christoph (1903–1963)
Matthew of Bologna (fl.1265/70)
Matthew of Gubbio (fl. early 14th cent.)S
Matthew of Vendôme (Fr.: Mathieu de Vendôme, d. *post* 1187)S
Matthews, G(eorge) Hubert (b.1930)

Matthews, James Brander (1852–1929)
Matthews, Peter H(ugoe, b.1934)
Matthews, *Rev.* Gordon (d.1947)
Matthews, Washington (1843–1905)
Matthews, William (1905–1975)
Matthiae, August Heinrich (1769–1835)
Matthias, Theodor (Alfred, 1859–1934)S
Matthiessen, Christian (b.1956)
Mattingly, Ignatius G. (b.1927)
Mattioli, Pietro Andrea (1500–1577)
Mattos, Francisco, S.J. (16??–1720)
Mattoso Câmara, Joaquim, Jr. (1904–1970)E
Mattusch, Hans-Jürgen (b.1931)K
Matuszewski, Józef (b.1911)
Matuz, Josef (1925–1992)
Matveev, Aleksandr K. (b.1926)
Matzel, Klaus (1923–1992)K
Mauderer, Michael (b.1950)K
Maugard, Antoine (1739–1817)
Mauger, Claude (*fl.*1690–1705)
Mauger, Gaston (1898–1998)
Maugüé, Jean (1904–1982)
Maunder, Samuel (1785–1849)
Maunsell, Robert (1810–1894)
Maupas, Charles (15??–1625?)
Maupas, Charles Cauchon de, *see* Cauchon de Maupas, Charles
Maupertuis, Pierre-Louis, Moreau de (1698–1759)
Maurenbrecher, Berthold (1868–*post* 1908)
Maurer, David W. (1906–1981)S
Maurer, Friedrich (1898–1984)S
Maurer, Theodore Henrique, Jr. (1906–1979)

Meile, Pierre (1911–1963)
Meillet, Antoine (Paul Jules, 1866–1936)S, E
Meineke, Eckhard (b.1953)K
Meiner, Johann Werner (1723–1789)S
Meiners, Christoph (1747–1810)
Meinhardt, Margarete (b.1943)K
Meinhof, Carl (Friedrich Michael, 1857–1944)E
Meinhold, Gottfried (b.1936)K
Meidinger, Johann Valentin (1756–1822)
Meinong, Alexius (*Ritter* von Handschuchsheim, 1853–1920)E
Meir b. David (late 13th cent. A.D.)
Meisel, Jürgen Michael (b.1944)
Meiser, Karl (1843–1912)
Meissner, Rudolf (d.1948)
Meister, Richard M. (1848–1912)
Mejstřík, Vladimir (b.1938)
Mekeel, Scudder (1902–1947)
Melancht(h)on, Philipp (*alias* Schwarzerdt, 1497–1560)E
Melander, Johan (d.1947)
Melazzo. Lucio (b.1950)K
Melby, Alan K(enneth, b.1948)
Melcer, Jozef (d.2000)
Melcher, Florian (1875–1913)
Melchers, Gunnel (b.1934)
Mel'čuk, Igor' A(leksandrovič, b.1932)E
Meli, Giovanni (1740–1815)
Melich, János (1872–1963)S
Melle, Jakob von (1659–1743)
Melle, Marinus Anthonie van (1872–1906)
Mellema, Elcie Edouard Leon (1544–1622)

Mel'ničuk, Aleksandr Savvič (in Ukrainian: Oleksandr Savyč Mel'nyčuk, 1921–1997)
Mel'nikov, Gennadij Prokopjevič (1928–2000)
Mel'nikova, Margarita Vasilievna (1934–1997)
Melo, Gladstone Chaves de (b.1917)
Melo, João de, S.J. (c.1525–1576)
Melzian, Hans-Jochim (1907–1945)
Mena, Juan de (1411–1456)
Ménage, Gilles (1613–1692)S
Menander (342?–289 B.C.)
Menantes, *see* Hunold, Christian Friedrich
Menaseh Ben Israel (1604–1656)
Mencken, Henry Louis (1880–1956)S, E
Mendelssohn, Moses (1729–1786)
Mendes, Valentino, S.J. (d.1759)
Mendieta, *Fray* Jerónimo, O.F.M. (c.1534–1604)
Mendoza, Bernardino de (1540–1604)
Menéndez (y) Pelayo, Marcelino (1856–1912)
Menéndez Pidal, Ramón (1869–1968)S, E
Meng, Katharina (b.1936)
Menges, Karl Heinrich (1908–1999)K
Meniński, Franciszek (*alias* François *or* Franz a Mesgnien, 1628–1698)
Menke, Hubertus (b.1941)K
Menner, Robert James (1892–1951)
Menšik, Jan (1885–1949)
Mensing, Otto (fl.1927–1935)
Méntrida, Alonso de, O.S.A. (1559–1637)

Mentrup, Wolfgang (b.1935)K
Mentzel, Christian (1622–1701)
Menudier, Jean (1636?–1690?)
Menzel, Peter (b.1931)K
Menzel, Wolfgang (b.1935)K
Menzerath, Paul (1883–1954)S
Mérandon, Albert Fortuné (18th
   cent.?)
Mercado, Nicolás, S.J. (1682–1763)
Mercado, Tomas de (d.1575)
Mercator, Arnold (1537–1587)
Mercator, Marius (c.400–450 A.D.)
Mercie, Alfred (1816–1894)
Mercier, Gustave L. S. (1874–1953)
Mercier, Jean (fl.1547–1570)
Mercier, Louis-Sébastien (1740–
   1814)
Mercurius, Jo(h)annes (alias Mor-
   sheymerus; Krämer, d. c.1567)
Mercy, Blanch (fl.1799–1803)
Merguet, (Peter Adalbert) Hugo
   (1841–1911)
Merian, Matthäus, the Elder (1593–
   1651)
Merian, André-Adolphe, baron de
   (1772–1828)
Meriggi, Piero (1899–1982)
Méril, Edelestand de (1801–1871)
Mérimé, Prosper (1803–1870)
Meringer, Rudolf (1859–1931)S, E
Merino de Jesucristo, Andrés (1730–
   1787)
Méritens, Eugène Herman Emmanuel
   (1835–post 1880)
Meriton, George (1634–1711)
Meritt, Herbert Dean (1904–1984)
Merkel, Carl Ludwig (1812–1876)
Merkel, Paul Johannes (1819–1861)
Merker, Paul (1881–1945)

Merle, Paul van, see Merula, Paulus
Merleau-Ponty, Maurice (1908–
   1960)
Merlet de la Boulaye, Gabriel Eléonor
   (1736–1807)
Merlette, Auguste Nicolas (pseud.
   Laruve et Fleury, 1827–post 1896)
Merlingen, Weriand (b.1907)K
Merle, Clemente (1879–1960)S
Merlo, Pietro (1850–1888)
Mermelstein, Paul (b.1939)
Merriam, C. Hart (1855–1942)
Merriam, George (1803–1880)
Merrick, James (1720–1769)
Merrifield, William R. (b.1932)
Merrilees, Brian (b.1938)
Merriott, Thomas (1589–1662)
Mersenne, le père Marin (pseud.
   Sieur de Sermes, 1588–1648)
Mersol, Stanley A. (1932–2004)
Mertens, Frans-Jozef (b.1928)
Mertian, Igna(t)z (1766–1843)
Mertner, Edgar (1907–1999)
Merton, Robert K(ing, 1910–2003)
Merula, Paulus (1558–1607)
Merx, (Ernst Otto) Adalbert (1838–
   1909)
Merzdorf, Reinhold (1854–1877)
Meščaninov, Ivan Invanovič (1883–
   1967)S
Meschonnic, Henri (b.1932)
Meščerskij, Nikita Aleksandrovič
   (1906–1987)
Mesgnien, François, see Meniński,
   Franciszek
Mesinus de'Codronchi (fl. late 14th
   cent. A.D.)S
Messel, John Andreas (1789–1850)

Miceli, Vincenzo (d.1781)

Michael of Marbais (Lat. Michael de Marbasio; Fr. Michel de Marbais, fl.1280–1300)S, E

Michael Psellos (1018–1078)

Michel Syncellus of Jerusalem (761/762–846 A.D.)

Michael, Ian (b.1915)

Michaelis, Adolf Th. F. (1835–1910)

Michaelis, Christian Benedict (1680–1764)

Michaelis, Christian Friedrich (1754–1814)

Michaelis, Gustav (1813–1895)

Michaelis, Johann David (1717–1791)

Michaelis, Johann Friedrich (1762–1810)

Michaelis, Johann Heinrich (1668–1738)

Michaelis (de Vasconcelos), Caroline (= Carolina Wilhelmina, 1851–1925)E

Michaelis, Salomon (1769–1844)

Michalov, M. A., *see* under Mixajlov, M. A.

Michailow, Leonid, *see under* Mixajlov, Leonid

Michałk, Frido (1927–1992)

Michalsky, Constantin (Konstanty Józef, 1879–1947)

Michalus, Štefan (1931–1995)

Michaud, Eugène (1839–1917)

Michaud, Joseph François (1767–1839)

Michaut, Gustave (1870–1946)

Michel de Marbais (fl.1280–1285)E

Michel le Syncelle (760/61–846 A.D.)

Michel, C.P.D. (pseud. Michel de Neuville, 1780–*post* 1854)

Michel, Francisque (1809–1887)

Michel, Georg (b.1926)K

Michel, L.–C. (fl.1834–1898)

Michel, Louis (1906–1944)

Michel, Xavier Francisque (1809–1887)

Michelant, Henri-Victor (1811–1874)

Michelena, Luis (*alias* in Basque: Koldo Mitxelena, 1915–1987)

Michelet, Jules (1798–1874)

Michelet, Karl Ludwig (1801–1893)

Michels, Leonardus Cornelius (1887–1984)

Michels, Viktor (1866–1929)

Michelson, Gunther (1920–2005)

Michelson, Truman (1879–1938)S

Micklesen, Lew R. (b.1921)

Micon, Francisco de Paula (alias Eugenio Sarmiento; Marquees de Meeritos, 1735–18110

Micyllus, Iacobus (*alias* Moltzer, Jacob, 1503–1558)

Middendorf, Ernst Wilhelm (fl.1890–1892)

Middendorff, Alexander Theodor von (1815–1894)

Middleton, George (1865–19??)

Midgley, Edward Graham (1923–1999)

Miechow, Matthias de (1456–1523)

Mieder, Wolfgang (b.1944)

Miège, Guy (1644–c.1718)S

Mielck, Hildemar (1840–1896)

Mielcke, Christian Gottlieb (c.1736–c.1805)

Mieleski, Augustyn (*alias* Augustinus Rotundus, c.1520–1582)

Mielle, Jean-François (1757–1839)
Mieses, Matthias (*alias* Matisyou, 1885–1945)
Miettinen, Erkki I. (b.1932)K
Migeod, Frederick William Hugh (1872–1952)
Migliorini, Bruno (1896–1975)S
Migne, *abbé* Jean-Paul (1800–1875)
Mignet, François-Auguste-Alexis (1796–1884)
Mignucci, Mario (d.2004)
Miguel (y Navas), Raimundo (1816–1878)
Mihaescu, Hăralambie (1907–1985)
Mihăilă, Gheorge (b.1931)
Mihailov, Georgii (1915–1991)
Mihm, Arend (b.1936)K
Mijangos, Juan de, O.S.A. (fl.1607–1624)
Mikami, Akira (1903–1971)S
Mikecs, László (d.1947)
Mikkelsen, Kristian Mathias (1845–1924)S
Mikkola, Jooseppi Julius (1866–1946)S
Miklas, Heinz (b.1948)K
Miklosich, Franz (Xaver, *Ritter* von; Slovene: Miklošić, Franc, 1813–1891)S, E
Mikola, Tibor (1936–2000)
Mikuš, Radivoj Francis(cus, 1906–1983)
Mikusev, A. K. (1926–1993)
Mikuta, Marian (1907–1996)
Milá y Fontanals, Manuel (1818–1884)
Milani, Lorenzo (1923–1967)S
Mailanovič, Branislav (1911–1997)

Milardet, Georges (1876–1953[?1937])
Milčetić, Ivan (1853–1921)
Milenbahs, Kārlis (German: Karl Mühlenbach, 1853–1916)S
Miles, Josephine Louise (1911–1985)
Milescu, Nicolae Spartarul (1625–1714)
Miletič, Ljubomir Georgiev (1863–1937)S
Milewski, Tadeusz (1906–1966)S
Mill, James (1773–1836)
Mill, John Stuart (1806–1873)E
Millar, Andrew (1707–1760)
Millardet, Georges (1876–1953)
Millares Cubas, Agustín (1863–1935)
Millares Cubas, Luis (1861–1925)
Miller, Aleksandr Aleksandrovič (1875–1935)
Miller, Charles William Emil (1863–1935)
Miller, Dayton Clarence (1866–1941)
Miller, D. Gary (b.1942)
Miller, Fedor Ivanovič (*alias* Gerhart Friedrich Müller, 19th cent.)
Miller, George A(rmitage, b.1920)E
Miller, James E(dward, "Jim", b.1942)
Miller, Robert Lee (b.1928)
Miller, Roy Andrew (b.1924)
Miller, Vsevelod Fedorovič (1848–1913)
Miller, Wick R. (1932–1994)
Mills, C. Wright (1916–1962)
Milne-Edwards, Henri (1800–1885)
Milner, George (1829–1914)
Milner, George B. (b.1918)
Milner, Jean-Claude (b.1941)

Morley, Sylvanus G. (1883–1948)
Moro, Andrea (b.1962)
Moroń, Bogusław (1905–1985)
Morpurgo Davies, *Dame* Anna
 (b.1937)E
Morris, Alice Vanderbilt (1874–
 1950)
Morris, Charles (1833–1922)
Morris, Charles W(illiam, 1901–
 1979)S, E
Morris, Edward Parmelle (1853–
 1938)
Morris, Lewis (*alias* Two Crows,
 1826?–1894)
Morris, Richard (1833–1894)
Morris-Jones, John (1864–1929)
Morrison, Robert (1782–1834)
Morsbach, Lorenz (1850–1945)
Mortgat, Michael (d.1954)
Mortillet, Gabriel de (1821–1898)
Morus, Samuel (1736–1792)
Moscherosch, Johann Michael
 (1601–1669)
Moschopulus, Manuel (13th cent.
 A.D.)
Mosel, Ulrike (b.1946)K
Mosellanus, Petrus (*alias* Peter
 Schade, 1493–1524)
Moser, Arthur Paul (1902–1987)
Moser, Hans (b.1939)K
Moser, Hugo (1909–1989)
Moses, Elbert Raymond (1908–*post*
 1976)
Moses ben Isaac, *see* ben Hanesi'ah
Mosher, Arthur D. (b.1948)K
Moskov, Mosko Dobrev (1927–
 2001)
Moskova, Violeta (b.1934)
Mossé, Fernand (1892–1956)

Mostowski, Andrzej (1913–1975)
Moszczeński, Stanisław Nałęcz
 (1731–1790)
Moszyński, Kazimierz (1887–1959)
Moszyński, Leszek (b.1919)
Moth, Matthias (1647–1719)
Motolinía, Toríbio de, S.J. (d.1568)
Motoori Haruniwa (1763–1828)S, E
Motoori Norinaga (1730–1801)S, E
Motorin, Jurij Aleksandrovič (1928–
 c.1978)
Motoya, Antonio Ruíz de, S.J. (1583–
 1652)
Motsch, Wolfgang (b.1934)K
Mott, Frank Luther (1886–1964)
Mott, *Sir* Nevill Francis (b.1905)
Mouchová, Buhumila (b.1933)
Moulton, James Hope (1863–1917)
Moulton, Jenni K(arding, b. c.1920)
Moulton, William G(amwell, 1914–
 2000)
Mounin, Georges (*alias* Louis Julien
 Leboucher, 1910–1993)E
Moura, Matheus, S.J. (d.1728)
Mourain de Sordeval, Charles (1800–
 1879)
Mourek, Václav Emanuel (1846–
 1911)
Moutier, François (1881–1961)
Mouw, Johan Andreas dèr, *see* Dèr
 Mouw, Johan Andreas
Movradjan, Arovsjak Nersesi
 (fl.1971)
Mowat, Robert (1823–1912)
Moxon, Joseph (1627–1700)
Mozart, Joseph (1805–1868)
Mozin, *abbé* Dominique Josephe
 (d.1840)
Mrázek, Roman (1921–1989)

Mulder, Jan (*alias* Johannes
  Wilhelmus Franciscus, b.1919)E
Mulder, M. J. (1923–1994)
Mulerius, Carolus (*alias* Des
  Muliers, 1601–1638)
Muljačić, Žarko (b.1922)K
Muller, Carl (Mulerus, Carolus, b.
  c.1600)
Muller, Charles (b.1909)
Muller, François (b.1948)
Muller, Henri-François (1879–1959)
Muller, Hendrik Clemens (1855–
  1927)
Muller, Jacob Wijbrand (1858–1945)
Muller Jzn. [= Jacobszoon], Frederik
  (1882–1944)
Mulligan, Kevin (b.1951)
Mullins, Nicholas C. (1939–1988)
Multatuli (*pseud.* of Eduard Douwes
  Dekker, 1820–1887)
Munch, Salmon (1803–1867)
Mundt, Theodor (1808–1861)
Munivar, Civañána, *see* Civañána
  Munivar
Muñiz y Vigo, Acisclo (1866–1941)
Munk, Salomon (1803–1867)
Munkácsi, Bernát (1860–1937)
Muno, Philippe (1932–2000)
Muñoz, Juan Bautista (1745–1799)
Muñoz Álvarez, Agustín (fl.1793–
  1799)
Múñoz Capilla, José Jesús, O.S.A.
  (1771–1840)
Muñoz y Manzano, Cipriano (el
  conde de la Viñaza, 1862–1933)
Munro, Pamela (Long, b.1947)
Munske, Horst Haider (b.1935)K
Muránsky, Jozef (1928–1989)

Muratori, Ludovico Antonio (1672–
  1750)S
Murayama, Shichiro (b.1908)E
Murdock, George Peter (1897–1985)
Muret, Eduard (1833–1904)
Muret, Ernst (Jules Rodolphe, 1861–
  post 1924)
Muret, Marc Antoine (Muretus,
  1526–1585)
Murethach (= Muridac, mid-9th cent.
  A.D.)S
Murgu, Eftimie (1805–1870)
Murguía, Manuel (1833–1923)
Murison, Alexander Falconer (1847–
  1934)
Murison, David (Donald, 1913–
  1997)
Murko, Matija (1861–1952)
Murme(l)lius, Jo(h)annes (*alias* Jan
  Murmel *or* Myrmeling, 1479–
  1527)
Murphy, James J(erome, b.1923)
Murr, Christoph Gottlieb von (1733–
  1811)
Murray, Alexander (1775–1813)E
Murray, David James (b.1940?)
Murray, (Katharine Maud) Elisabeth
  (1909–1998)
Murray, Gilbert (1966–1957)
Murray, (*Sir*) James Henry Augustus
  (1837–1915)S, E
Murray, Lindley (1745–1826)S, E
Murray, Stephen O(mar, b.1950)
Murray, William Vans (fl.1792)
Murry, John Middleton (1889–1957)
Murzaev, Èduard M. (1908–1998)
Musgrave, Alan (20th cent.)
Mus(ch)ler, Johannes (1501/1502–
  1555)

N.

Nabokov, Vladimir Vladimirovič (1899–1977)

Nachersberg, Johann Heinrich Ernst (1775–1841)

Nachtigal, Gustav (1834–1885)

Nadel, Siegfried F. (1903–1956)

Nadeljaev, Vladimir M. (1912–1985)E

Nadesdin, Nikolaj Ivanovič (1804–1856)

Nad'kin, Dmitri Timofeevič (1934–1992)

Näf, Anton (b.1946)K

Naert, Pierre (1916–1971)E

Næs, Olav (1901–1984)S

Nägelsbach, Karl Friedrich von (1806–1859)

Nagano, Masaru (b.1922)

Nagao, Makoto (b.1936)

Nagata, Hôsei (1838–1911)S

Nagel, Peter (b.1938)K

Nagera Yanguas, *Licendiado* Diego de (16th cent.?)

Nagnajewicz, Marian (1911–1987)

Nāgojībhaṭṭa (*alias* Nagésa, d.1755)S, E

Nagucka, Ruta (b.1930)

Nagy, Gregory (b.1942)

Nagy, József (1958–1996)

Nagy, Kálmán (1939–1971)

Nagy, Pál Beregszászi (c.1750–1828)

Nagykin, Dmitrij Tyimofevics, *see* Nad'kin, D. F.

Naharro, Vicente (1750–1823)

Naḥḥās, Abū Ǧaᶜfar Aḥmad ibn Muḥammad an- (d.338/950)S

Nahtigal, Rajko (1877–1958)S

Naigeon, Jacques André (1738–1810)

Nájera, Manuel de San Juan Crisótomo (1803–1853)

Nájera Yanguas, Diego de (1560–1635)

Nakajima, Fumio (1904–1999)

Nakao, Toshio (1934–2000)

Nałęcz-Moszczeński, Stanisław (fl.1779; d.1790)

Nandriş, Grigore (1895–1968)

Nandris, Octavian (1914–1987)

Nanjio, Bunyiu (1849–1927)E

Nanni, Giovanni (*alias* Annius of Viterbo, 1432?–1502)

Nantes, P. Bernardo de, O.F.M., cap. (fl.1709)

Napier, Arthur Sampson (1853–1916)

Napoli, Donna Jo (b.1948)E

Nardi, Bruno (1884–1968)

Nares, Robert (1753–1829)S

Nāṣif, Ḥafnī (1855?–1919/20)S

Naro, Anthony J(ulius, b.1943)

Narten, Johanna (b.1930)K

Nascentes, Antenor (1886–1972)

Nash, Helen Elizabeth (b.1921)

Nash, June (1911–1979)

Nash, Leonard K. (b.1918)

Nash, Rose (b.1924)

Nasović, Ivan Ivanovič (1788–1877)

Nasser, Johan Adolph (1753–1828)

Nast, Johann (172–1807)

Nasyri, Kajum (d.1947)

Natalis, Hervaeus, *see* Hervæus Natalis

Natalis, Franciscus (*alias* František Božičević, c.1465–c.1530)
Nātan ben Yĕḥi'ēl (1035–c.1110)S
Natter, Leonhard (c.1493–1544/45)
Nattiez, Jean-Jacques (b.1945)
Naudé, Gabriel (1600–1653)
Naumann, Bernd (b.1938)K
Naumann, Hans (1886–1951)
Naumann, Hans-Peter (b.1939)K
Naumann, Horst (b.1925)K
Naumova, Tat'jana (b.1946)
Nausester, Walter (fl.1901)
Nauton, *abbé* Pierre (1912–1970)
Navagero, Andrea (1483–1529)
Návalar, Arunmuka, *see* Návalar Arunmuka
Navarro, João de Azpilcueta, S.J. (c.1522–1570)
Navarro, Martín de Azpilcueta (1492–1586)
Navarro, Miguel (1563–1627)
Navarro Tomás, Navarro (1884–1979)E
Naveros, Jacobus (fl. c.1533)
Naville, (Henri) Adrien (1845–1930)
Naylor, Kenneth E. (1937–1992)
Nazarova, Tetjana V. (d.1996?)
Nazet, Jacques (1944–1996)
Neale, John Mason (1818–1866)
Neander, Michael (1525–1595)
Nebel, Arthur (1888–1981)
Nebreda y López, Carlos (d.1876)
Nebrija, Elio Antonio de (also Nebrixa, Lebrixa; pseud. for Antonio Martínez de Cala y Xarava, 1441/44?–1522)S,E
Nebrissensis, Aelius Antonius, *see* Nebrija, Elio Antonio
Nechutová, Jana (b.1938)

Neckam, Alexander, *see* Alexander Nequam
Nedjalkov, Vladimir Petrovič (b.1928)K
Needham, Roger Michael (b.1935)
Neep, Johann (1767–1843)
Negelen, Julius von (1872–1932)
Nehls, Dietrich (1941–1994)K
Nehring, Alfons (1886–1968)
Nehring, Johann Christoph (c.1635–1697?)
Nehring, Władysław (*alias* Walter, 1830–1909)
Neilson, William Allen (1869–1946)
Neira, Alonso de, S.J. (c.1680–1730)
Neisser, Walter (1860–1941)
Neithart, Hans (c.1430–*ante* 1499)
Nekes, Hermann (1875–1948)
Nekrasov, Nikolaj Petrovič (1828–1913)
Nelde, Peter H. (b.1942)K
Nencioni, Giovanni (b.1911)
Nemnich, Philipp Andreas (1764–1822)
Neogrammarians, *see Junggrammatiker*
Neoral, Josef (1852–19??)
Nepote, Fernando (fl.1460–1492)
Neppert, Joachim M. H. (b.1934)K
Nerius, Dieter (b.1935)K
Nerlich, Brigitte (b.1956)K
Nerval, Gérard (de, 1808–1855)
Nesfield, John C. (*fl.*1895–1903)
Nesheim, Asbjørn (1906–1989)
Nespital, Helmut (b.1936)K
Nesselmann, Georg (Heinrich Ferdinand, 1811–1881)
Neu, Erich (1936–1999)K
Neubauer, Adolf (1832–1907)

Nicolaus of Cusa (Cusanus *alias*
   Nikolaus Krebs of Kues, 1401–
   1464)
Nicolaus Sophianus (c.1500–*post*
   1545)
Nicole, Pierre (1625–1695)
Nicolson, *Bishop* William (1655–
   1727)
Nicot, Jean (*sieur* de Villemain,
   c.1530–1604)S
Nicolova, Ruselina (b.1931)
Nida, Eugene A(lbert, b.1914)E
Niebaum, Hermann (b.1945)K
Niebuhr, Barthold Georg (1776–
   1831)
Niebuhr, Carsten (Karstens, 1733–
   1815)
Niederehe, Hans-Josef ("Hanno",
   b.1937)K
Niedermann, Max (1874–1954)
Niedźwiedzki, Władysław (1849–
   1930)
Nielsen, Hans Fredrik ("Frede",
   b.1943)
Nielsen, Jørgen Erik (b.1933)
Nielsen, Konrad (Hartvig Isak
   Rosenvinge, 1875–1953)S
Nielsen, Niels (Christian, b.1921)
Nielsen, Peter Heinrich (1905–1984)
Niemeier, Susanne (b.1960)
Niemeyer, Manfred (b.1947)K
Niemeyer, Max (1841–1911)
Nieminen, Eino (Vilho Kalervo,
   1891–1962)S
Nienaber, Gabriël Stephanus (1903–
   1994)
Nies, Fritz (b.1934)K
Nietzsche, Friedrich (Wilhelm, 1844–
   1900)

Nieuhof, Johan (1618–1672)
Nigidius Figulus, Publius (*ante* 99–
   45 B.C.)S
Nigidius, Petrus the Elder (1501–
   1583)
Nigol, Salme (b.1923)
Nijhoff, Martinus (1826–1894)
Nikiforov, Stepan Dmitrievič (1891–
   1951)
Nikitin, Afanasi (d.1472)
Nikolaeva, Tatjana Mixajlovna
   (b.1933)E
Nikolić, Svetozar (1921–2000)
Nikolov, En'o (1887–1966)
Nikol'skij, Aleksandr Sergeevič
   (1755–1834)
Nikol'skij, Vladimir Kapitonovič
   (1894–1953)
Nikonov, Vladimir A. (1904–1988)
Nikula, Henrik (b.1942)K
Nilson, Don L(ee) F(red, b.1934)
Nimuendajú, Curt (*pseud.* Un(c)kel,
   1883–1945)
Nipperdey, Thomas (1927–1992)
Nirenburg, Sergei (b.1950)
Nirvi, Ruben Erik (1905–1986)
Nisard, Désiré (1806–1888)
Nisbet, Robert A. (1913–1996)
Nishida, Tatsuo (b.1928)E
Nissilä, Viljo Johannes (1903–1986)
Nītiņa, Daina (b.1942)K
Nitsch, Kazimierz (1874–1958)S
Nitsch, Karl Wilhelm (1818–1880)
Nitze, William Albert (1876–1957)
Nižnanský, Jozef R. (1925–1996)
Nizolius, Marius (Nizolli, Mario,
   1498–1566)
Nketia, Joseph H. Kwabena (b.1921)

Nobel, Julius Adolf Johannes (1887–1960)
Nobili, Roberto de, S.J. (1579–1656)
Noble, Shlomo (1905–1986)
Noboa, *Bachiller* Antonio Martínez de (b. c.1800; fl.1839)S
Nóbrega, Manoel da, S.J. (1517–1570)
Noceda, Juan de, S.J. (1681–1747)
Nodal, John Howard (1831–1909)
Nodier, Charles (1780–1844)
Noël, François-Joseph-Michel (1755–1841)
Noeldeke, Georg Justus Friedrich (1768–1843)
Nöldeke, Theodor (1836–1930)E
Nöth, Winfried (b.1944)K
Noiré, Ludwig (1829–1889)
Nokl-Armfield, George (IPA member 1908–1913)
Noll, Volker (b.1958)
Nolst Trenite, Gerard (1870–1946)
Nolte, Johann Friedrich (1694–1754)
Nolte, Johann Wilhelm Heinrich (1767–1832)
Nomoto, Kikuo (b.1922)
Nonius Marcellus (6th cent. A.D.)
Noordegraaf, Jan (b.1948)
Noorduyn, Jacobus (1926–1994)
Norberg, Dag (1909–1996)
Nord, Lennart (1947–1999)
Norden, Eduard (1868–1941)
Nordfelt, A. (d.1943)
Nordgård, Torbjørn (b.1959)
Nordmeyer, George (1912–1995)
Nordmeyer, Henry Waldemar (1891–*post* 1977)
Noreen, Adolf (Gotthard, 1854–1925)S, E

Noreen, Erik (d.1947)
Norman, Frederick (1897–1968)
Normand, Claudine (b.1934)
Norment, Clarence Forbes (1856–19??)
Norrick, Neal R. (b.1948)K
Norris, John (1657–1711)
North, Douglass Cecil (b.1921)
North, *Sir* Dudley (1641–1691)
North, Sterling (1906–1974)
North, *Sir* Thomas (1535–1601?)
Norton, Thomas (1532–1584)
Nøs, Olav (1901–1984)
Nosek, Jiří (b.1919)
Nosović, Ivan Ivanovyč (1788–1877)
Noss, Richard B. (b.1923)
Nothofer, Bernd (b.1941)K
Notker (Labeo 'Teutonicus', c.950–1022)
Noüel, François (Joseph Michel, 1755–1841)
Novák, Bořivoj (1906–1973)
Novák, L'udovit (1908–1992)
Nováková, Julie (1909–1991)
Novaković, Stojan (1842–1915)
Novalis (= Georg Philipp Friedrich Leopold, *Freiherr* von Hardenberg, 1772–1801)
Novikiv, Lex Alekseevič (1931–2003)
Nowak, Henryk (b.1933)
Nowak, Zbigniew Jerzy (d.1994)
Nowell, Laurence (c.1514–1576)
Noydens, Benito Remigio (1630–1685)
Noyes, Gertrude (b.1905)
Noyes, George R. (1873–1952)
Nuchelmans, Gabriel (Reinier Franciscus Maria, 1922–1996)
Nugent, Christopher (1544–1602)

Nuijtens, Emile Theophile Gerardus
(fl.1962)
Nuñes de Arenas, Isaac (1812–
1869)S
Nuñes de Leão, Duarte (1528–1608)
Nuñes de Taboada, Manuel? (1741–
1808)
Nuñes de Taboada, Melchor Manuel
(b.1786; fl.1812)
Nunes, Leonardo, S.J. (d.1554)
Nunes, Placido (d.1755)
Nunes de Leão, Duarte (c.1530–
1608)
Núñez, José María (1812–1856)
Núñez, Pedro Juan (1522–1602)
Núñez de Arce, Gaspar (1834–1903)
Núñez de Prado, José, S.J. (1666–
1743)
Nurm, Ernst (1896–1983)
Nurse, Derek (b.1942?)
Nuttal, Zelia (1858–1933)
Nutting, Rufus (1793–1878)
Nuutinen, Olli (1939–1995)
Nyberg, Henryk Samuel (1889–
1974)
Nyerup, Rasmus (1750–1829)
Nygaard, Marius (1838–1912)
Nyholm, Kurt (b.1932)K
Nyíri, Antal (1907–2000)
Nykl, Alois Richard (1895–*post*
1953)
Nyloë, Jacobus (1670–1714)
Nyrop, Kristoffer (1858–1931)S
Nysted, Hans Olufsøn (1664–1740)

O.

Oakden, James Parker (1904–1988)
Obenauer, Karl Justus (1888–1973)
Oberhuber, Karl (b.1915)K
Oberlin, Jeremias Jacob (1735–1806)
Oberpfalcer-Jílek, František (1890–1973)
Obicini, Thomas, O.F.M. (1585–1632)
Oblak, Vatroslav (Ignaz, 1864–1896)
Obnorskij, Sergej Petrovič (1888–1962)S
Obrębska-Jabłońska, Antonina (1901–1994)
Ombredane, André (1898–1959)
O'Brien, Michael A. (1896–1962)
Obry, Jean Baptiste François (1793–1871)
Obst, Ulrich (b.1946)K
Ocahasa, Guillermo (fl.1681)
O'Cain, Raymond Kenneth (b. c.1940)
Ó Carrigáin, Éamonn (b.1942)
Occioni, Onorato (1829–1925)
Ochs, Elinor [Keenan] (b.1940?)
Ockham, William, *see* William of Ockham
O'Connor, J[ames] Desmond ("Doc", b.1919)
O'Connor, Patricia (b.1931)
O'Connor , Michael Patrick (d.2007)
Ó Crónín, Donncha A. (1920–1990)
Odier, Henri (Charles Agenor, 1873–1938)

Odum, Howard W. (1884–1954)
Öhlschläger, Günther (b.1947)K
Öhmann, Emil (1894–1984)S
Öhmann, Sven (b.1936)
Öhrling, Emanuel Johan (1718–1779)
Ölberg, Hermann (b.1922)K
Ölinger, Albert (fl.1574–1587)
Oellacher, Hans (d.1949)
Oellinger, Georg Erasmus (d.1664)
Oelsner, Joachim (b.1931)K
Oertel, Hanns (1868–1952)
Oertelius Winshemius, Vitus (from Winsheim, 1501–1578)
Oesterreicher, Wulf (b.1942)K
Oesterle, John A. (1912–1977)
Oettinger, Anthony G(ervin, b.1929)
Oettinger, Norbert (b.1949)K
Offelen, Heinrich (*alias* Henry, fl.1686–1687)
Ofeigsson, Jón (1881–1938)
Oftedal, Magne (1921–1985)
Ogawa, Hiroshi (b.1942)
Ogburn, William Fielding (1886–1959)
Ogden, Charles Kay (1889–1957)E
Ogilvie, John (1797–1867
Ogier, François (d.1670)
Ogle, Richard A. (b.1947?)
O'Grady, Geoffrey N. (b.1928)
O'Grady, William Delaney (b.1952)
Ogura, Michiko (b.1949)
Ogura, Mieko (b.1948)
Ohala, John J(erome, b.1941)
O'Hearn, Edna M. (b.1919)
Ohijenko, Ivan Ivanovič (*Metropolitan* Illarion, 1882–1972)
Ohlshausen, Justus (1800–1882)
Ohly, Friedrich (b.1914)K

P.

Paardekooper, Petrus Cornelis ("Piet", b. 1920)

Paasonen, Heikki (1865–1919)S

Pabst, Karl (1810–1873)

Pacconio, Francesco, S.J. (1589–1641)

Pace, Richard (c.1482–1536)

Páclová, Ilona (1933–1988)

Pacnerová, Ludmila (b.1925)

Padilla, Francisco de (1527–1607)

Padilla, Manuel, S.J. (1715–1785)

Padley, George Arthur (1924–1986)

Padučeva, Elena Viktorovna (b.1935)E

Paepcke, Fritz (1916–1990)K

Paets, Jan Jacobszoon (fl.1608)

Pätzold, Margita (b.1947)

Pagden, Anthony (b.1945)

Page, Raymond Ian (b.1924)

Pagés, Aniceto de (1843–1902)

Paget, *Sir* Richard Arthur Surtees (*Baronet*, 1869–1955)E

Pagliaro, Antonino (1898–1973)S

Pagnini, Santi (1470–1536)

Pai, Ti-Chou (1900–1934)

Paillard, Denis (b.1945)

Paine, Thomas (1737–1809)

Pais, Cidmar Teodoro (b.1940)

Pais, Dezső (1886–1973)

Pak Sŭngbin (*alias* Hakpŏn, 1880–1943)S

Palacio Fontán, Eduardo del (1872–*post* 1928)

Palaemon, Quintus Remmius (mid-1st cent. A.D.)

Palafox y Mendoza, Juan de, *bishop* of Osma (1600–1659)

Palamarčuk, Leonid Sydorovyč (1922–1985)

Palavestra, Vlajko (1927–1993)

Palencia, Alfonso de (1423–1492)

Palet, Jean (fl.1604–1608)

Palkovič, Konštantin (b.1919)

Palladio, Andrea (1508–1580)

Palladius (pseudo-Probus, 4th cent A.D.)

Pallas, Peter Simon (1741–1811)S, E

Pallavicino, Pietro Sforza (1607–1667)S

Pallottino, Massimo (1909–1995)

Palmer, *Rev.* Abram Smythe (fl.1876–1913)

Palmer, Frank R(obert, b.1922)

Palmer, Harold Edward (1877–1949)E

Palmer, Leonard Robert (1906–1984)

Palmer, Thomas (fl.1380–1410)

Palmireno, Juan Lorenzo (1514–1580)S

Palmotić, Junjie (1608–1657)

Pálóczi Horvát, István (1784–1846)

Palomares, Francisco Javier de Santiago (1728–1796)

Palomino de Castro y Velasco, Antonio (1655–1726)

Palsgrave, John (1480?–1554)S, E

Palva, Heikki (b.1935)

Pamp, Bengt (1928–2001)

Panagl, Oswald (b.1939?)

Panckoucke, Charles-Joseph (1736–1798)

Parmenides (of Elea, c.515–*post* 440 B.C.)S

Parmenter, Clarence Edward (1888–1982)S

Parmentier, Léon Joseph (1863–

Parodi, Ernesto Giacomo (1862–1923)S

Parol, Urszula Zofia (1942–1998)

Paroli, Teresa (b.1939)

Parra, Caracciolo (1901–1939)

Parra, *Fray* Francisco de la, O.F.M. (d. c.1560)

Parret, Herman (b.1938)

Parry, Milman (d.1935)

Parsons, Elsie Claws (1875–1941)

Parsons, F. W. (1908–1993)

Parsons, James, M.D. (1705–1770)

Parsons, Talcott (1902–1979)

Partee, Barbara H(all Corey, b.1940)E

Parthey, Gustav (1798–1872)

Partridge, Astley Cooper (b.1901)

Partridge, Eric (Honeywood, 1894–1979)E

Pascal, Blaise (1623–1662)

Pasch, Renate (b.1942)K

Paschall, Andrew (c.1630-c.1696)

Pasius, Curius Lancillotus (fl.1504)

Pasolini, Pier Paolo (1922–1975)S

Pasor, Matthias (1599–1658)

Pasquali, Giorgio (1885–1952)S

Pasquier, Estiennne (1529–1615)S

Passen, Robert van (1923–2002)

Passerieu, Jean-Claude (b.1950)

Passin, Herbert (b.1916)

Passmore, John (Arthur, b.1914)

Passow, Franz (Ludwig Carl Friedrich, 1786–1833)S

Passy, Paul (Édouard, 1859–1940)S, E

Pastarnek, František (1853–1940)

Pasternak, Boris Leonidovič (1890–1960)

Pastor, Julio Rey, *see* Rey Pastor, Julio

Pastor, Ludwig von (1854–1928)

Pastrana, Luis de (1540?–*post* 1583)S

Páta, Josef (1886–1942)

Patañjali (2nd cent. B.C.)S, E

Pathy, *Capt.* C.S.K. (1895–1976)

Patin, Henri Joseph Guillaume (1793–1876)

Patois, Charles (Joseph Émile, 1888–1947)

Patón, Bartolomé Jiménez (1569–1640)

Patri, Sylvain (b.1959)

Patrick, George Zinovei (d.1946)

Patrick, Simon (1626–1707)

Pătruţ, Ioan (1914–1992)

Patru, Olivier (1604–1681)

Pattanayak, Debiprasanna (b.1931)

Patterson, Calvin (1847–1902)

Paues, Anna Carolina (1867–1945)

Paufler, Hans-Dieter (b.1935)K

Paul Diacre, of Genoa ('the Deacon', d. c.1100)

Paul of Venice (Paulus Nicolettus Venetus, c.1369–1429)S

Paul, Hermann (Otto Theodor, 1846–1921)S, E

Paul, Jean-Honoré-Robert de, *chevalier* de La Manon (1752–1787)

Paul, Vincent de (c.1580–1660)

Porras Barrenechea, Raúl (1897–1960)
Porsanger, Anders (1735–1780)
Porsch, Peter (b.1944)K
Porson, Richard (1759–1808)
Port-Royal Grammar/School (17th cent.)
Porte, Arnaldo de la (17th cent.)S
Porter, Noah (1811–1892)
Porter y Casanate, Pedro (1613–1655)
Porthan, Henrik Gabriel (alias Purtanen, 1739–1804)S
Portus, Aemilius (alias Porto, Emilio, 1550–1614/15)
Portus, Franciscus (Porto, Francesco, 1511–1581)
Porzeziński, Jan Wiktor (alias Viktor Karlovič Poržezinskij, 1870–1929)S
Porzig, Walter (1895–1961)S
Pos, Hendrik J. (Henricus Josephus, 1898–1955)S
Poška, Dionizas (1765–1830)
Posener-Krieger, Paule (1925–1996)
Posner, Rebecca (b.1926?)
Posner, Roland (b.1942)K
Posodippus of Pella (3rd cent. B.C.)
Possel, René de (1905–1972)
Post, Emil L. (1897–1954)
Post, Hendrik Howens (1904–1986)
Post, Friedrich (1710–1785)
Postal, Paul M(artin, b.1936)
Postel(lus), Guillaume (1510–1581)E
Postgate, John Percival (1853–1926)
Posti, Lauri (Albert, 1908–1988)S
Postman, Neil (1931–2003)

Potebnja, A(leksandr) A(fanas'evič; Ukr.: Oleksandr Opanasovyč, 1835–1891)S, E
Potgieter, Everhardus Johannes (1808–1875)
Potier, Pierre-Philippe, S.J. (1708–1781)
Potken, Johannes (late 15th–early 16th cent.)
Potocki, Jan (1761–1815)
Pott, August Friedrich (1802–1887)S, E
Potter, Ralph Kimball (1894–19??)
Potter, Simeon (1898–1976)
Pottier, Bernard (b.1924)
Potts, Rev. John (1775–1837)
Pougens, Charles-Marie-Joseph de (1755–1833)
Pouillet, Claude (Servais Matthias Marie Roland, c.1790–1868)
Poultney, James Willson (1907–1993)
Pound, Ezra (1888–1972)
Pound, Louise (1872–1958)S, E
Pouchenis, Andres (1693–1748)
Poutsma, Hendrik (1856–1937)S, E
Považaj, Metej (b.1941)
Povejšil, Jaromír (b.1931)
Powdermaker, Hortense (1900–1970)
Powell, Major John Wesley (1834–1902)S
Powell, Thomas George Eyre (b.1916)
Poznański, Samuel (1869–1921)
Pozo, Antonio, O.P. (d.1623)
Pozzi-Escot Zapata, Inés (1923–1997)
Prabhākara (7th cent. A.D.)S
Prado, Pablo de, S.J. (1576–1651)

Praetorius, Franz (1847–1927)
Prager, Johann Christian (d.1796)
Prager, William (1903–1980)
Prantl, Carl von (1820–1888)
Prasch, Johann Ludwig (1637–1690)
Prat, Jean-Marie (1809–1891)
Pratt, Robert Armstrong (1907–1987)
Pražak, Josef (1860–1938)
Prędota, Stanisław (b.1944)K
Preece, *Sir* William Henry (1834–
1913)
Preinersdorfer, Rudolf (b.1933)
Prémaire, Joseph Henri Marie de, S.J.
(1666–1736)
Premk, Francka (b.1943)
Prémontval, André-Pierre le Guay de,
see Le Guay de Prémontval, André-
Pierre
Prendergast, Thomas (1806–1886)
Presocratics (c.625–c.450 B.C.)
Preston, Henry (fl.1606–1703)
Preston, Richard Joseph (b.1931)
Preston, William D. (d.1954)
Preti, Giulio (1811–1872)S
Pretnar, Tone (1945–1992)
Pretorius, Michael (1571/72–1621)
Pretten, Johann (1634–1708)
Preuss, Theodor (fl.1912–1932)
Prévost, *abbé* Antoine-François
(1697–1863)
Prévost, Marcel Eugène (1862–1941)
Prévost, *abbé* Pierre (1751–1839)
Preyel, Adam (fl.1655)
Price, Aubrey Charles (d.1939)
Price, Derek J. de Solla (1922–1982)
Price, Henry Habberly (1899–19??)
Price, Owen (c.1632–1671)
Price, Thomas (1599–1685)
Price, William (1780–1830)

Prichard, Harold Arthur (1871–1947)
Prichard, James Cowles, M.D.
(1786–1848)
Pride, John Bernard (1929–1993)
Priestley, Joseph (1733–1804)S, E
Priestly, Tom M. S. (b.1937)
Prieto, Luis Jorge (1926–1996)
Prietze, Rudolf (1854–1933)
Prignel, Maurice (1903–1987)
Prigogine, Ilya (1917–2003)
Prijs, Leo (b.1920)K
Prilutski, Noyekh (1882–1941)
Prince, Alan (b. c.1950)
Prince, Ellen (b. c.1945)
Prince, Della (Henry, 1877–1962)
Prince, John Dyneley (1868–1945)
Prins, Anton Adriaan (1902–19??)
Printz, Wilhelm (1887–1941)
Priscian(us Caesariensis, 'of
Cesarea', late 5th–early 6th cent.
A.D.)S, E
Pritchard, James Bennett (b.1909)
Probus Palladius (c.305 A.D.)
Probus, Marcus Valerius (fl.60 A.D.)
Proclus (c.411–485 A.D.)
Profous, Antonín (1878–1953)
Prodikos of Keos (c.460–390 B.C.)
Prokosch, Eduard (1876–1938)S
Prokosch, Erich (b.1935)K
Pronko, Nicholas Henry (b.1908)
Propp, Vladimir Jakovlevič (1895–
1970)E
Proschan, Frank (b.1953)
Protagoras (of Abdera, c.485–411
B.C.)S
Proudhon, Pierre-Joseph (1809–
1865)
Proulx, Paul (Martin, 1942–2005)
Provinse, John (1897–1965)

Proyart, *abbé* Lievain Bonaventure (c.1743–1808)

Prudentius (= Aurelius Prudentius Clemens, 348–405 A.D.)

Pruner-Bey, Franz (1808–1882)

Prutz, Robert (1816–1872)

Prym, Eugen (1843–1913)

Prys, Edmund (*c*.1541–1624)

Przełęcki, Marian (b.1923)

Przetacznik-Gierowska, Maria (1920–1995)

Przybylski, Jacek (1756–1819)

Przyluski, Jean (1885–1944)

Przywara, Michal (1867–1906)

Psammetichus, Egyptian king (664-610 B.C.)

Pseudo-Albertus Magnus (c.1280)

Pseudo-Apuleus (fl. 2nd cent. A.D.)

Pseudo-Augustinus, Divus Aurelius (fl.1508)

Pseudo-Cato (4th cent. A.D.)

Pseudo-Probius, *see* Palladius

Pseudo-Robert Grosseteste (c.1260?)

Pseudo-Scotus (13th cent. A.D.)

Psichari, Jean (*alias* Ioannis Psucharis, 1854–1929)

Ptolemaios ('Ptolemy the Peripatetic', 2nd cent. B.C.)

Ptolemy (fl.127 A.D.)

Puchmayer, Anton Jaroslav (1769–1820)

Pudor, Christian (17th cent.)

Puech, Christian (b.1950)

Puerta Cansxeco, Juan de la (1827–1902)

Püschel, Ulrich (b.1943)K

Pütz, Martin (b.1955)K

Pufendorf, Samuel *Freiherr* von (1632–1694)

Puhvel, Jaan (b.1932)

Puig y Xoriguer, Salvador (1719–1793)

Puigblanch, Antonio (1775–1842)

Pulgar, Hernando del (1451–1531)

Pulgram, Ernst (1915–2005)K

Pulleyblank, Edwin G(eorge, b.1922)

Pulleyblank, Douglas (b. c.1952)

Pullum, Geoffrey K(eith, b.1945)

Pulsiano, Phillip (1947–2000)

Pumnul, Arune (*or* Aron, 1818–1866)

Pumpjanskij, Lev (1891–1940)

Puoti, Basilio (1782–1847)S

Puppel, Stanisław (b.1947)

Purchas, Samuel (1575?–1626)

Purczinsky, Julius O., Jr. (b.1925)

Purkyně, Jan Evangelista (1787–1869)

Purnell, Thomas C. (b.1963)

Purșottama (12th cent. A.D.)S

Pușcariu, Sextil (1877–1948)S, E

Pussendorfer, Artur (1864–1936)

Puteanus, Erycius (*alias* Hendrik van der Putten, 1574–1646)

Putilov, Boris Nikolaevič (1919–1997)

Putnam, Frederic Ward (1839–1915)

Putnam, George N(elson, 1909–1991)

Putnam, Hilary (b.1926)E

Putschius, Helias (1580–1606)

Putschke, Wolfgang (b.1937)K

Puttamittran̠ (11th cent. A.D.)

Puttenham, George (1530–1590)

Puzynina, Jadwiga (b.1928)

Pylades (*alias* Buccardus, Ioannes Franciscus = Gianfrancesco Boccardo, d.1506)

Q.

Qālī, Abū ᶜAlī Ismāᶜīl ibn Qasim al-
(288/901–356/967)S

Qian, Daxin (1728–1804)

Qimḥi, David, *see* Kimḥi, David

Qinh, Kia (1796–1821)

Quackenbos, George Payne (1826–
1881)

Quaegebeur, Jan (1943–1995)

Quadri, Bruno (1917–1997)

Quadrio, Francesco Saverio (1695–
1756)

Quandt, Christlieb von (1740–1824)

Quatrefages de Breau, Armand de
(1810–1892)

Quatremère, Étienne Marc (1782–
1857)

Queixalos, Francisco (b.1947)

Quemada, Bernard (b.1926)

Quemada, Gabrielle Josette (b.1925)

Quentin, Jacques, S.J. (1572–1647)

Quer y Martínez, José (1695–1764)

Quesnay, François (1694–1774)

Quicheret, Jules (1814–1882)

Quick, Edith E. (1877–1949)

Quiehl, Karl (1857–*post* 1912)

Quilis, Antonio (1933–2003)E

Quiller-Couch, *Sir* Arthur (1863–
1944)

Quillian, M. Ross (b.1931)

Quin, Ernest Gordon (1910–1986)

Quine, Willard Van Orman (1908–
2000)E

Quinet, Edgar (1803–1875)

Quinette, Nicolas-Marie (c.1761–
1821)

Quinquarb(o)r(eu)s, Jean (1514–
1587)

Quintescu, Nicolae (1841–1913)

Quintilian(us), Marcus Fabius (c.35–
c.95 A.D.)S,E

Quintin, Hervé (b.1952)K

Quirk, (Charles) Randolph (*Lord
Quirk of Bloomsbury*, b.1920)E

Qŭnabay-ŭlï, Abay (1845–1904)

Quraysh, Yehuda Ibn, *see* Ibn
Qurayš, Yēhūdāh

Quṭrub, Abū ᶜAlī Muḥammad ibn
Mustanīr (d.206/821)S

Qvigstad, Just Knud (1853–1957)S

R.

Rabbinowicz, Israel Jehiel Michael (1818–1893)

Rabelais, François (1494–1553)

Rabin, Chaim (b.1915)

Rabiner, Lawrence (b.1943)

Rabot, Guillaume (1530?–1589)

Rabouin, Paul (1828–1896)

Rachel, Joachim (1618–1669)

Racine, Jean Baptiste (1639–1699)

Rackham, Harris (1868–1944)

Radau, Rodolphe (1835–1911

Radbruch, Gustav (1878–1949)

Radhakrishnan, Sarvepalli (1888–1975)

Radcliffe-Brown, Alfred Reginald (1881–1955)

Radden, Günter (20th cent.)

Rademaker, Cornelis S(imon) M(aria, b.1930)

Radice, Betty (1912–1985)

Radin, Paul (1883–1959)S

Radtke, Edgar (b.1952)K

Radlof, Johann Gottlieb (1781–1846)

Radloff, (Friedrich) Wilhelm (*alias* Vasilij Vasil'evič Radlov, 1837–1918)S

Radlov, V. V., *see* Radloff, Wilhelm

Radonvilliers, Claude-Franç(o)is Lyzarde de, S.J. (1709–1789)S

Radouant, René (1862–*post* 1922)

Radulescu, Ión Eliad(e) (19th cent.)

Radulphus Brito (c.1275–1320)S, E

Radwańska-Williams, Joanna (b.1961)

Rafinesque(-Schmalz), Constantine Samuel (1783–1840)

Raffles, *Sir* Thomas Stamford (1781–1826)

Ragusa, Paul (18th cent.)

Raible, Wolfgang (b.1939)K

Raidt, Edith Hildegard (b.1932)K

Raith, Josef (1903–1991)K

Raietit, Erich (1920–1992)

Rajandi, Edgar (1902–1978)

Rājarājavarma, A. P. (1863–1918)E

Rajna, Pio (1847–1930)

Raleigh, *Sir* Walter (1552?–1618)

Ralph of Beauvais (fl. c.1175)S

Ralph Strode (d.1387)S

Ralston, William S. R. (1828–1889)

Ramanujan, Attipat K. (b.1929)

Ramaswami Aiyar, L. Vishwanātha (1895–1948)E

Ramat, Paolo (b.1936)E

Rambaud, Jean-Jacques-Arnaux (fl.1853)

Rambaud, Honorat (fl.1580)

Rambeau, Adolphe (1852–*post* 1907)

Rambosson, Jean Pierre (1827–1886)

Rameau, Jean Philippe (1683–1764)

Ramírez, Diego (1589–1647)

Ramírez de Carrión, Manuel (1579–*post* 1652)

Ramler, Karl Wilhelm (1725–1798

Ramm, Bernard L. (b.1916)

Ramos, Domingos, S.J. (d.1728)

Ramos, Teodoro (1895–1937)

Ramovš, Fran (1890–1952)S

Ramsey, Frank Plumpton (1903–1930)

Ramsey, Robert L(ee, b.1929)

Ramshorn, (Johann Gottlieb) Ludwig (1786–1837)

Ramson, John Crowe (1888–1974)
Ramson, William Stanley (b.1933)
Ramstedt, Gustaf John (1873–
    1950)S, E
Ramult, Stefan (1859–1913)
Ramus, Petrus (*alias* Pierre de La
    Ramée, 1715–1772)S, E
Rand, Asa (1783–1871)
Randall, Robert A. (b.1942)
Rangel, Alonso (c.1500–1547)
Ranjina, Dinko (1536–1607)
Ranke, Hermann (1878–*post* 1939)
Ranke, Leopold (von, 1795–1886)
Rankin, Joseph H. (b.1951)
Rankova, Marija (1914–1989)
Raoul le Breton, *see* Randulphua
    Brito
Rapet, Jean-Jacques (1805–1882)
Raphelengius, Franciscus (*alias*
    Ravelingen, 1539–1597)
Rapin, René (1621–1687)
Rapola, Martti (1891–1972)S
Rapp, Eugen Ludwig (1904–1977)
Rapp, Karl Mori(t)z (1803–1883)
Rappaport, David (1911–1960)
Raqueneau, Paul, S.J. (1608–1660)
Raquette, Gustaf (d.1945?)
Rasadin, Valentin Ivanovič (b.1939)E
Rask, Rasmus Kristian (1787–
    1832)S, E
Rasles, Sébastien (*alias* Râles, also
    Rale, 1657–1724)
Rasmussen, Jens Elmegård (b.1944)
Rasmussen, P0ul Bøggild (1942–
    1996)
Rastell, John (1475–1536)
Rastier, François (b.1945)
Rāta, Anna (1904–1993)
Ratclifffe, John (fl.1540)

Rath, Rainer (b.1934)K
Rathmayr, Renate (b.1947)K
Ratichius, *see* Ratke, Wolfgang
Ratke, Wolfgang (Ratichius, 1571–
    1635)S, E
Ratzel, Friedrich (1844–1904)
Rattell, J.-A.-A. (fl.1896)
Rau, Joachim Justus (1713–1749)
Raub, Albert Newton (1840–1904)
Rauch, Christian Heinrich (1718–
    1763)
Rauch, Irmengard (b.1933)K
Raudnitzky, Hans (1887–19??)
Rauh, Gisa (b.1947)K
Raulin, Petrus (c.1443–1514)
Raumer, Karl Otto von (1805–1859)
Raumer, Rudolf (Heinrich Georg)
    von (1815–1876)S, E
Raup, Hallock F. (1901–1985)
Ravaisson-Mollien, (Jean Gaspard)
    Félix Lacher (1813–1900)
Ravalière, P.-A., Levesque de la, see
    Levesque de la Ravalière, P.-A.
Ravila, Paavo Ilmari (1902–1974)S
Ravis, Christian (*alias* Raue, 1613–
    1677)
Rawlinson, Henry Creswicke (1810–
    1895)
Ravn, Hans Mikkelsen (1610–1663)
Rawson, Elizabeth Donata (b.1934)
Ray, John (1627–1705)
Ray, Verne Frederick (b.1905)
Rayleigh, John William Strutt, *baron*
    (1842–1919)
Raymundus Lullus, *see* Lullus,
    Raimundus
Raynal, *abbé* Guillaume Thomas
    François (1713–1796)

Ribeiro, Antonio, S.J. (d.1744)
Ribeiro de Andrade Fernandes, João
 Batista (1860–1934)
Ribeiro, Emmanuel (d.1745)
Ribeiro, Darcy (b.1922)
Ribot, Théodule Armand (1839–
 1916)
Ricardo, Antonio (d.1606)
Ricci, Matteo, S.J. (1552–1610)
Rice, David Storm (*alias* Sigismund
 Reich, d.1962)
Rice, Howard Croby, Jr. (1904–
 1980)
Rice, John (fl.1765)
Rice, Keren (Dichter, b.1949)
Rice, Stuart A. (1889–1969)
Richard Billingham (14th cent.)S
Richard Brinkley (2nd half of 14th
 cent.)S
Richard de Mediavilla (1249–c.1302)
Richard Kilvington (c.1305–1361)S
Richard Lavenham (d. c.1400)
Richard of Campsall (c.1285–c.1355)
Richard of Hambury (fl.1290)
Richards, Ivor Armstrong (1893–
 1979)E
Richardson, Alexander (c.1563–
 1629)
Richardson, Brian (b.1945?)
Richardson, Charles (1775–1865)
Richardson, Edward (c.1618–c.1677)
Richardson, Irvine Whaley (b.1934)
Richardson, Ivor Lloyd Morgan
 (b.1930)
Richardson, John (1664–1747)
Richardson, John (1741–1811?)
Richardson, Jonathan (1665–1745)
Richardson, Samuel (1689–1761)
Richat, Alfred (1833–1910)

Richelet, César-Pierre (1626–1698)S
Richelieu, Armand Jean du Duplessis,
 cardinal, duc de (1585–1642)
Richens, Richard Hook (1918–1984)
Richepin, Jean (1849–1926)
Richet , Charles (1850–1935)
Richey, Michael (1678–1761)
Richmond, (Winthrop) Edson
 (b.1916)
Richter, Elise (1865–1943)S, E
Richter, Jean (*alias* Hans) Paul
 (1763–1825)
Richter, Wolfgang (b.1926)K
Richthofen, Karl, *Freiherr* von
 (1811–1888)
Ricius, Paulus (d.1541)
Ricken, Ulrich (b.1926)K
Rickford, John Russell (b.1949)E
Ricoeur, (Jean) Paul (Gustave, 1913–
 2005)
Ridenour, Louis Nicot (1911–1959)
Ridington, W(illiam) Robin (b.1939)
Ridley, Mark (1560–1624)
Ridley, Nicholas (c.1500–1555)
Ridruejo, Emilio (b.1949)
Rieber, Robert W(olf, b.1934)
Riedel, Gabriel (1781–1859)
Riederer, Friedrich (c.1450–c.1510)S
Riederer, Johann Friedrich (1678–
 c.1732)
Riedlinger, Albert (1883–1978)
Riffaterre, Michel (1924–2006)
Riegel, Herman(n, 1843–1900)S
Rieger, Burghard (b.1937)K
Rieger, Janusz (b.1934)
Rieger, Max(imilan, 1828–1909)
Riehl, Wilhelm Heinrich (1823–
 1897)
Riemann, Othon (1853–1891)

Roždestvenskij, Jurij Vladimirovič (1926–1999)

Rozen, Viktor Romanovič (1849–1908)

Rozencveijg, Viktor Jul'evič (1911–1998)

Rozière, Eugène de (1820–1896)

Rozniecki, Stanisław Walenty (1865–1921)

Rozov, Volodymyr (1876–1940)

Rozwadowski, Jan (Michał alias Johannes von Rozwadowski, 1867–1935)S, E

Rubenstein, Herbert (b.1920)

Rudbek, Olof ("the Elder",1630–1702)

Rudelle, Lucien de (1804–1877)

Rudenko, Sergej Ivanovič (1885–1969)

Rudjakov, Mykola Oleksandrovyč (1926–1993)

Rudnicki, Mikolaj (1881–1978)

Rudnyc´kyj, Jaroslav Bohdan (1910–1995)

Rudwick, Martin J(ohn) S(pencer, b.1932)

Rudzka(-Ostyn), Brygida (1939–1997)

Rudzīte, Marta (1924–1996)

Rück, Heribert (b.1930)

Rückert, Friedrich (1788–1866)

Rückert, Heinrich (1823–1875)

Rüdiger, Johann Christian Christoph (1751–1822)

Ruelle, Pierre (1911–1993)

Rüppell, Wilhelm Peter Eduard Simon (1794–1884)

Rues, François des (c.1625)

Ruesch, Jurgen (b.1909)

Ruffin, Pierre-Jean-Marie (1742–1824)

Rufinus (345–406 A.D.)

Ruge, Arnold (1802–1880)

Ruggieri, Michele, S.J. (1543–1607)

Ruhlen, Merritt (b.1944)

Ruhnken(ius), David (1723–1798)

Ruiz, Gaspar, S.J. (1564–1624)

Ruíz Blanco, Matías, O.F.M. (1643–1705)

Ruiz de Corral, Fray Felipe (17th cent.)

Ruiz de Montoya, Antonio, S.J. (1585–1652)

Ruíz de Vergara, Pedro (1453–1509)

Ruland, Martin (1532–1602)

Rumelhart, David E. (b.1942)

Rummani, Abū l-Ḥasan ᶜAlī ibn ᶜÎsa ar- (296/909–384/994)S

Rumpelt, Hermann Berthold (1821–1881)

Rumpelt, Hermann Berthold (1821–1881)

Runciman, Sir Steven (b.1903)

Rundhovde, Gunnvor (1918–1987)

Runze, Georg (1852–1938)

Ruong, Israel (1903–1996)

Ruoppila, Veikko (1907–1993)

Rupp, Julius (1809–1884)

Ruprecht, Hans-Georg(e, b.1936)K

Ruscalla,Vergezzi Giovenale (1799–1865)

Ruscelli, Gerolamo (d.1566)

Rusek, Jerzy (b.1930)

Rusev, Rusi (1900–1988)

Rush, James (1786–1869)

Rusiewicz, Zygmunt (1911–1954)

Rusinov, Rusin (1930–1998)

Rusínová, Zdenka (b.1939)

S.

Sá, Antônio de (1620–1678)

Saadya Gaon (*alias* Saadya ben
 Joseph al-Fạyyūmi, 882–942
 A.D.)E

Saareste, Andrus (1892–1964)

Saari, Henn (1924–1999)

Śabara (between 350 and 500
 A.D.?)S

Sabatier, Paul (1858–1928)

Sabbadini, Remigio (1850–1934)

Sabban, Annette (b1953)K

Sablé, Madeleine de Souvré,
 marquise de (1598–1678)

Sabol, Ján (b.1933)

Šabršula, Jan (b.1918)

Såby, Viggo (1835–1898)

Sacer, Gottfried Wilhelm (*alias*
 Hartmann Reinhold, 1635–1699)

Sacerdos, Marcius Plotius, *see*
 Plotius Sacerdos, Marius

Sachau, Eduard (1845–1930)

Sachs, Hans (1494–1576)

Sachs, Michael (1808–1864)

Sackmann, Robin (b.1962)

Sacks, Harvey (1935–1975)E

Sacleux, Charles, C.S.Sp. (1856–
 1943)

Saco y Arce, Juan Antonio (1835–
 1881)

Sacy, Silvestre de, *see* Silvestre de
 Sacy, Antoine-Isaac

Saddock, Jerrold M. (b.1935?)

Sadeniemi, Matti (1910–1989)

Sadler, Victor (b.1937)

Sadnik, Linda (1910–1998)

Sadvakasov, G. S. (1929–1991)

Sæbø, Kjell-Johan (b.1956)

Safarewicz, Jan (1904–1992)

Safařík, Pavel Jozef (1795–1861)

Safir, Kenneth J. (b.1950)

Safronov, German Ivanovič (1924–
 1997)

Sag, Ivan A(ndrew, b.1949)

Sager, Naomi (b.1927)

Sagard (-Théodat), *frère* Gabriel,
 O.F.M. (Recollect, c.1600–1650)

Sagart, Laurent (b.1950)

Sagen, Trygve (1924–1977)

Sager, Juan Carlos (b.1929)K

Sager, Sven Frederik (b.1948)K

Sahagún, *Fray* Bernardino, O.F.M.
 (1499–1590)

Sahlgren, Jöran (1884–1971)S

Sahlstedt, Abraham (1716–1776)S

Sahlin, Gunvor (b.1905)

Said, Edward Wadie (*alias* William,
 1935–2003)

Said Ali Ida, Manuel (1861–1953)E

Sainéan, Lazare (*alias* Lazăr
 Şăineanu; *originally*: Eliezer
 Schein, 1859–1934)S

Sainliens, Claude de (*alias* Claudio a
 Sancto Vinculo, *alias* Claudius
 Hollyband, c.1540–1597)E

Saint-Cyran, *abbé* (17th cent.)

Saint-Gelais, Octavien de (1468–
 1502)

Saint-Hilaire, Jules Barthélémy
 (1805–1895)

Saint Isidore, *see* Isidore of Seville

Saint-Jorre, Danielle de (d.1997)

Saint-Martin, Antoine-Jean (1791–
 1832)

Saint-Martin, Louis Claude, *marquis* de (1743–1803)

Saint-Simon, Maximilien Henri, *marquis* de (1720–1799)

Saint-Quentin, Auguste de (d.1875)

Saint-Réal, César Vichard de (1639–1692)

Sainte-Beuve, Charles Augustin (1804–1869)

Saito, Hidesaburo (1866–1929)

Saito, Haruyuki (b.1953)K

Saito, Mamoru (b.1953)

Saito, Shizuka (1891–1970)

Sajavaara, Kari (b.1938)

Sajnovics, Janós, S.J. (1735–1785)E

Śākaṭāyana (6th cent. B.C.)S

Sakayan, Dora (b.1931)K

Saker, Alfred (1814–1880)

Sakkākī aš- (d.626/1229)

Šakun, Leū M. (d.1997)

Sala, Marius (c.1925–*post* 1997)

Salas, Pedro de, S.J. (1584–1664)

Salat, Johannes (1498–1561)

Salazar, Ambrosio de (1575?–*post* 1622)S

Salemann, Karl (1849–1916)

Salernitano, Masuccio (c.1410–1475)

Salesbury, William (c.1520–1584?)

Saleski, Reinhold Eugen(e) August (1890–1971)

Salevsky, Heidemarie (b.1944)K

Salisbury, Edward Elbridge (1814–1901)S

Salisbury, Stephen (1835–1905)

Sall, Andrew (1612–1682)

Salleras, Matias (c.1840–*post* 1885)S

Sallwürk, Ernst von (1839–1926)

Salmasius, Claudius (Saumaise, Claude, 1588–1653)

Salmon, Paul Bernard (1921–1997)

Salmon, Vivian G(ladis, b.1921)

Salmons, Joseph C(urtis, b.1956)

Salnikov, Nikolai (b.1932)K

Salter, Thomas (1548–1625)

Saltveit, Laurits (1913–1999)

Saltzmann, Philipp (d.1666)

Salum, Isaac Nicolau (1913–1993)

Salus, Peter H(enry, b.1938)

Salutati, Colucio (1331–1406)S

Salvá y Pérez, Vicente (1786–1849)S

Salvador, Gregorio (b.1927)

Salvador, Joseph (1793–1883)

Salvador, *Frei* Vicente do (*alias* Vicente Rodrigues Palha, 1564–1636)

Salvandy, Narcisse-Achille, *comte* de (1795–1856)

Salverda de Grave, Jean Jacques (1863–1947)

Salviati, Lionardo (1539–1589)S

Salvini, Anton Maria (1653–1729)S

Salvioni, Carlo (1858–1920)S

Salys, Antanas (1902–1972)S

Samaniego, Diego de, S.J. (1541–1626)

Samaragdus (9th cent. A.D.)

Samarin, William John (b.1926)

Samedo, Alvaro (fl.1654)

Sampson, Geoffrey (b.1945)

Sampson, Thomas (14th cent.)

Samson, *Abbot* of Bury St. Edmund (1135–1211)

Samuels, Michael Louis (b.1920)

Sanada, Shinji (b.1946)

San Augustín, Andrés de, O.F.M. (17th cent.)

San Augustín, Gasparo de, O.S.A. (1646–1724)

Sappok, Christian (b.1941)K
Saqueniza, Jacobo (anagram for
    Joaquín Cabezas, see there)
Sara, Solomon Ishu, S.J. (b.1930)
Śaraṇadeva (12th cent. A.D.)S
Sarauw, Christian (1865–1925)
Saravia, Adrian (1531–1613)
Sardou, Antoine-Léandre (1803–
    1894)
Sarles, Harvey (b.1933)
Sarmiento, Domingo Faustino
    (1811–1888)
Sarmiento, Martín, O.S.B. (1695–
    1771)
Sarmiento González, Ramón (b.1947)
Sarpi, Paolo (1552–1623)S
Sarrazin, Gregor (1857–1915)
Sartorius, Ioannes (alias Snijders,
    c.1500–1557)
Sartre, Jean-Paul (1905–1980)
Śarvavarman (4th cent. A.D.)S
Sasabe, Hideo (b.1926)
Sasaki, Tatsu (1904–1986)
Sasse, Hans-Jürgen (b.1943)K
Sasse, Werner (b.1941)K
Sassen, Albert (1921–1999)
Sassen, Ferdinand Léon Rudolphe
    (1894–1971)
Sassetti, Filippo (1540–1609)
Sathasivam, Arumugam (b.1926)
Sato, Charlene Junko (1951–1996)
Sato, Shuji (b.1938)
Sattler, Johann Rudolf (genannt
    Weissenburger, 1577–1628)
Šarṭūnī, Saᶜīd al- (1849?–1912)
Saturnio, Agostino (Lazaroneus,
    d.1533)
Satzinger, Helmut (b.1938)K
Sauer, August (1855–1926)

Sauer, Hans (b.1946)K
Sauer, Helmut (b.1929)K
Sauer, Lucia (b.1942)
Sauer, Walter (b.1942)K
Sauer, Wolfgang (b.1944)K
Saulcy, F. C. de (1807–1880)
Saumaise, Claude, see Salmasius
Šaumjan (Shaumyan), Sebastian
    Konstantinovič (b.1916)
Saunders, Ross (alias Dimitri R.,
    1938–2005)
Saur, Abraham (1545–1593)
Šaur, Vladimír (b.1938)
Sauseuil, Jean Nicolas Jouin de
    (fl.1783)
Saussure, Ferdinand (-Mongin) de
    (1857–1913)S, E
Saussure, Léopold de (1866–1925)
Saussure, René de (1868–1943)
Sauter, Roger (b.1943)K
Sauveur, Lambert (1826–1907)
Sauzé, Émile Blais de (1878–c.1950)
Sauvageot, Aurélien (1897–1988)
Savart, F. (1791–1841)
Savary, Claude Étienne (1750–1788)
Savigny, Friedrich Carl von (1779–
    1861)
Saville-Troike, Muriel R(enee,
    b.1936)
Savickij, Petr Nikolaevič (pseud. P.
    V. Logovikov and S. Lubinskij,
    1895–1968)
Sawaie, Mohammed (b.1941)
Sawashima, Masayuki (b.1927)
Sawr, Abraham (1545–1593)
Sawyer, Jesse O. (1918–1986)
Saxarnij, Leonid Vol'kovič (1934–
    1996)

Saxarov, Andrej Dmitrievič (1921–1989)

Šaxmatov, Aleksej Aleksandrovič (1864–1920)S

Šaxnarovič, Aleksandr Markovič (1944–2001)

Say, Jean Baptiste (1757–1832)

Sayce, *Rev.* Archibald H(enry, 1845–1933)E

Saz, Antonio, O.F.M. (17th cent.)

Sbarbi, José María (1834–1910)

Sbiera, Ion G. (1836–1916)

Scaglione, Aldo (Domenico, b.1925)

Scaliger, Joseph Justus (1540–1609)S,E

Scaliger, Julius Caesar (*pseud.* for Giulio Bordone, *dit* Scaligero, Giulio Cesare, 1484–1558)S, E

Ščaranskij, Anatolij Borisovič (b.1948)

Scaravelli, Luigi (1894–1967)S

Scargill, Mathew H. (d.1997)

Scarpa, Cristoforo (fl.1430–1450)

Scartazzini, Giovanni Andrea (1837–1901)

Scaurus, Quintus Terentius (first half of 2nd cent. A.D.)S

Ščepkin, V(iktor?) N(ikolaevič?) (1863–1920)

Ščerba, Lev Vladimirovič (1880–1944)S, E

Ščerbatskij, Fedor Ipolitovič (c.1946)

Scerbo, Francesco (1849–1927)

Schaank, Simon Hartwich (1861–1935)

Schaar, Johannes van der (1912–1984)

Schaarschmidt, Gunter (Herbert, b.1929)

Schabowska, Maria (1925–1995)

Schabram, Hans (b.1928)

Schach, Paul (1951–1998)

Schachermeyr, Fritz (1895–1987)

Schachter, Paul (Morris, b.1927)

Schack Rasmussen, Lone (1944–1996)

Schade, Benjamin (fl.1835)

Schade, Egon (b.1913)

Schade, Oskar (1826–1906)

Schächter, Josef (1901–19??)

Schädel, Bernhard (1878–1926)

Schaeder, Burkhard (b.1938)K

Schaeder, Hans Heinrich (1896–1957)

Schäfer, Jürgen (1933–1985)

Schäfer-Prieß, Barbara (b.1955)

Schaf(f)arik, Josef, *see* Šafařík, Pavel Josef

Schaffroth, Elmar (b.1958)

Schaffter, Albert (1823–1897)

Schall, Anton (b.1920)K

Schall, Hermann (1908–1986)

Schaller, Helmut (b.1940)K

Schane, Sanford A(lvin, b.1937)

Schanen, François (b.1938)K

Schank, Roger C(arl, b.1946)E

Scharf, Siegfried (b.1932)K

Scharfe, Hartmut (b.1930)

Scharnhorst, Jürgen (b.1929)K

Scharten, Carel (1878–1950)

Schasler, Max (Alexander Friedrich, 1819–1903)

Schatte, Christoph (b.1947)

Schatte, Czesława (b.1947)K

Schebesta, *Pater* Paul, SVD (1887–1967)

Schecker, Michael (b.1944)K

Scheel, Willy (1869–c.1908)

Scholes, Robert J. (b.1932)
Scholmeijer, Harrie (b.1960)
Scholtz, Christian (1697?–1771)
Scholvin, Robert (1850–1929)
Scholz, Friedrich (b.1928)K
Scholz, Heinrich (1884–1956)
Schomerus, Hilko Wiardo (1879–1945)
Schoolcraft, Henry Rowe (1793–1864)
Schooneveld, Cornelis Hendrik van (1921–2003)
Schooten, Frans van (1615–1660)
Schopenhauer, Arthur (1788–1860)
Schopf, Alfred (b.1922)K
Schoppe, Caspar, *see* Scioppius, Gaspar
Schorer, Christoph (1618–1671)
Schorr, Mojzesz (1874–1943)
Schorta, Andrea (1905–1990)K
Schorus, Henricus (2nd half of 16th cent.)
Schoterman, Jan Anthony (1948–1989)
Schott, Andreas (1552–1629)
Schott, Albert (fl.1940)
Schott, Wilhelm (1807–1889)
Schottel(ius), Justus Georg (1612–1676)S, E
Schrader, Eberhard (1836–1908)
Schrader, Friedrich Otto (1876–1961)
Schrader, Hans (1869–1948)
Schrader, Johannes (1721–1783)
Schrader, Otto (1855–1919)
Schramm, Gene (b.1929)
Schrant, Johannes Matthias (1783–1866)

Schreiber, Alois Wilhelm (1763–1841)
Schreiber, Georg (1882–1962)
Schreven, J(an?) van (1791–1859)
Schreyer, Rüdiger (b.1941)K
Schrieck(ius), Adriaan van (*alias* Scrieckius *or* van Schrieck [seigneur de] Rodornus, Adrianus, 1560–1621)S
Schrijnen, *Mgr.* Jozef (Karel Frans Hubert, 1869–1938)
Schroderus, Ericus (1608?–1639)
Schroderus, Ericus Joannes (1570–1647)
Schrodt, Richard (b.1948)K
Schröder, (Friedrich Wilhelm) Ernst (1841–1902)
Schröder, Carl (1802–1867)
Schröder, Konrad (b.1941)
Schröder, Edward (1858–1942)S
Schröder, Ernst (1841–1902)
Schröder, Franz Rolf (1893–1979)
Schröder, Hartmut (b.1954)K
Schröder, Jochen (b.1938)K
Schroeder, Johannes (1600–1664)
Schröder, Konrad (b.1941)K
Schroeder, Leopold von (1851–1920)
Schroeder, Manfred (b.1926)
Schroeder, Nicolaus Wilhelm (1721–1798)
Schröer, Arnold (Michael Martin, 1857–1935)
Schröpfer, Johann (d.1996)
Schubert, Klaus (b.1954)K
Schubinger, Maria (1902–1985?)
Schubring, Walther (1881–1969)
Schuchardt, Hugo (Ernst Mario, 1842–1927)S

Sédillot, Jean-Jacques-Emmanuel (1777–1832)
Sedulius Scottus (*alias* Sedulius de Liège, 9th cent. A.D.)S
Seebold, Elmar (b.1934)K
Seelbach, Dieter (b.1941)K
Seelen, Johann Heinrich von (1688–1762)
Seely, *Sir* John Robert (1834–1895)
Seetzen, Ulrich Jasper (1767–1811)
Seger, Johann (1582?–1637?)
Segner, Johann Andreas von (1704–1777)
Segond, Louis (1810–1885)
Segre, Cesare (b.1928)
Seguin, Pedro, O.S.B. (fl.1636)
Seguy, Jean (1914–1972)
Sehrt, Ernst Theodor (1911–1983)
Seibicke, Wilfried (b.1931)K
Seidel, Anna (1938–1991)
Seidel, August (1863–*post* 1941)
Seidel, Caspar (c.1700)
Seidel, Eugen (1906–1981)
Seidelmann, Christian Friedrich (fl.1724)
Seidenstücker, Johann Heinrich Philipp (1765–1849)
Seidl, Johann Gabriel (1804–1875)
Seidler, Herbert (1905–1983)
Seifert, Lester Wilhelm Julius ("Smoky", 1915–1996)
Seiffert, Leslie (1934–1990)K
Seiler, Hansjakob (b.1920)K
Seip, Didrik Arup (1884–1963)S
Šejn, Pavel Vasil'evič (1826–1900)
Sejong, *King* (1397–1450)
Sekereš, Stjepan (1912–1996)
Selbor, León (1836–1902)
Selden, John (1584–1654)

Seldeslachts, Herman (b.1959)
Seler, Eduard (Georg, 1849–1922)
Selfridge, Oliver G. (b.1926)
Selig, Maria (b.1959)
Seligman, Carl G. (1873–1940)
Selinker, Larry (b.1937)
Seliščev, Afanasij Matveevič (1886–1942)S
Selivestova, Olga N. (1934–2001)E
Selkirk, Elisabeth O. (b.1945)
Sells, Peter (b.1957)
Selmer, Ernst W. (1890–1971)
Selting, Margret (b.1955)K
Selz, Otto (1881–1943)
Šembera, Alois Vojtěch (1807–1882)
Semeleder, Friedrich (*alias* Federico, 1832–1901)
Semenjuk, Natalija (b.1925)K
Semkowicz, Władysław (1878–1949)
Semmedo, Alvarez (1585–1658)
Semon, Richard (1859–1918)
Sen(-Jasanoff), Sheila (b.1944)
Sen, Sukumar (1900–1992)E
Sénart, Émile (1847–1928)
Sendlmeier, Walter F. (b.1955)K
Seneca, Lucius (or Marcus) Annaeus ('the Elder', c.55 B.C.–40 A.D.)
Seneca, Lucius Annaeus ('the Younger', c.5 B.C.–65 A.D.)
Senn, Alfred (1899–1978)S
Senn, Fritz (b.1928)
Sennett, Richard (b.1943)
Sentmenat, *marqués* de (1697–1762)
Seppänen, Lauri (b.1924)K
Sequeira, Inácio de, S.J. (1581–1644)
Sequoyah (*alias* George Gist, 1760–1843)
Seraphim, Peter Heinz (1902–1998?)
Serbat, Guy (1918–2001)

Spiegelberg, Wiilhelm (1870–1930)
Spieghel, Hendrik Laurenszoon
(1549–1612)
Spi(e)ker, Samuel Heinrich (1786–
1858)
Spier, Leslie (1893–1961)
Spies, Heinrich (1873–1962)
Spiewok, Wolfgang (b.1929)K
Spillner, Bernd (b.1941)K
Spina, Franz (1868–1938)
Spinden, Herbert Joseph (1879–
1967)
Spindler, George Dearborn (b.1920)
Spinoza, Baruch (*alias* Benedict(us)
de, 1632–1677)
Spira, Theodor (1885–1961)
Spiridovič, Efim (1891–1935)
Spitaler, Anton (b.1910)
Spitta, Wilhelm (1853–1883)
Spitzbardt, Harry (b.1926)K
Spitzer, Leo (1887–1960)S, E
Spitzner, Ernst Franz Heinrich
(1787–1841)
Splett, Jochen (b.1938)K
Spolsky, Bernard (b.1932)
Sponcius Provincialis (13th cent.
A.D.)
Spore, Palle (1931–2002)
Sporschil, Johann (1800–1863)
Sportiche, Dominique (b.1952)
Spranger, Eduard (1882–1953)
Sprat, Thomas (1635–1713)
Sprenger, Aloys (1813–1893)
Sprincl, Jan (1917–1989)
Springer, Otto (1905–1991)S
Spurzheim, Johann Gaspar (1776–
1832)
Šrámek, Rudolf (b.1933)

Sreznevskij, Izmail Ivanovič (1812–
1880)S
Śridhara (fl. 10th cent.)
Srivastava, Ravindra Nath (1936–
1992)
Staal, Fritz (*alias* Johan Frederik,
b.1930)
Stabler, Edward (b.1955)
Stache-Rosen, Valentina (1925–
1980)
Stachowitz, Rolf Armin (b.1934)
Stachowski, Stanisław (b.1929)
Stachurski, Edward (b.1942)
Stackhouse, Thomas (1677–1752)
Staden (von Homberg), Hans
(c.1525–1576)
Staël, Madame de (*alias* Anne Louise
Germaine Necker, *baronne* de
Holstein, 1766–1817)
Stählin, Wilhelm (1883–1975)
Staevanović, Mihailo (1903–1991)
Stahl, Georg Ernst (1660–1734)
Ståhl, Harry (1905–1991)
Stahl, Heinrich (Henricus, c.1600–
1657)
Ståhle, Carl Ivar (1913–1980)S
Stalder, Franz Josef (1757–1833)
Stalder, Kurt (1914-1996)
Stalin, Josef (*alias* Iosiv Vissariono-
vič Dzugasvili, 1879–1953)
Stamenov, Maxim I(van, b.1952)
Stammerjohann, Harro (b.1938)K
Stammler, Gerhard (1898–1977)
Stammler, Wolfgang (1886–1965)
Standop, Ewald (b.1921)
Stang, Christian Schweigaard (1900–
1977)S, E
Stanislav, Ján (1904–1977)S
Stankiewicz, Edward (b.1920)

Stendal (*alias* Marie Henri Beyle, 1783–1842)
Stender, Gotthard Friedrich (1714–1796)
Stengel, Edmund (1845–1935)
Stenton, *Sir* Frank Merry (1880–1967)
Stenzler, Adolf Friedrich (1807–1887)
Stepanov, Georgij Vladimimirovič (1919–1986)
Stensen, Niels (*alias* Nicolaus Steno, 1638–1686)
Stenton, *Sir* Frank (1880–1967)
Stepanova, María D. (1899–1990)
Stephan, Fredrick F. (1903–1971)
Stephani, Heinrich (1761–1850)
Stephanius, Stephanus Johannis (1599–1650)
Stephany, Ursula (b.1937)K
Stephanus (4th–5th cent. A.D.)
Stephanus of Byzantium (7th cent. A.D.)
Stephanus, Henricus, *see* Estienne, Henri
Stephanus, Robertus, *see* Estienne, Robert
Stephens, George (1813–1895)
Stephens (*or* Stevens), Thomas, S.J. (*alias* Esteuão, 1549?–1619)
Steriade, Donca (b. c.1950)
Štern, Alla Solomonova (1941–1995)
Stern, Clara (née Joseephy, 1877–1948)
Stern, H[ans] [Heinrich] ("David", 1913–1987)
Stern, Joseph Peter Maria (1920–1991)
Stern, (Nils) Gustaf (1882–1948)

Stern, (Louis) William (1871–1938)
Stern, Ludwig Christian (1846–1911)
Stern, Salomon Gottlieb (d.1883)
Sternemann, Reinhard (b.1930)K
Stetson, Raymond Herbert (1872–1950)
Stetter, Christian (b.1943)K
Steettler, Eduard (1880–1940)
Steube, Anita (b.1939)K
Steudel, Friedrich (1779–1837)
Steuvechius, Godescalcus (*alias* Gottschalk Steewech, c.1556–c.1599)
Stevanović, Mihajlo (1903–1991)
Stevens, André (1913–2001)
Stevens, Joan (1918–1986)
Stevens, Kenneth N(oble, b.1924)
Stevens, Stanley Smith (1906–1973)
Stevenson, Charles Leslie (1908–19??)
Stevenson, James (d.1888)
Stevenson, Rev. John, D.D. (1798–1858)
Stevenson, Matilda Coxe Evans (1849–1915)
Stevenson, William Barron (b. c.1885–d. *post* 1945)
Stevin, Simon (1548–1620)
Steward, Julian H(aynes, 1902–1972)
Stewart, Alexander (1764–1821)
Stewart, Dugald (1753–1828)
Stewart, George R. (1895–1980)
Stewart, J. A. (d.1949)
Stewart, John M. (b.1926)
Stewart, William A. (1930–2002)
Stibitz, George Robert (b.1904)
Stickel, Gustav (1805–1897)
Stieber, Zdzisław (1903–1980)
Stiebitz, Ferdinand (1894–1961)

T.

Ṯa ᶜālibī, Abū Manṣūr ᶜAbd al-Malik ibn Muḥammad at- (c.350/960–429/1078)S

Tabakowska, Irena (1908–1990)

Taber, Charles Russell (b.1928)

Tachard, Guy (c.1650–1712)

Tachon, Fr. Alphonse (1847–1928)

Tadadjeu, Maurice (b.1950),E

Tacitus, Publius *or* Gaius Cornelius (c. 55–117 A.D.)

Tafazzoli, Ahmad (1937–1997)

Taffel, Abram (1906–1995)

Taffin, Pierre F. (18th cent.)

Tagamlicka, Galina (b.1926)

Tagliavini, Carlo (1903–1982)S, E

Tagore, Rabindranath (1861–1941)

Täntzer, Johann (c.1633–1690)

Ṭahṭāwī, Rifāᶜa Rāfi' Bek aṭ- (1801–1873)S

Taillander, Saint-René (1817–1879)

Taine, Hippolyte-Adolphe (1828–1893)

Tajima, Matsuji (b.1942)

Takács, Etel (1921–1992)

Takahashi, Yumiko (b.1951)K

Takahashi, Terukazu (b.1944)K

Takamiya, Toshiyuki (b.1944)

Takenobu, Yoshitaro (1863–1930)

Taᶜlab, Abū l-ᶜAbbās Aḥmad Ibn Yaḥyā (200/815–291/904)S

Talavera, Hernando de (1428–1507)

Talbert, Ferdinand (1823–1894)

Tallement, Paul (1642–1712)

Talleyrand-Périgord, Charles-Maurice de (1754–1838)

Tallqvist, K. L. (d.1949)

Talmon, Rafael (b.1936?)

Talvj (pseud. *Theresa Albertina Luise von Jacob*-Robinson, 1797–1870)

Tam, Jacob b. Meir (c.1100–1171)

Tamara, Francisco, *see* Thamara, Francisco

Tamás, Lajos (1904–1984)S

Tamayo y Baus, Manuel (1829–1898)

Tamba(-Mecz), Irène (b.1940)

Tambiah, Stanley J. (b.1929)

Tamony, Peter (19??–1985)

Tamura, Suzuko (b.1934)

Tanaka, Hiroyuki (b.1931)K

Tang, Lan (1900–1979)S

Tannen, Deborah (orig. Tannenbaum, b.1945)E

Tanner, Thomas (1674–1735)

Tantaquidgeon, Gladys (1899–2005[*sic*])

Tany, Thomas (fl.1649–1655)

Tanzer, Helen H. (1876–*post* 1937)

Tapia y Zenteño, Carlos de, *bachiller* (fl.1753–1767)

Tappolet, Ernst (1870–1939)

Taraldsen, Knut Tarald (b.1948)

Taranovsky, Kiril (1911–1993)

Tarbell, Frank Bigelow (1853–1920)

Tarbell, Horace Sumner (1838–1904)

Tarde, (Jean) Gabriel (de, 1843–1904)

Tardivel, Jules-Paul (1851–1905)

Tareporewala, I. G. (1884–1956)

Tarnowska, Wanda (1906–1990)

Tarski, Alfred (1902–1983)E

Tarvainen, Kalevi (1932–1993)

Tase, Pano (1903–1978)
Taszycki, Witold (1898–1978)S
Tatarkiewicz, Władysław (1886–
1980)
Tatian (2nd cent. A.D.)
Tatiščev, Vasilij Nikitič (1686–1750)
Tatlock, John Strong Perry (1876–
1948)
Tatwine of Mercia (d.734 A.D.)S
Tatzreiter, Herbert (b.1938)
Taube, Mortimer (1910–1965)
Tauler, Johannes (c.1300–1361)
Tauli, Valter (1907–1986)
Tauriscus (2nd cent. B.C.)
Tauste, *Frei* Francisco de, O.F.M.
cap. (d.1698)
Taverner, Richard (1505–1575)
Tavernier-Vereecker, Cecile (1915–
2000)
Tavoni, Mirko (b.1949)
Tavora, Francisco de (fl.1566)
Tax, Sol (b.1907)
Taylor, Archer (1890–1973)
Taylor, Bayard (1825–1878)
Taylor, Charles Mundy (1890–19??)
Taylor, Daniel J(ennings, b.1941)
Taylor, Douglas (1901–1979)
Taylor, Isaac, Jr. (1829–1901)
Taylor, *bishop* Jeremy (1613–1667)
Taylor, Orlando L. (b.1937)
Taylor, Talbot J. ("Tolly", b.1952)
Taylor, William (1765–1836)
Taszycki, Witold (1898–1979)
Tebaldus (Theobaldus, fl. 10th or
11th cent.)S
Techmer, Friedrich (Heinrich
Herrmann, 1843–1891)
Técikar, Cuvámináta, *see* Técikar
Cuvámináta

Técikar, Vaittiyanáta, *see* Vaittiyanáta
Técikar
Tedesco, Paul (Maximilian, 1898–
1980)
Tedlock, Dennis (b.1939)
Teepe, Paul (1924–1989)
Teeter, Karl V(an Duyn,1929–2007)
Tegnér, Esaias (Henrik Vilhelm,
1843–1928)
Teichmeyer, Hermann Friedrich
(1680–1746)
Teit, James A. (1864–1922)
Teixeira, Bento (1545–1618)
Teixeira de Castilho, Ataliba (b.1937)
Tejeda, Jerónimo (Hierosme) de
(1581–*post*-1629)
Tejnor, Antonín (1923–1997)
Tekavčić, Pavao (b.1930)
Telegdi, Zsigmond (1910–1996)
Telesio, Bernardino (1509–1588)
Tell, Julien (1807–*post* 1874)
Tellier, André René (b.1924)
Téma, Bedřich (b.1913)
Temesi, Mihály (1914–1988)
Temple, *Sir* Richard Carnac, 2nd
baronet (1850–1931)
ten Kate (Hermansz.), Lambert
(1674–1731)
Téné, David (1922–1997)
Teng, Ssu Yu (b.1906)
Tengstrand, Erik (1898–1984)
Tentzel, Wilhelm Ernst (1659–1707)
Teodorov-Balan, Aleksandăr
Stojanov (1859–1959)S
Terasawa, Yoshio (b.1928)
Terence (= Publius Terentius Afer,
c.190–159 B.C.)
Terentianus Maurus (late 2nd cent.
A.D.)

Terentianus Scaurus (early 2nd cent. A.D.)

Tereščenko, Natalija (1908–1987)

Termayer, Raimondo Maria de (1738–17??)

Ternes, Elmar (b.1941)K

Terreros y Pando, Esteban de, S.J. (1707–1782)

Teruo, Hirayama (b.1909)

Terracher, Adolphe Louis (1881–1955)

Terracini, (Aron[ne]) Benvenuto (1886–1968)S, E

Terreos y Pando, Esteban (1707–1782)

Terrien de la Couperie, Albert (1845–1895)

Terrien-Poncel, Albert (1819–1899)

Terry, Robert R. (b.1934)

Teruel, Luis de, S.J. (d.1670)

Teruo, Hirayama (b.1909)

Tesauro, Emanuele, S.J. (1592–1675)S

Tesnière, Lucien (Valérius, 1893–1954)S, E

Tessmann, Günter (1884–*post* 1969)

Tetens, Johann Nikolaus (1737–1807)

Tetzlaff, Gerhard (b.1923)

Tetzner, Franz Oskar (1863–1919)

Teubner, Benedictus Gotthelf (1784–1856)

Teuchert, Hermann (1880–1972)S

Teutleben, Kaspar von (1567–1629)

Tevenar, Gerhard von (1912–1943)

Tevfik Bey, *see* Esenç, Tevfik

Te Winkel, Jan (1847–1927)

Texeda, Jerónimo de (1581–*post* 1629)

Teyssier, Jacques (1926–1973)S

Teyssier, Paul (1915–2002)

Teza, Emilio (1831–1912)

Thalbitzer, William (Karl, 1873–1958)

Tham, Karl Ignaz (*alias* Václav, 1763–1816)

Thámara, *Bachiller* Francisco (mid-16th cent.)S

Thausing, Moritz (1838–1884)

Thelwall, John (1764–1834)E

Themistius (4th cent. A.D.)

Theobaldus, *see* Tebaldus

Theodektes (c.380–c.340 B.C.)

Theodore (of) Gaza (c.1400–c.1475)

Theodoros Prodromus (c.1098–1156/58)

Theodosius Alexandrinus (Greek: Theodósios, 346?–395 A.D.)S

Theodosius, *see* Macrobius, Ambrosius Theodosius

Theodulf of Orleans (c.800 A.D.)

Theon, Aelius (Gk. Aillos Théōn, first cent. A.D.)S

Theophrastus (c.372–287 B.C.)

Theophrastus ('of Eresus', c.371–286 B.C.)

Thévenot, Jean (1633–1665)

Thevet, *Frei* André, O.F.M. (*alias* Andreas, 1502–1590)

Thibaut, Georg Friedrich Wilhelm (1848–1914)

Thiébault, Dieudonné (1733–1807)

Thiedemann, Dietrich (1748–1803)

Thiele, (Friedrich Karl) Johannes (1865–1918?)

Thiele, Johannes (b.1935)K

Thiele, Wolfgang (b.1942)K

Thieme, Paul (1905–2001)

Thiemer-Sachse, Ursula (b.1941)
Thierfelder, Franz (1896–1962)
Thierry, Amédée-Simon Dominique
   (1797–1873)
Thierry of Chartres (c.1100–
   c.1157)S
Thierry, Guichard (fl.1610)
Thiersch, Craig (b.1944)
Thiersch, Friedrich Wilhelm von
   (1784–1860)
Thode, Henry (1857–1920)
Thomas à Kempis (*alias* Thomas
   Hemerken, c.1379–1471)
Thomas Aquinas, St. ('Doctor
   angelicus', c.1221–1274)S
Thomas Bradwardine (1295?–1349)S
Thomas Maulfelt (Thomas Anglicus,
   14th cent. A.D.)
Thomas of Erfurt (fl.1300)S, E
Thomas, Alex (1895–1971)
Thomas, Antoine (1851–1935)
Thomas, Calvin (1854–1910)
Thomas, Cyrus (1825–1910)
Thomas, David D. (b.1930)
Thomas, Dorothy Swaine (1899–
   1977)
Thomas, Homer (Leonard, b.1913)
Thomas, Jakob Ludwig (1752–1796)
Thomas, Jacqueline (b.1930)
Thomas, John Jacob (1840–1889)E
Thomas, Lawrence L(eslie, b.1924)
Thomas, Robert (fl.1894–1896)
Thomas, Werner (b.1923)K
Thomas, William Clifford Elvet
   (1905–1994)
Thomas, William I. (1863–1947)
Thomasius, Christian (1655–1728)
Thomason, Richmond H(unt, b.1939)

Thomason, Sarah Grey ("Sally",
   b.1940?)
Thomasius, Christian (1655–1728)
Thomassin, Louis (1619–1695)
Thomopoulos, Giankos A. (1911–
   1988)
Thompson, John George (fl.1859)
Thompson, Laura Maud (b.1905)
Thompson, Laurence C(assius, 1926–
   1983)E
Thompson, Laurence Roger (1906–
   1973)
Thompson, Sandra Annear (b.1942)
Thompson, Stith (1885–1976)
Thoms, Dorothy Swaine (1900–
   1977)
Thomsen, Vilhelm (Ludvig Peter,
   1842–1927)S, E
Thomson, Cyrus (d.1910)
Thomson, James (1700–1748)
Thomson, Joseph (1858–1895)
Thomson, Thomas (1773–1852)
Thorbecke, Heinrich (1837–1890)
Thordarson, Olafr (hvitaskald,
   c.1212–1259)
Thorellier d'Olivet, *abbé* Pierre
   Joseph (1682–1768)
Thor Helle, Anton (1683–1748)
Thorie, John (*alias* Thorius, fl.1590–
   1611)
Thorkelin, Grimur Jónsson (1752–
   1829)
Thorndike, Ashley Horace (1871–
   1933)
Thorndike, Edward Lee (1874–1949)
Thorne, Barrie (b.1942)
Thorne, James Peter (1933–1988)
Thornton, William (1759–1828)
Thorowgood, Thomas (1595?–1669)

Tristram, Luise Charlotte Hildegard (b.1941)K
Trithemius, Johannes (*alias* von Trittenheim, 1462–1516)
Trithen, Franz Heinrich ("Frederick", 1820–1854)
Trivikramadeva (13th cent.)S
Trivolis, Michele, *see* Maxim the Greek
Trivunac, Miloš (1876–1944)
Trnka, Bohumil (1895–1984)S, E
Troc, Michał Abraham (*alias* Michael Abraham Trotz; c.1689–1769)
Trocin, Dumitrv (1936–1986)
Trömel-Plötz, Senta (b.1939)K
Trofimov, M. V. (d.1948)
Trofimovyč, Kostjantyn Kostjantynovyč (1923–1993)
Troickij, Matvej Mixajlovič (1835–1889)
Troike, Rudolph C(harles, b.1933)
Trojanskij, Petr Petrovič Smirnov-(1894–1950)
Trojański, Jan Kajetan (1796–1850)
Trombetti, Alfredo (1866–1929)S
Tronskij, Iosif M. (1897–1970)
Trost, Klaus (b.1934)K
Trost, Pavel (1907–1987)
Trotz, Michael Abraham, *see* Troc, Michał Abraham
Trotzendorf, Valentin (*alias* Trocedorfius, 1490–1556)
Troxymenko, Mykola F. (1899–1937)
Trubacev, Oleg Nikolaevič (1930–2002)
Trubert, Pierre (1793–1879)
Trubetzkoy (Trubeckoj), Nikolaj S(ergeevič, *Prince*, 1890–1938)S, E

Trubetzkoy, Vladimir S(ergeevič, *Prince*, 1891–1937)
Trübner, Karl J. (1846–1907)
Trübner, Nikolaus (later: Nicholas, 1817–1888)
Trudeau, Danielle (b.1951)
Trudgill, Peter J(ohn, b.1943)
Trudinger, Ronald M. (1918–2002)
Trumbull, James Hammond (1821–1897)
Trumpp, Ernst (1828–1885)
Trusler, *Rev.* John (1735–1820)
Truszkowski, Witold (1912–1994)
Tryphon of Alexandria (c.60-10 B.C.)S
Ts'ai, Yuan-P'ei (1867–1940)
Tschauder, Gerhard (b.1947)K
Tscherning(ius), Andreas (1611–1659)
Tschischka, Franz (1786–1855)
Tschudi, Aegidiu (1505–1572)
Tschudi, Johann Jacob von (fl.1846–1884)
Tsen, Qixiang (1903–1989)
Tsuda, Aoi (b.1944)
Tsuda, Umeko (1864–1929)
Tsukahara, Tetsuo (1912–1997)
Tsurumine Bôshin (1788–1859)
Tsurumine Shigenobu (1786–1859)
Tsuzaki, Stanley M(amoru, 1930–1991)S
Tuaillon, Gaston (b.1921)
Tucker, Allen B(rown), Jr. (b.1942)
Tucker, Archibald Norman (1904–1980)E
Tucker, G. Richard (b.1942)
Tucker, Thoma George (1859–1946)
Tudoran, Romulus (1918–1993)
Tuinman, Carolus (1659–1728)

U.

Ubrjatova, Elizaveta Ivanova (1907–1990)E

Uc Faidit (fl.1210/40)S

Uchita, Sataro (b.1926)K

Udall, John (c.1560–1592)

Udall, Nicholas (1505–1556)

Udalrich (= Ulrich of Augsburg, 890–973 A.D.)

Udayana (c.1000 A.D.)S

Udino, Antonio, *see* Oudin, Ant(h)oine

Udull, John (c.1560–1592)

Ueda, Kazutoshi (1867–1937)E

Ueberweg, Friedrich (1826–1871)

Ülkü, Vural (b.1938)K

Ünal, Ahmet (b.1943)K

Uexküll, Jakob von (1864–1944)

Uffenbach, Zacharias Conrad von (1683–1734)

Ulfilas (= Wulfila, *bishop* of the Goths, c.311–383 A.D.)

Ughelli, Ferdinando (1594–1670)

Uguccione da Pisa (Hugutio de Pisa, 1130/40–1210)S

Uhland, Ludwig (1787–1862)

Uhlár, Vlado (1912–1996)

Uhle, Max (1856–1944)

Uhlenbeck, C(hristiaan) C(ornelis, 1866–1951)S

Uhlenbeck, Eugenius M(arius, "Bob", 1913–2003)

ᶜUkbarī, Abū l-Baqā ᶜAbdallāh ibn Ḥusayn, al- (538/1143–616/1219)S

Uhlig, Gustav (1838–1914)

Uhlisch, Gerda (b.1937)K

Uitti, Karl D(avid, b.1933)

Ujfalvy, Charles de (1842–1904)

Ułaszyn, Henryk Kazimierz (1874–1956)

Ulrich, Rolf (b.1920)K

Ulbricht, Elfriede (1910–1984)

Uldall, Elizabeth T(heodora "Betsy", *née* Anderson, 1913–2004)

Uldall, Hans Jørgen ("Jan", 1907–1957)S, E

Ulfilas (*or* Wulfila), Bishop of the Goths (c.311–381?)E

Ul'janov, G. K. (1859–1912)

Ullendorff, Edward (b.1920)E

Ullmann, Stephen (*alias* István, 1914–1976)

Ulloa, Antonio de (1716–1795)

Ulqinaku, Hafiz Ali (1855–1913)

Ulrich, Jakob (1856–1906)

Ulrich, Winfried (b.1941)K

Ulrix, Eugène (1876–1936)

Uluxarov, Igor' Stefanovič (b.1935)

Ulvydas, Kazys (1910–1996)

Umeda, Noriko (b.1933)

Umiker(-Sebeok), Donna Jean (b.1946)

Umlenski, Ivan Vasilev (1917–1992)

Unbegaun, Boris Ottokar (1898–1973)

Unckel, Kurt, *see* Nimuendajú, Curt

Underhill, Ruth (1884–1984)

Ungeheuer, Gerold (1930–1982)S

Unger, Carl Richard (1817–1897)

Unger, Heinz (b.1914)

Ungnad, Artur (1879–1947)

Univere, Aili (1901–1994)

Uno, Yoshikata (b.1919)

V.

Vāaspati Miśra (fl. between 850–980 A.D.)S
Văcărescu, Ienăchtiţă (1740–1799)
Vachek, Josef (1909–1996)E
Vachros, Igor´(1917–1996)
Vaerman, Jan (1653–??)
Värri Haarmann, Anna-Liisa (1938–1985)
Váez, Domingo Augustín, S.J. (c.1565)
Vahlen, Johannes (1830–1911)
Vahylevyč, Ivan (1811–1866)
Vaihinger, Hans (1852–1933)
Vailati, Giovanni (1863–1909)S
Vaillant, André (1890–1977)S
Vaimberg, Solomon (1930–2000)
Vairasse d'Allais, Denis (c.1630–1682)
Váiyapuri Pillai, S. (1891–1956)
Vaittiyanáta Técikar (17th cent. A.D.)
Vajda, Edward J. (b.1958)
Vajda, Georges (1908–*post* 1980)
Vajs, *Mgr.* Josef (b. c.1888–*post* 1948)
Vakk, Feliks (1930–1987)
Valaczkai, László (b.1939K
Valade, Y(ves) L(éonard) Rémi (1809–1890)
Val Alvaro, Josee Francisco (b.1952)
Val Buena, Manuel (d.1821)
Valckenaer, Lodewijk Caspar (1715–1785)
Valdastri, Idelfonso (1762–1818)S

Valdés, Juan de (c.1495–1541)
Valdivia, Luis de, S.J. (1561–1642)
Valdman, Albert (b.1931)
Vale, Leonardo do, S.J. (1534–1591)
Vale, Salvador, S.J. (1628–1676)
Valence, Pierre (fl.1515–1555)
Valente, Christóvão, S.J. (1566–1627)
Valentin, Paul (b.1934)K
Valentine, Lisa Philips (b.1954)
Valera, Blas, S.J. (1551–1597)
Valera, Cipriano de (1532?–1625)
Valera, Juan (1824–1905)
Valeriano, Piero (1499–1588)
Valerius ab Auduater, Cornelius (*alias* Woutersz, Cornelis, 1512–1578)
Valerius Probus, Marcus (1st cent. A.D.)
Valéry, Paul (1871–1945)
Valett, Johann Jakob Meno (1758–1850)
Valfells, Sigríður (1938–1998)
Valiente, José Hipólito (José Ipólito Baliente, fl.1731)
Valignano, Alessandro, S.J. (1539–1606)
Valin, Roch (b.1918)
Valjavec, Matija K. (1831–1897)
Valkhoff, Marius François (1905–1980)E
Valla, Laurentius (*alias* Lorenzo della Valle, 1405–1457)S
Valladares Nuñez, Marcial (1823–1903)
Vallancey, Charles (1721–1812)
Vallange, ? de (fl.1719–1730)
Vallart, *abbé* Joseph (1698–1781)
Valle, José del (b.1964)

Velius Longus (early 2nd cent. A.D.)S

Velleman, Barry L(eonard, b.1946)

Velloso, *Frei* José Mariano da Conceição (1742–1811)

Velo, Giambattista (1752–1819)

Veloso, Xavier José Mariano da Conceição (1742–1811)

Velten, Harry de Veltheyme (1897–1967?)

Ven'aminov, Ivan Evsejevič (since 1977: Saint Innokenti,1797–1867)S

Venator Anglicus, Johannes (*alias* John Hunt(e)man, fl.1373–1414)

Vendryes, Joseph (Jean Baptiste Marie, 1875–1960)S

Venegas del Busto, Alejo (1493–*post* 1572)

Venelin, Jurij (1802–1839)

Veneroni, Giovanni di (*alias* Jean Vigneron, 1642–1700/1708)

Venezky, Richard Lawrence (b.1938)

Vengerov, Semen Afanas'evič (1855–1920)

Venier, Victor-Augustin (1769–1845)

Venn, John (1843–1923)

Vennemann (*genannt* Nierfeld), Theo (b.1937)K

Ventris, Michael (George Francis, 1922–1956)E

Venzky (Venski, Venzke), Georg (1704–1757)

Vera, Fernando de (d.1638)

Vera Zúñiga y Figueroa, Juan Antonio (1588–1658)

Veras, Gonçalo de, S.J. (1629–1686)

Verbeck, Guido Herman Fridolin (1830–1898)

Verbickaja, Ludmilla Alekseeva (*née* Bubnova, b.1936)

Verburg, Pieter Adrianus (1905–1989)

Vercoullie, Jozef (1857–1937)S

Verdeyen, René (d.1949)

Verdier, Roger (1899–1995)

Verduga, Andrés (d.1656)

Ver(r)epaeus, Simon (*alias* Vereept, 1522–1598)

Verenič, Vjačeslav L. (1924–1999)

Vergilius, *see* Virgil

Vergnaud, Jean-Roger (b.1947)

Vergote, Jozef (1910–1992)

Verhaar, Johannes Wilhelmus Maria ("John", 1925–2001)

Verheijen, Jilis A J., SVD (1908–1997)

Verlato, Micaela (b.1955)

Vermouzek, Rotislav (1911–1993)

Vernadskij, Vladimir Ivanovič (1863–1945)

Vernant, Jean-Pierre (1914-2007)

Verner, Karl (Adolf, 1846–1896)S

Verney, Luís Antonio (1713–1792)

Vernon, Edward Johnston (1814?–1848)

Veron, Jean (d.1563)

Veronese, Guarino (1374–1460)

Verrac, Monique (b.1947)

Verrier, Paul (fl.1909)

Verrius Flaccus, Marcus (c.50 B.C.–c.25 A.D.)S

Verseghy, Ferenc (1757–1822)

Versor, Johannes (c.1410–1485)

Versteegh, Kees (*alias* Cornelis Maria Henricus, b.1947)

Versteeghan, Richard (Rowlands, c.1565–1620)

Vert, Wilhelmus (*alias* Weert or Zenderus, late 15th cent.)
Vértes, András (1911–1997)
Vértes, Edit (1919–2002)
Vervaetermeulen, Antoon (1870–1949)
Verwer, Adriaen ("Anonymus Batavus", 1654–1717)
Verwey, Albert (1865–1937)
Verwijs, Eelco (1830–1880)
Verxrats'kyj, Ivan Hryhor'evyč (1846–1919)
Vescu, Victor (1928–1991)
Vesdin, Filip (*alias* Philipp Wesdin), *see* Paulinus a Bartholomaeo
Veselovskij, Aleksandr Nikolaevič (1838–1906)
Veselovskij, Aleksej Nikola'evič (1843–1918)
Vesikansa, Jouko (1915–1987)
Veske, Mixail P. (1843–1910)
Veski, Johannes V. (1874–19??)
Vetancourt, *Frei* Augustín de, O.F.M. (1620–1700)
Vetter, Emil (1878–1963)
Vetter, Ferdinand (1847–1924)
Vetter, Theodor (1853–1922)
Vettori, Pietro (*alias* Ptrus Victorius, 1499–1585)
Vetuxiv, Oleksa (1869–1941)
Vetvickij, V. G. (1924–1999)
Veyne, Paul (1930–1992)
Veyrenc, Charles Jacques (1925–1985)
Veysière de la Croze, Maturin (1661–1739)
Vhael, Barthold (*alias* Pärttyli, 1667–1723)

Viana, Aniceto dos Reis Gonçalves, *see* Gonçalves Viana, Aniceto dos Reis
Viana, Gonçalves (d.1939?)
Viano, Carlo Augusto
Vianu, Tudor (1897–1964)
Vicente, Gil (1465?–1536)
Vicente, *archbishop* Lourenço (d.1397)
Vickroy, Thomas Rhys (1833–*post* 1895)
Vico, Domingo de, O.P. (d.1555)
Vico, Giambattista (Giovanni Battista, 1668–1744)S
Victorinus, (Gaius) Marius (3rd–4th cent. A.D.)
Victorinus Maxim(inian)us (6th cent. A.D.?)S
Vicq d'Azyr, Félix (1748–1794)
Vicuña Mackenna, Benjamin (1831–1886)
Vidal de Besalú, Raimon (early 13th cent.)
Vidales, Luis, O.F.M. (fl.1644–1648)
Vidigal, José (1674–1748)
Vidman, Ladislav (1924–1989)
Vidoeski, Božidar (1920–1998)
Vidos, Benedek Elemér (1902–1989)
Vidossi, Giuseppe (1878–19??)
Vidović, Radovan (1924–1994)
Vidović-Muha, Ada (b.1940)
Viegas, Antonio, S.J. (d.1729)
Viegas, Manuel, S.J. (1533–1608)
Viehoff, Heinrich (1804–1886)
Viehweg, (Hans) Friedrich (1761–1835)
Viehweger, Dieter (1936–1991)
Viel, Michel (b.1946)

Viel, Nicholas, O.F.M. (Recollect, d.1625)

Viera, Antônio, S.J. (1608–1697)

Viereck, Wolfgang (b.1937)K

Viëta, François (alias Viete, 1540–1603)

Viëtor, Karl (1892–1951)

Viëtor, Wilhelm (1850–1918)S, E

Vietze, Hans-Peter (b,1939)K

Vigfússon, Guðbrandur (1827–1889)

Vignal, Pierre (fl.1592–1640)

Vigny, Alfred de (1797–1863)

Vigón, Branlio (1849–1914)

Viires, Helmi (1919–1984)

Viitso, Tiit-Rein (b.1928)

Vijvere, Gerard van den, see Vivre, Gérart de

Vikár, Béla (1859–1945)

Vilāns, Otomārs (1911–1987)

Vilemarqué, Théodore-Claude-Henri Hersat, vicomte de (1815–1895)

Villalón, Cristóbal de ("el Licenciado", c.1510–1562)S

Villalpando, Fray Luis de (d.1552)

Villanova, Francisco Alberti di (1733–1801)

Villanueva, Joaquín Lorenzo (1757–1837)

Villar, Juan, S.J. (1596–1660)S

Villareal, Federico (1850–1923)

Villedieu, Alexandre, see Alexandre de Villedieux

Villemain, Abel François (1790–1870)

Villena, Enrique de (1384–1434)

Villers, Charles (1756–1815)

Villotte, Jacques (d.1743)

Vin, Adriaan de (1916–1994)

Vinaver, Eugène (1899–1979)

Vinay, Jean-Paul (1910–1999)

Viñaza, Conde de la (1862–1933), see Muñoz y Manzano, Cipriano

Vincent Ferrer (c.1350–1419)

Vince, Zlatko (1922–1994)

Vincent of Beauvais (1190–c.1264)

Vincent, Nigel (b.1947)

Vincenz, André (alias Andrzej,) de b.1922)K

Vinet, Alexandre (1797–1847)

Vinja, Vojmir (b.1921)

Vinnikov, Isaak Natanovič (1897–1973)

Vinogradov, Viktor Vladimirovič (1895–1969)S

Vinokur, Grigorij Osipovič (1896–1947)S

Vinokur, Tat'jana (1924–1992)

Vinson, (Élie Honoré) Julien (1843–1926)S

Vintr, Josef (b.1938)K

Vio, Tommaso Cajetan de (1469–1534)

Viqueira, Juan Vicente (1886–1924)

Víracóliyam (11th cent. A.D.)

Virchow, Rudolf (1821–1902)

Virey, Julien-Joseph (1775–1846)

Virgil (Publius Virgilius Maro, 70–19 B.C.)

Virgilius Maro Grammaticus (late 6th–early 7th cent. A.D.)S

Virtadanta, Pērtti (1918–1997)

Vis, Henri de (1885–1949)

Vischer, Friedrich Theodor (1807–1887)

Vising, Per Johan (1855–1942)

Visscher, Lodewijk Gerard (1797–1859)

Visscher, Roemer (1547–16720)

W.

Waag, Albert (1863–1929)

Waard, Jan de (b.1931)

Wachler, Johann Friedrich (1767–1838)

Wachsmuth, Curt (1837–1905)

Wachsmuth, Ernst Wilhelm Gottlieb (1784–1866)

Wachter, Johann Georg (1673–1757)S

Wack, Johann Konrad (fl.1713)

Wackernagel, Jacob (1853–1938)S

Wackernagel, Wilhelm (1806–1869)E

Wackernell, Josef Eduard (1850–1920)

Wada, Hiroshi (b.1914)

Waddington, Conrad Hall (1905–1975)

Waddington, Rodolphus (Ralph, fl.1575)

Wade, Ira Owen (1896–1983)

Wade, *Sir* Thomas Francis (1818–1895)

Wadstein, N. Elis (d.1942)

Wadsworth, James (1604–1656?)

Wächtler, Kurt (b.1920)K

Wagener, Zacharias (1614–1668)

Wagenvoort, Hendrik (1886–1976)

Wagley, Charles (1913–1993)

Wagnalls, Adam Willis (1843–1924)

Wagner, Albrecht (1850–1909)

Wagner, Ewald (b.1927)K

Wagner, Heinrich (Hans, 1923–1988)E

Wagner, Karl Franz Christian (1760–1847)

Wagner, Max Leopold (1880–1962)S, E

Wagner, Philipp (fl.1888–1914)

Wagner, Robert Léon (1905–1982)S

Wagner, Rudolf (1805–1864)

Wagner, Zdzisław (1933–1992)

Wahl, Samuel Friedrich Günther (1760–1834)

Wahle, Ernst (1889–1981)

Wahlert, Georg Erich (Ernst) Adam (1782–1850)

Wahlgren, Eric (b.1911)

Wahlgren, John Howard (b.1921)

Wahlund, Carl (1846–1914)

Wahn, Hermann (b.1678)

Wahrig, Gerhard (1923–1978)

Wahrman, Paula (1881–1945)

Wailly, Noël-François de (1724–1801)

Waismann, Friedrich (1896–1959)

Waitz, Theodor (1821–1864)

Wajskop, Max (d.1994)

Wakefield, Robert (d.1537)

Wakelin, Martyn Francis (1935–1988)

Wakita, Hisashi (b.1934)

Wal, Marijke van der (b.1949)

Walahfrid Strabo (808/809–848 A.D.)S

Walch, Johann Georg (1693–1775)

Walch, Johann Ernst Immanuel (1725–1778)

Walcott, Charles (1850–1927)

Walczak, Bogdan (b.1949)

Walczak, Placyd (*alias* Placidus de Valcio, fl.1703)

Wald, Benji (b.1944)

Wald, Samuel Gottlieb (1762–1828)
Walde, Alois (1869–1924)
Waldman, Nahum M. (b.1931)
Walker, Douglas C(harles, b.1944)
Walker, D. P. (1914–1985)
Walker, Elkanah (1805–1877)
Walker, John (1732–1807)E
Walker, William (1623–1684)
Wall, Charles William (1783?–1862)
Wall, Robert Eugene (b.1936)
Wallace, Alfred Russell (1823–1913)
Wallace, Anthony F. C. (b.1923)
Wallach, Luitpold (b.1910)
Wallenius, Jacob (1761–1819)
Wallensköld, Axel Gabriel (1869–1924)
Wallerand, Gaston (fl.1908)
Walleser, Max Gerhard Lebrecht (1874–1954)
Wallin, Georg August (1811–1852)S
Wallis, John (1616–1703)S
Wallis, Wilson D. (1886–1970)
Wallon, Henri (1879–19??)
Walpole, Hugh R. (1905–19??)
Walter of Ascoli (Lat. Gualterius Esculanus, fl. first half of 13th cent.)S
Walter of Bibbesworth (13th cent.)
Walter Burleigh or Burley (Latin name: Gualterus de Burley or Burlaeus, c.1275–c.1345)S
Walter of Henley (13th cent.)
Walter, Ernst (b.1925)K
Walter, Henriette (b.1929)
Walter, Hilmar (b.1923)
Walter, Max (1857–c.1935)
Waltereit, Richard (b.1967)
Walters, John (1721–1797)

Walther, Christian Theodor (1699–1741)
Walther, Christoph (1841–1914)
Walton, Brian (1600–1661)
Waltz, Heidi (b.1960)
Walzel, Oskar (1864–1944)
Wandelaincourt, Antoine Hubert (1731–1819)
Wander, Karl Friedrich Wilhelm (1803–1879)
Wandruszka, Mario (1911–2004)K
Wandruszka, Ulrich (b.1941)K
Wang, Kuo-Wei (or Guowei, 1877–1927)S
Wang Li (1901–1986)S, E
Wang Nian-Sun (1744–1832)E
Wang, William S(hi)-Y(uan b.1933)
Wang, Yi (b.1919)
Wang Yin-zhi (1766–1834)
Wanley, Humfrey (1672–1726)
Warburton, William (1698–1779)
Warchoł, Stefan (b.1930)
Ward, Ida Caroline (1880–1949)E
Ward, James (1843–1925)
Ward, John (1679?–1758)
Ward, Lester Frank (1841–1913)
Ward, Ralph L(awrence, b.1910)
Ward, Seth (1617–1689)
Ward, William (1708/09–1772)S
Wardrop, Oliver (1864–1948)
Wardhaugh, Ronald (b.1932)
Ware, Jonathan (1767–1838)
Warnant, Léon (1919–1996)
Warner, William Lloyd (1989–1970)
Warner, Walter (c.1558–1643)
Warnke, Karl (d.1948)
Warnock, Geoffrey (b.1923)
Warren, Donald William (b.1935)

X.

Xaburgaev, Georgij Aleksandrovič
(1931–1991)
Xarcijev, Vasil' (1866–1937)
Xavier, *Saint* Francis(co), S.J. (a*lias*
Franciscus Javier, 1506–1552)
Xenocrates (c.395–313 B.C.)
Ximénez, Francisco, O.F.M. (d.
1537)
Ximenéz, *Frei* Francisco, O.P.
(1666–1723)
Xenophon (c.450–354 B.C.)
Xie, Qikun (1737–1802)
Xolodovič, Aleksandr Aleksandrovič
(1906–1977)S
Xolovac'kyj, Jakiv (1814–1888)
Xomjakov, Aleksej Stepanovič
(1804–1860)
Xomonov, Mixail P. (1913–1993)
Xovanskij, Aleksej Andreevič (1814–
1899)
Xu, Daming (b.1951)
Xu, Jialu (b.1937)
Xu, Shen (d. c.149 A.D.)E
Xulkov, Mixail Dmitrievič (1740–
1793)
Xub Kuang (c.313–238 B.C.)
Xun Zi (c.313–238 B.C.)

Y.

Yaḥyā ibn ᶜAdī, Abū Zakariyyā'
  (280/893–363/974)S
Yalman, Nur (b.1931)
Yamada, Toshio (b.1922)
Yamada, Yoshio (1873–1958)S, E
Yamagiwa, Joseph K. (1906–1968)
Yamamoto, Tadao (1904–1991)
Yan, Zhitui (531–c.591 A.D.)S
Yang, Shuda (1885–1956)S
Yang, Shih-feng (d.1989)
Yang Xiong (53 B.C.–18 A.D.)S, E
Yangues, Manuel de, O.F.M. (1630–
  1676)
Yāqīt, Abū ᶜAbd Allāh (d.626/1229)
Yarborough, Ralph W. (b.1903)
Yar-Shater, Ehsan (b.1920)E
Yāska (5th cent. B.C.)S, E
Yasu y Xavier, Francisco de (*alias*
  Franciscus Xaverius, 1506–1552)
Yasuhara, Sadamuro (1610–1673)
Yates, Edward (1829–1864)
Yates, (*Dame*) Frances Amelia
  (1899–1981)
Yāzigī, Ibrāhīm b. Nāṣif al- (1847–
  1906)S
Yāzigī, Nāṣif ibn ᶜAbdallāh al-
  (1800–1871)S
Yehuda b. David, *see* Ḥayyj, Judah
Yeong, Jiang (1681–1762)
Yeves, Carlos (1822–1882)
Yngve, Victor H(use, b.1920)
Yong Jiang (1618–1662)
York, Brantley (1805–1891)

Young, Edward (1683–1765)
Young, John (1730–1820)
Young, John (1879–1932)
Young, Karl (1879–1943)
Young, Linda Wai-Ling (b.1954)
Young, Robert W. (1887–1974)
Young, Robert W(endell, b.1912)
Young, Thomas (1773–1829)E
Ypeij, Annaeus (1760–1837)
Yu Hūi (1773–1837)S
Yu Kilchun (*alias* Sŏngmu and
  Kudang, 1856–1914)S
Yu, Xingwu (1896–1984)S
Yu Yue (1821–1907)
Yule, George Udny (1871–1951)
Yuyama, Akira (b.1933)
Yvon, Henri (1873–1963)

Z.

Zaᶜba (byname of Zainal ᶜAbidin Bin Ahmad, 1895–1973)

Žába, Zbyněk (1917–1971)

Zabani, Matiáš (17th/18th cent.)

Zabarella, Jacopo (*also* Giacomo, 1533–1589)S

Zabīdī, Murtāza al- (1732–1790)

Zabīdī, as-Sayyid Abū l-Fayḍ Muḥammad Murtaḍā az- (1145/1732–1206/1791)S

Žabkar, Louis V. (1914–1994)

Zaborowski(-Moindron), Sigismond (1851–1928)

Zaborski, Andrzej (b.1942)K

Zabrocki, Ludwik (1907–1977)S, E

Zabrocki, Tadeusz (b.1948)

Zachariae, Theodor (1851–1934)

Zacher, (Ernst) Julius (August, 1816–1887)

Zacher, Konrad (Erich Hartmut, 1856–1907)

Zachrisson, Robert Eugen (1880–1937)

Zadeh, Lotfi Asker (b.1921)

Zadovsky, Otto von (b. c.1930)

Zaefferer, Dietmar (b.1947)K

Zaenen, Annie (b.1941)

Zagurskij, Leonard Petrovič (1827–1891)

Zaǧǧāǧī, Abū Isḥāq Ibrāhīm ibn as-Sarī az- (230/844–311/923)S

Zaǧǧāǧī, Abū l-Qāsim ᶜAbd ar-Raḥmān ibn Isḥāq az- (d.337/948)S

Zahn, Johann Christian (Matthias, 1767–1818)

Zaimov, Jordan Dimov (1921–1987)

Zajączkowski, Stanisław (1890–1977)

Zajączkowski, Włodzimir (1914–1982)

Žakov, Kallistrat F. (1866–1926)

Zakrevs'ka, Jaroslava (1931–1999)

Zaleski, Jan (1926–1981)

Zales´kyj, Anton Mykolajovyč (1936–1989)

Zaliznjak, Andrej Anatoljevič (b.1935)

Zalkind-Hurwicz (*dit* Hourwitz, 1738–1812)

Załuski, Józef Andrzej (bishop of Kiev, 1702–1774)

Zamahsari, Ġār Allāh Abū l-Qāsim Maḥmūd ibn ᶜUmar az- (467/1057–538/1144)S

Zamenhof, Ludwik Lazarus *or* Lejzer (1859–1917)

Zamora, Al(f)onso (fl.1512–1515)

Zamora, Bernardo Agustín de, OCarm (1730–1785)

Zamora (Munné), Juan C(lemente, b.1930)

Zamora, Santiago de (1670–1737)

Zamora Vicente, Alonso (1916–2006)

Zampolli, Antonio (1937–2003)E

Zamputi, Injac (1910–1998)

Zander, Johann Wilhelm (1716–1781)

Zandvoort, Reinard Willem (1894–1990)

Zánthó, Róbert (1933–2000)

Zaręba, Alfred (1921–1988)

Zaрębina, Maria (b.1924)

Zarechnak, Michael M. (b.1920)

Zünd-Burguet, Adolphe (1870–*ante* 1919)
Zujevskyj, Oleh (1920–1996)
Žukov, Vlas Platonovič (1921–1991)
Žukovskaja, Lidija Petrovna (1920–1994)
Žukovskij,Valentin (1858–1918)
Žukovskij,Vasilij Andreevič (1783–1852)
Zuloaga, Santiago Augustín (1715–1780)
Zumarán, José Ángel de (fl.1634)S
Zumpt, Karl Gottlob (1792–1849)
Zumthor, Paul (1915–1994)
Zúñiga, *Frei* Dionisio de, O.P. (c.1580–1636)
Zuntz, Günther (1892–1992)
Zunz, Leopold (1794–1886)
Zupitza, Ernst (1875–1917)
Zupitza, Julius (1844–1895)S
Zutphen, Gerard Zerbold van (1367–1398)
Žurinskij, Al'fred Naumovič (1938–1991)
Zvegincev, Vladimir Andreevič (1910–1988)
Zvelebil, Kamil Veith (b.1927)E
Zwaardemaker, Hendrik (1857–1930)
Zwartjes, Otto (b.1958)
Zwicky, Arnold M(elchior, b.1940)
Zwingli, Huldrych (1481–1531)
Zwirner, Eberhard (1899–1984)S
Zwirner, Kurt (1903–*post* 1982)
Zwoliński, Przemysław (1914–1982)
Zyhlarz, Ernst (1890–1964)
Žylko, Fedot Trofymovyč (1908–19??)
Zytec'kyj, Pavel Ignat'evič (1837–1911)

Zyzanij, Lavrentij, *see* Zizani, Lavrentij

STUDIES IN THE HISTORY OF THE LANGUAGE SCIENCES

E. F. K. Koerner, Editor

Zentrum für Allgemeine Sprachwissenschaft, Typologie
und Universalienforschung, Berlin
efk.koerner@rz.hu-berlin.de

The series *Studies in the History of the Language Sciences* (SiHoLS) has been established as a companion to the journal *Historiographia Linguistica*. The series intends to meet the revival of interest in the history of linguistic thought and to provide an organized reservoir of information concerning our heritage of linguistic ideas of more than two millennia. SiHoLS will publish book-length scholarly studies on (the evolution of) human reflection about the nature of language and the many ways in which it can be analyzed and used. These studies may concern particular aspects of language study, entire traditions, or special periods of their development. In addition, the series will include re-editions or entirely new translations into English of 'classic' works in the field that have been out of print for many years. These new editions will be introduced by a present-day specialist who places the book in its intellectual and socio-historical context, and highlights its significance in the evolution of our thinking about language. A complete list of titles in this series can be found on the publishers website, **www.benjamins.com**

96 JOSEPH, John E.: Limiting the Arbitrary. Linguistic naturalism and its opposites in Plato's *Cratylus* and modern theories of language. 2000. x, 224 pp.

95 CRAM, David, Andrew R. LINN and Elke NOWAK (eds.): History of Linguistics 1996. Volume 2: From Classical to Contemporary Linguistics. 1999. xx, 390 pp.

94 CRAM, David, Andrew R. LINN and Elke NOWAK (eds.): History of Linguistics 1996. Volume 1: Traditions in Linguistics Worldwide. 1999. xx, 341 pp.

93 COBLIN, W. South and Joseph A. LEVI: Francisco Varo's Grammar of the Mandarin Language (1703). An English translation of 'Arte de la lengua Mandarina'. With an Introduction by Sandra Breitenbach. 2000. liv, 282 pp.

92 KOERNER, E.F.K.: Linguistic Historiography. Projects & prospects. 1999. x, 236 pp.

91 NIEDEREHE, Hans-Josef: Bibliografía cronológica de la lingüística, la gramática y la lexicografía del español (BICRES II). Desde el año 1601 hasta el año 1700. 1999. vi, 472 pp.

90 ESPARZA TORRES, Miguel Ángel and Hans-Josef NIEDEREHE: Bibliografía Nebrisense. Las obras completas del humanista Antonio de Nebrija desde 1481 hasta nuestros días. 1999. vi, 374 pp.

89 JONES, William J.: Images of Language. Six essays on German attitudes to European languages from 1500 to 1800. 1999. x, 299 pp.

88 KOERNER, E.F.K. (ed.): First Person Singular III. Autobiographies by North American scholars in the language sciences. 1998. x, 267 pp.

87 STEIN, Dieter and Rosanna SORNICOLA (eds.): The Virtues of Language. History in language, linguistics and texts. Papers in memory of Thomas Frank. 1998. viii, 232 pp.

86 DARNELL, Regna: And Along Came Boas. Continuity and revolution in Americanist anthropology. 1998. xviii, 333 pp.

85 TAYLOR, Daniel J.: De Lingua Latina X. A new critical text and English translation with prolegomena and commentary. 1996. x, 205 pp.

84 VERBURG, Pieter A.: Language and its Functions. A historico-critical study of views concerning the functions of language from the pre-humanistic philology of Orleans to the rationalistic philology of Bopp. Translated by Paul Salmon in consultation with Anthony J. Klijnsmit. 1998. xxxiv, 577 pp.

83 WOLLOCK, Jeffrey: The Noblest Animate Motion. Speech, physiology and medicine in pre-Cartesian linguistic thought. 1997. l, 461 pp.

82 BEKKUM, Wout Jac. van, Jan HOUBEN, Ineke SLUITER and Kees VERSTEEGH: The Emergence of Semantics in Four Linguistic Traditions. Hebrew, Sanskrit, Greek, Arabic. 1997. ix, 322 pp.

81 LEE, Penny: The Whorf Theory Complex. A critical reconstruction. 1996. x, 324 pp.

80 NERLICH, Brigitte and David D. CLARKE: Language, Action and Context. The early history of pragmatics in Europe and America 1780–1930. 1996. xiv, 497 pp.

79 KOERNER, E.F.K.: Professing Linguistic Historiography. 1995. viii, 274 pp.

78 JANKOWSKY, Kurt R. (ed.): History of Linguistics 1993. Papers from the Sixth International Conference on the History of the Language Sciences (ICHoLS VI), Washington DC, 9–14 August 1993. 1995. xx, 380 pp.

77 SALMON, Vivian: Language and Society in Early Modern England. Selected essays 1982–1994. 1996. viii, 276 pp.

76 NIEDEREHE, Hans-Josef: Bibliografía cronológica de la lingüística, la gramática y la lexicografía del español (BICRES). Desde los principios hasta el año 1600. 1994. vi, 457 pp.

75 VERSTEEGH, Kees: The Explanation of Linguistic Causes. Az-Zaǧǧāǧī's Theory of Grammar. Introduction, translation, commentary. 1995. xvi, 310 pp.

74 FORMIGARI, Lia and Daniele GAMBARARA (eds.): Historical Roots of Linguistic Theories. 1995. viii, 309 pp.

73 GOLDZIHER, Ignaz: On the History of Grammar among the Arabs. Translated and edited by Kinga Dévényi and Tamás Iványi. 1994. xx, 153 pp.

72 RADWAŃSKA-WILLIAMS, Joanna: A Paradigm Lost. The linguistic thought of Mikołaj Kruszewski. 1994. xii, 200 pp.

71 LAW, Vivien A. (ed.): History of Linguistic Thought in the Early Middle Ages. 1993. viii, 255 pp.

70 FORMIGARI, Lia: Signs, Science and Politics. Philosophies of language in Europe 1700–1830. 1993. x, 218 pp.

69 MURRAY, Stephen O.: Theory Groups and the Study of Language in North America. A social history. 1994. xx, 598 pp.